TAROT
and the
PSYCHOLOGY
of the
SOUL

EXPLORING THE ARCHETYPAL MIRRORS
OF THE PSYCHE

MARIANA LOUIS

WEISER BOOKS

This edition first published in 2026 by Weiser Books, an imprint of
Red Wheel/Weiser, LLC
With offices at:
65 Parker Street, Suite 7
Newburyport, MA 01950
www.redwheelweiser.com

Copyright © 2026 by Mariana Louis
All rights reserved. No part of this publication may be reproduced or transmitted in any form or by any means, electronic or mechanical, including photocopying, recording, or by any information storage and retrieval system, nor used in any manner for purposes of training artificial intelligence (AI) technologies to generate text or imagery, including technologies that are capable of generating works in the same style or genre, without permission in writing from Red Wheel/Weiser, LLC. Reviewers may quote brief passages.

ISBN: 978-1-57863-898-7

Library of Congress Cataloging-in-Publication Data
Names: Louis, Mariana, 1989- author   Title: Tarot and the psychology of the soul : exploring the archetypal mirrors of the psyche / Mariana Louis. Description: Newburyport, MA : Weiser Books, 2026. | Includes bibliographical references and index. | Summary: "This is part classic guidebook and part provoking how-to, with a dash of stirring tarot philosophy. With a focus on inspiration and inclusivity for all tarot levels, it begins by establishing how we can view the cards as reflections of the psyche via depth psychology, and it walks readers through how to use the cards for inner work and shadow work to answer the question: "How am I meant to live?""-- Provided by publisher.
Identifiers: LCCN 2025042963 | ISBN 9781578638987 trade paperback | ISBN 9781633413948 ebook   Subjects: LCSH: Tarot | Divination | BISAC: BODY, MIND & SPIRIT / Divination / Tarot | SELF-HELP / Spirit

Cover image is an adaptation of Rothschild Tarot, 15th century (Louvre, Paris), public domain. Interior photos credits on page 305. Diagrams by the author.
Interior by Ashley McKevitt, Happenstance Type-O-Rama
Typeset in Adobe Caslon Pro, Ofelia Display, and OPTI Bauer Text

Printed in the Unites States of America
IBI
10 9 8 7 6 5 4 3 2 1

*To my late grandfather, the emblem of Logos,
whose dusty paper treasures became the seeds of my
seeking; and to my late grandmother, the embodiment
of Eros, who taught me that life is holy when
each day is dressed, fed, and lived.*

CONTENTS

Introduction 1

PART 1
Depth Psychology and the Archetypal Approach

Chapter 1: Roots of the Psyche 17
Chapter 2: Archetypal Methods and Techniques 33

PART 2
The Minor Arcana

Chapter 3: The Multifaceted Power of the Pips 49
Chapter 4: The Pips 69
Chapter 5: The Many Faces of the Tarot Court 103
Chapter 6: The Court Cards 113

PART 3
The Major Arcana

Chapter 7: The Trumps and the Story of
           Individuation. 141
Chapter 8: The Primordial Powers—Archetypes of
           the Masculine and Feminine. 149
Chapter 9: Birth of Selfhood—Archetypes of the Developing
           Ego 181

Chapter 10: Encountering the Shadow—Archetypes
of Descent 205

Chapter 11: Approaching Wholeness—Archetypes
of Transcendence. 229

PART 4
Reading with a Psycho-Spiritual Lens

Chapter 12: The Ritual of the Reading 261
Chapter 13: Archetypal Tarot Spreads 275

Afterword 289
Acknowledgments 291
Notes. 293
Bibliography 299
Image Credits 305
Index 307
About the Author 313

INTRODUCTION

Humanity, take a good look at yourself. Inside, you've got heaven and earth, and all of creation. You're a world—everything is hidden in you.
—HILDEGARD VON BINGEN

I had my first tarot reading on a yoga retreat in the late summertime woods of Rhinebeck, New York. I was twenty-six, pinned to that liminal place between childhood fantasies and the adult burden of choosing how to live. Behind me, my decade-long dream of Broadway stardom lay abandoned, and ahead a master's degree in a jobless field loomed wide and bleak. I was bookended by terror of the unknown.

The reader's name was Autumn, and in her Long Island brogue she asked for my question. I felt my face flush as I gave it: "What am I meant to do with my life?"

Three years earlier this question would have been inconceivable to me. I had spent my entire young life training to become a musical theater performer, and I had thoroughly believed it was Broadway or bust. And then, on a lazy spring afternoon rummaging through my grandfather's attic library, I happened upon a little book called *The Undiscovered Self* by Carl Jung. Barely ten pages into that book I realized that it was true—I had yet to discover my *Self*. Suddenly there was no other choice but to put down old dreams and begin the search for my soul.

Autumn nodded, unfazed by the enormity of my question, and laid out the cards. First she asked about debts—of which I had none—and then about traveling somewhere near mountains—to which I shrugged that I'd recently been to the West Coast. As card after card only vaguely connected, I feared that my anxiety had somehow skewed them or that my stubborn faith in this sort of thing was being proven ridiculous.

Autumn came to the final card—the outcome. My heart throbbed as she blinked at it, popped a bubble in her gum, and said, "Are you planning on becoming a yoga teacher?"

Gutted, I quietly answered no. I liked yoga but certainly would never pursue it beyond my Tuesday morning class. She looked at the card again, tapping her red manicured finger on it as she replied, "The High Priestess is a big card. She tells you you're meant to be a teacher, like a spiritual guide. That's what you're meant to do."

I stared down at that High Priestess card in the shimmering summer dusk, examining her prayerful face and solemn pose, the scroll of wisdom held lightly in her hand, the crescent moon shining underfoot, and I brushed up against her shocking archetypal power. Though it would take me years to understand, the High Priestess spoke to me in that moment, communicating in that serene, wordless way: *Here it is, the path you've been seeking. This is the moment it opens before you. It is your choice, now, to follow.*

The more I learned about the cards, the more I realized that the ones Autumn had pulled could not have been more right. The Four of Pentacles was not about debt, but about my inherited fear of poverty; the Page of Wands was not about travels, but about reawakening my sense of vitality and passion; and the High Priestess did not tell me to train as a yoga teacher, but confirmed that my choice to radically upend my life had risen from my deepest wisdom. The tarot had indeed answered my question. What I was meant to do was courageously pursue the life of soul I had discovered in my grandfather's dusty attic.

The following years were a storm of study. I worked to earn my master's degree in Western intellectual traditions with a focus in archetypal theory, while simultaneously devouring everything I found on Jungian psychology and the tarot. After a decade of exploring, reading, and learning, I weaved the principles of depth psychology with the cards into what I call the archetypal tarot approach, which I have since taught to thousands of students all over the world. In this approach, which you will be guided through in this book, we do not read the cards for predictive divination or even encouraging self-care, but as a tool to support our individuation, the psycho-spiritual process of self-becoming.*

---

* *Psycho-spiritual* meaning the meeting point of psychology and spirituality.

In my years of tarot teaching and counseling, I have come to learn that the only question we bring to the cards is the one I asked on that summertime evening: *How am I meant to live?* While the lure to glimpse what the future holds is undeniable, we don't really want to know what's going to happen as much as we want to know what promise we hold and how to meet it. We ask whether to move, to go on that date, to quit that job, but actually we want to find out which path is leading us to the most authentic, fulfilled experience of our individual selves. We may (and usually do) intuitively sense what is right; still we cannot help but doubt. Essentially, we do not want the cards to *tell* us how to live, but to help us *trust* how we live.

This doubt doesn't come from a lack of will but a lack of wisdom. Society's overinsistence on rigid empiricism and rationality has usurped the intuitive relationship with our depth, and the vital communication between our conscious and unconscious halves has diminished. As Laurens van der Post writes, without the natural exchange between the conscious and unconscious minds, "man becomes sick and deprived of meaning." More than ever we are a world suffering the sickness of meaninglessness, confusion, and inner chaos, and we often seek desperate guidance from outside oracles (be they cards, self-help gurus, or Google searches). If the answers we find are not sourced from our own unconscious wisdom, however, we will never feel sated. We will continue to ask and ask and ask, *How am I meant to live?*

Rather than use the cards to solve our meaninglessness and confusion, we can employ them to mend this divide between the conscious and unconscious sides of our psyche. This is why depth psychology is such a natural companion to tarot. Unlike many other branches of psychology, depth psychology does not teach us how to categorize or cope in life. It unveils the road into the wilderness of the unconscious, showing us how to listen to the insights of our dreams, the whispers of our shadows, the longings of the essential Self that pulls us in with its primordial gravity. It teaches us how to intentionally cultivate and protect that exchange between our waking conscious minds and the mystery of our unconscious souls.

In the archetypal tarot approach, the cards are windows of communication between the conscious and unconscious. We read them as constellations of wisdom already extant within us, and seek the archetypal tapestry they weave in every spread. Our intention in this approach is always to move further along the path of individuation, learning to trust our alignment with the center of our being—what Jung called that capital-*S* Self and we might equally call soul. If we're willing to listen and learn, the tarot offers us the framework for conscious living in communion with our depths.

What Is the Tarot?

Two decades into the twenty-first century, there is still tremendous confusion about the tarot. Most think of it as a scam of false promise of the future, and many of those who do accept it believe it to be a key to the great cosmic secrets, passed down like commandments from ancient, faceless gods. The truth is, of course, that the tarot is simply a collection of seventy-eight images printed onto cardstock, created perhaps this week, one hundred years ago, or half a millennium ago.

This truth does not minimize the immense psycho-spiritual properties of the tarot. In fact, its seemingly ordinary origins emphasize its archetypal potency. In its standardized form, the tarot is a deck of seventy-eight cards divided into two groups: the Major and Minor Arcana. The Major Arcana ("greater secrets") is composed of twenty-two illustrated cards that progress in a numbered order from zero to twenty-one. The Minor Arcana ("lesser secrets") is fifty-six cards subdivided into four suits (Cups, Swords, Pentacles, and Wands), containing both numbered cards known as the pips (Ace through 10) and the court cards (Page, Knight, Queen, and King).

Though the historical origins of the deck are fairly well-established, there are many legends about its genesis that persist from early bad research. Some say it arose from ancient near-eastern hermeticism, others the Egyptian *Book of Thoth*, and still others argue it was created by the mystical Sufi, Romani, and Cathar traditions. While it is certainly possible that it was distantly influenced by any or all of these sources, the tarot's earliest incarnation was in the artwork of a fifteenth-century set of cards collectively known today as the Visconti-Sforza Tarot. Much is still unknown about these early cards, but we do know that there are at least two iterations of the Visconti tarot. Considered the oldest of these decks is the Visconti di Modrone (c. 1442), likely commissioned by Duke Filippo Maria Visconti of Milan. The second deck (c. 1450), may have been commissioned to commemorate the marriage of the Duke's daughter Bianca Visconti to Francesco Sforza, who became the Duke's successor.

Before it was known as the game *tarocchi*, the tarot was called *carte da trionfi*, or cards with triumphs. The triumphs—today called the trumps—are the defining attribute that has survived through history, and they distinguish the tarot from the typical playing card deck. Rather than depict value or rank as the pips and courts, the trumps tell an internal story. The original trumps of the fifteenth century were not named; they were pictorial representations of virtues, concepts, and societal fascinations (such as judgement, charity, strength, love, death, and visions of the divine). Over time, the cards were referenced by their image (such as *l'Imperatrice del mazzo*, or "the Empress of the deck") and eventually evolved into the names that have stuck with us: the World, Judgement, Strength, the Empress, the High Priestess, and so forth. Ultimately there is no historical record indicating that the trumps were intended to have deeper meaning, yet the centuries-long collective instinct that they do refuses to be washed away.

Figure 1. The cards "rise for judgement," "fortitude," and "charity" (a nod to both High Priestess and Hierophant) from the Visconti di Modrone tarot, Milan, 15th century.

A rule we hold in archetypal scholarship is that meaning is not determined by causal connection (i.e., *this* influenced *that*), but in energetic symbiosis. In other words, rather than being preoccupied with proving direct links, we are focused on tracing cultural patterns. These patterns illuminate the archetypal motifs active within the collective unconscious. At the beginning of the Renaissance in the fifteenth century, Europe was brimming with archetypal vitality; it was a landscape dedicated to seeking the unseen powers, recovering hidden wisdom and divine beauty, journeying into the unknown and back. Those who deny the tarot's deeper meaning because there's no surviving "proof" and those who insist on its deeper meaning by defending the fallacy of legendary origins are both missing its true value.

Whether its first authors intended it or not, they birthed a deck of cards that depict archetypes of life, with all of their power and potential. Through a simple compilation of illustrations, the cards communicate human experience, ranging from the universally mundane to the utterly inexpressible. They show us the mortal moments of joy, fear, peace, rage, hope, creativity—folding back the image just a little to reveal the glimmer of the immortal truth within. As tarot scholar Sallie Nichols writes, "It seems apparent that these old cards were conceived deep in the guts of human experience, at the most profound level of the human psyche. It is to this level in ourselves that they will speak."[1]

The tarot has gone through countless iterations across several hundred years, but we can directly trace the development of the deck as we know it today. After a few decades of prominence in the fifteenth century, the tarot fell out of fashion until the rise of the printing press in the eighteenth century. With the printing of the Tarot de Marseille, the tarot formula was settled and quickly resparked continental curiosity. Interest in occultism spread through Europe, and the cards were adapted to be used not only for gameplay but fortune-telling. By the late nineteenth century the tarot's obvious mystery and depth caught the attention of esoteric thinkers, and in particular the Hermetic Order of the Golden Dawn. Two of its members—Pamela Colman Smith and Arthur Edward Waite—collaborated to create a new iteration of the deck, which today remains the most popular version. With Smith's astounding intuitive artistry and Waite's profound knowledge of the

Figure 2. The continuing evolution of the tarot as seen in the Magician, the Lovers, and Death cards. Top row: the Tarot de Marseille (c. 1760). Bottom row: the Rider-Waite deck, 1909.

cards, the Rider-Waite-Smith deck persists as a fixture of mainstream consciousness.*

Of course, it's not the historical past of the cards that enchants us but their innate living mysteries. Through all their transformations, the Star presents the same hopeful glow, the Empress the same maternal power, and Death the same eerie gloom. From its mysterious incarnation half a

---

* Though the decks that have been produced since are largely modeled after the Rider-Waite-Smith, the two other well-known tarot schools are the Tarot de Marseille and the Thoth Tarot, the creation of Golden Dawn member Aleister Crowley. However, for the purposes of this book we are focused solely on the Waite-Smith school.

millennium ago, the tarot's hidden wisdom continues to mystify us, and it is this wisdom we seek.

Jung and Depth Psychology

Depth psychology may conjure images of Freudian couches and thick diagnostic manuals, but in reality it is an approachable study that is in many ways highly intuitive. Drawn from the Greek words *psyche*, meaning "soul," and *logia*, the "study of," psychology began in the nineteenth century as an investigation of the hidden relationship between the conscious and the unconscious sides of the personality. Though modern psychology has largely moved on, centering this split remains at the core of depth psychology and its branches. Depth psychology's primary interest is uncovering the hidden dynamics of the psyche, exploring how unconscious and transpersonal experience (meaning that which extends beyond the limits of personal identity) relate to and influence the conscious mind. And in Jungian depth psychology, beyond focusing solely on our thoughts and feelings, or even on our neuroses and complexes, we go deeper, working with the dreamscape, the imagination, mythology, and mystery. It is, at its core, the psychology of the soul.

Carl Jung was a pioneer in the science of psychoanalysis alongside Sigmund Freud, though the center of his psychology was not repressed sexuality but a fascination with what he called the numinous—the spiritual, the awe-inspiring, the divine. It was this fascination that inspired many of his theories, including those of the collective unconscious, synchronicity, and archetypes. Jung saw the psyche not as something to be fixed or cured, but as something to be explored, embraced, and made whole. In this way, psychology to Jung was not merely a pathological science but a road to unity with the soul. This is the same mystical truth at the heart of the tarot: We embark on a long and meandering journey, rife with both darkness and brilliance, which ultimately brings us to the center of who we are. There we embrace all of ourselves and are made vibrantly whole.

In this book, we are not interested in analytical or clinical applications of depth psychology, but philosophical and practical ones. We can use its principles to illuminate what depth psychologist James Hillman calls "soul-making": the pursuit of developing a faith and intimacy with the soul.* Our goal in studying depth psychology is to better understand the psyche and thus better understand ourselves. With this knowledge of its mechanisms and processes, we can revive the numinous potency of our inner world and attempt to unify our split halves of consciousness and unconsciousness into an essential Self, a unified soul.

The tarot offers us a tool to guide this effort, but we should not think to use it to psychoanalyze ourselves. There is a tendency in our contemporary world to self-pathologize and self-therapize, which can be misguided and even psychologically dangerous. If we are thoughtful and conscientious about our approach, however, we can use these depth psychology principles to support and guide our own intuitive and therapeutic self-inquiry.† As Hillman puts it:

> Therapy, or analysis, is not only something that analysts do to patients; it is a process that goes on intermittently in our individual soul-searching, our attempts at understanding our complexities, the critical attacks, prescriptions, and encouragements that we give ourselves. We are all in therapy all the time insofar as we are involved with soul-making.[2]

Using depth psychology as the bedrock upon which we build our relationship to the cards, we can formulate an approach that is grounded in the realities of the psyche while also prompting a relationship with our depth, the source of soul.

---

* Although there are certain depth psychology nuances between them, for the purposes of this book we will use the terms *Self* and *soul* somewhat interchangeably.

† It is essential to make clear that this is not at all suggesting tarot can replace therapy or licensed psychological help. In fact, I would argue that tarot is best used in tandem with psycho-therapeutic containers like analysis.

Divination vs. Individuation

For most, when they think of the tarot, they can't help but picture a dark-haired woman behind a red curtain, her gold bracelets clanging as she flips over the cards. This image, which we've carried for centuries, paints the tarotist not as a reader of symbols but as a diviner of fortunes. Of course, as a divinatory device, we view tarot as a method of foretelling future or unknown events, but the truth is that divination is also a practice of real depth. It is a rich, nuanced, and ancient art form of interpreting the unseeable nature of our world.

The word *divination* derives from the same Latin root as *divine*—*divinare*, "to be inspired by a god." The act of divining is not so much seeing what has not yet come to pass as it is peering into the unknown with god-blessed vision, uncovering what is hidden or obscure from mortal sight. While we understand divination as the practice of glimpsing the external unknowns, it is equally a practice of discovering the internal ones. Furthermore, if divination is the practice of seeing inwardly through the eyes of a god, then its purview is the realm of the unconscious. As Jung famously said, "The world of gods and spirits is truly 'nothing but' the collective unconscious inside me."

We will explore these concepts more fully in chapter 1, but we can understand the collective unconscious as the deepest realm of the psyche which houses the archetypes, the universal "thought-forms" of humanity. Jungian Marie-Louise von Franz suggests that it is indeed the archetypes, the inner "gods and spirits," that we are engaging when we use divinatory practices. As von Franz puts it, the divination oracle (in our case the tarot) is a medium for contacting "the dynamic load of an archetypal constellation to give it a reading pattern of what it is."[3] In other words, the tarot's divinatory power is to offer a selection of cards that represent an archetypal source within us and draw up its "dynamic load"—its potency and meaning—within our lives.

This is not to discount using the cards for traditional divination. There are many readers who excel at this practice, and it is undeniable that sometimes the cards have that spooky way of warning us about things. I do believe, however, that reading the tarot predictively can be both difficult and dangerous. In predictive reading we may feel pressured by divined information that scares, tricks, or confuses us, and in the worst cases, we surrender our agency and make choices that violate our own intuitive wisdom.

Therefore, rather than thinking of the tarot as a tool of divination, we should think of it as one of *individuation*. Individuation is the core of Jungian psychology and the end goal of the tarot. Jung defines *individuation* as the process of embracing "our innermost, last, and incomparable uniqueness, it also implies becoming one's own self. We could therefore translate individuation as 'coming to selfhood.'"[4] In the work of individuation we are becoming who we most authentically are; we are becoming whole. It is the effort of embracing our extraordinary multiplicity and complexity, accepting and appreciating it all profoundly, and integrating it into a unified, centered experience of selfhood.

The work of individuating is not only psychological but inherently spiritual. Ultimately, it is about learning how to live in communion with the soul. When we use the tarot to support this psycho-spiritual process of self-knowing and self-unifying, rather than asking it to give us blocking cues like actors on a stage, it supports our agency to live in ever more empowered, unique, and authentic ways.

If we wish to use the cards for our individuation, we should not ask them to reveal answers but to amplify truth. Rather than ask what to do, what we should know, or what will happen, we must ask them only to help us discover what we don't yet know about ourselves, to offer possibilities, insights, and symbols to guide us to the resolutions we already hold within. (We'll discuss exactly how to do this in chapter 2.) Then each card you pull becomes a personal and intimate encounter, a cipher for the unconscious wisdom seeking conscious understanding.

With this depth approach to the tarot, we must be willing to slow down and get lost. We must let the cards challenge and disappoint us, trusting that they are speaking to a revelation that will—inevitably—come. Though this way of using the tarot requires commitment, faith, and humility, it may indeed become one of the greatest tools you have for change and growth.

Seeking Meaning

At the height of the pandemic, when life seemed to come to a shuddering halt, a trend emerged on social media to "romanticize your life." TikTok was rife with videos of people swirling their lattes on rainy Sunday mornings or reading thick Russian novels on European terraces. Ostensibly, the trend is an unconscious rebellion against the ugliness of stuckness and stagnancy, but there is also something archetypal at its core. The idea of romanticizing life is not merely about its beautification, but its *centralization*. We are encouraged to once again become the "main character" and experience life as a *romance*—in the original medieval meaning of the word as a story of love and adventure in which we are the great hero. To reengage with life as our own romance means taking up the incredible adventure of living and seeing it as such. Therefore, it seems that what we really mean by *romanticizing* life is *mythologizing* it.

Myths are the archetypal shapes of life that constellate within each individual into a story of selfhood. As existential psychologist Rollo May writes:

> Myths are narrative patterns that give significance to our existence. Whether the meaning of existence is only what we put into life by our own individual fortitude, as Sartre would hold, or whether there is a meaning we need to discover, as Kierkegaard would state, the result is the same: myths are our way of finding this meaning and significance. Myths are like the beams in a house: not exposed to outside view, they are the structure which holds the house together so people can live in it.[5]

We are the heroes of our living myths, and it is in these myths we find meaning. Being in a society divorced from our own unconscious imagination, however, we may find initiating this task of personal mythmaking seemingly impossible. This is why the tarot is one of the most valuable psycho-spiritual tools we have today. It presents us with the symbols and archetypes that make up our living myth, and thus offers a method of reimbuing our lives with the meaning we've lost.

As tarot scholar Mary K. Greer puts it, the tarot zooms us out of our "little story" and into our "big story." It functions as the mirror that reflects this moment of our personal myth. When we pull cards and then scour our guidebooks, reciting our anxious prayer *but what does it mean?*, we can be sure it's not information or skill we're lacking, but depth. While keywords are helpful, the cards' meaning does not come from some great mind of the past who cracked the code of the unknown; the cards' meaning comes from our question guiding the quest into the unknown within ourselves. If we can use the cards to explore our myth rather than determine how it will end, we will indeed be blessed with the meaning we seek.

The Contemplative Path

The Cloud of Unknowing, a famous Christian mystical text on contemplation of the fathomless mystery of God (written one century before the first known tarot deck was commissioned), begins not by inviting new readers but by rejecting them:

> I charge and beg you, with all the strength and power that love can bring to bear, that whoever you may be who possesses this book ... you should, quite freely and of set purpose, neither read, write, or mention it to anyone, nor allow it to be read, written, or mentioned by anyone unless that person is ... in your estimation, one who has for a long time been doing all that he can to come to the contemplative life by virtue of his active life. Otherwise the book will mean nothing to him.[6]

The author does not discriminate against potential readers because he believes them unworthy, but because they are unready. If the reader is not fully primed for the contemplative path and eager to bring it into active life, then the wisdom of the book will ultimately be wasted on them.

Similarly, if you come to this book unready or uninterested in contemplating the psycho-spiritual path, it will also be mostly meaningless for you. The aim of this book is to act as a guide into greater self-knowledge via the cards, not as a manual for how the cards can fix your life nor as a quick dose of someone else's interpretive wisdom to stand in for your own. Its true purpose is to guide you both toward a deeper relationship with the tarot and toward a deeper relationship with yourself.

Contemplation is the key to inner work of any kind, but particularly so with the tarot. In the medieval Christian world, the contemplative life was one of solitude and serenity devoted to the knowledge and love of God. In our contemporary world, we can see it as one of intuitive presence, accepting the invitation to listen before we act, remaining faithful to a source within ourselves that holds every answer we seek. To live contemplatively means to wonder at what is whole and sacred within us and to approach our lives as the inward journey toward it.

This book will guide you through big ideas and encourage you to flex your cerebral muscles, but ultimately this information is meant to support your own contemplative psycho-spiritual work. I encourage you to embrace being a novitiate (even if you are a longtime tarotist) and to engage with this book as an exercise of revelation with the cards and relationship with yourself. Move intentionally through these pages. Be curious in your investigation of the psyche and its symbolic language. Be uncomfortable, confused, and challenged. Question parts of yourself you've yet to consider. Wander aimlessly through the mystery of the archetypes. Follow the pull of the soul.

Finally, the task of contemplation requires intentionality. This book is crafted to mindfully guide you through not only the cards, but your own depths. My hope is that it helps you learn to trust your own immanent powers of interpretation and inspires you to seek the endless potentialities of the cards within your life. If used as such, it can be a rich resource in the journey of becoming.

Borrowing the words of our sharp-tongued fourteenth-century mystic, I ask that above all you approach the content of this book with an open, contemplative heart: "not continually, maybe, as in the case of true contemplatives, but now and then willing to share in the deep things of contemplation. If such people see this book, by the grace of God they should be much inspired by it."[7]

PART 1

DEPTH PSYCHOLOGY AND THE ARCHETYPAL APPROACH

CHAPTER 1

ROOTS OF THE PSYCHE

Your vision will become clear only when you can look into your own heart. Without, everything seems discordant; only within does it coalesce into unity. Who looks outside dreams; who looks inside awakes.

—CARL JUNG

Jung's greatest psychological discovery came to him in a dream. He found himself in a house decorated as a nineteenth-century salon, filled with Baroque furniture and antique paintings. He descended to the lower floor which brought him into the dark gloom of a medieval manor. He then made his way down yet again and stepped into an ancient Roman cellar. From that level he believed he could go no further, until he spotted a hatch in the stone floor. Opening it, he found a ladder and descended once more into a rough-hewn cave scattered with the bones and pottery shards from a lost primitive world.

What Jung understood from this dream is that the psyche is not two-storied as Freud had argued, split between what we consciously know and what we've unconsciously repressed. Instead, the psyche is layered and deep, descending below the personal into the collective, the ancient, the primordial. This inspired his theories of the collective unconscious and the archetypes, which drew his psychology out of the narrow cell of the consulting room and into the greater world of myth, symbol, and our human heritage.

Because Jung explored these metaphysical and spiritual realities of the psyche, his work is often disregarded as being more mystical than scientific, and though Jung himself avidly denied it, there is a kernel of truth in this criticism. His psychology is not based on replicable data as much as a profound, intuitive comprehension of human nature, but for many this is what makes it so potent and alive. In our modern world exhausted by empirical absolutism, we are eager to validate not what can be proved to us, but what can *move* us. In our bleak contemporary landscape of technological dominion, listless consumerism, and corporate burnout, we have become a world yearning to remember its inherent mystery, magic, and meaning—its *depth*.

Still, Jung's psychology is a psychology. It is built upon discernible psychological phenomena and methodologies, and to understand its significance for our own inner work, we must have a foundation in its core principles. In this chapter we will explore the key tenets of Jungian thought essential for our understanding of the cards, including the process of individuation, the strata of the psyche, the archetypes, and synchronicity.

The Process of Individuation

Jungian depth psychology is, at its core, about the process of individuation, the endeavor of coming to selfhood. Individuation has two complementary aims. On one hand, it is the practical effort of differentiating our unique selves from the masses by pushing back external influence and centering internal direction. On the other, it is the mystical pursuit of reconciliation between ego and Self—the small I and the big I—to become a unified, whole being.

We often focus on objectives such as "personal growth" or "raising our vibration," the core idea being a linear, even teleological development from a lower state to a higher one. However, in Jung's concept of individuation we reject this linear path. Instead we view inner development as a spiral, moving us up and down, back and forth, always rotating around the unchanging center of who we are. Thus, individuation is not about progress but *process*. It is the gradual maturation of the psyche as it slowly integrates unconscious contents (such as complexes, archetypes, and shadow) into consciousness. In this process we are not aiming to correct parts of ourselves but to embrace all of ourselves. We seek a state of wholeness in which we achieve harmony between the inner and outer, our conscious and unconscious halves. With each hard-won moment of self-reckoning in which we reconcile these fragments of ourselves, we are both closer to that state of wholeness and closer to the central, unchanging truth of who we are. As Jung writes:

> Individuation appears, on the one hand, as the synthesis of a new unity which previously consisted of scattered particles, and on the other hand, as the revelation of something which existed before the ego and is in fact its father or creator and also its totality.[1]

In its two capacities, individuation reveals our particular uniqueness, our specialness, our individuality, while also reuniting us with that primordial essence of our selfhood, which we may call soul or Self or even God.

Individuation occurs continually and naturally in all of us, but dedicated therapeutic tools like the tarot can support the process. With each card we find ourselves plugged into an archetypal or psychological experience that reveals something about ourselves, that unearths one of these "scattered particles." The tarot provides symbols and reflections that act as a mirror through which we might better recognize and ultimately embrace what has been hidden, misunderstood, or neglected within us.

Individuation is not a process of ascension. We should not romanticize it, picturing ourselves picking up seeds of enlightenment along the forest path. Individuation comes from the work of holding what Jung called the tension of the opposites—the ceaseless series of inner conflicts between who the ego tells us we are and what the Self knows we are. It is this tension that creates both suffering and the spark of life, cracking through to let in new insight and usher us along that ceaseless spiral.

The Strata of the Psyche

Let us now excavate Jung's dream levels of the psyche. First, we should reiterate that the psyche is split between the two complementary but opposing realms: consciousness and unconsciousness. Consciousness is, in essence, all the psychic (meaning psychological) processes and information that is known to us. Unconsciousness, on the other hand, is all the psychic material that is unknown, forgotten, obstructed, repressed, or otherwise hidden, rendering it invisible though nonetheless present.

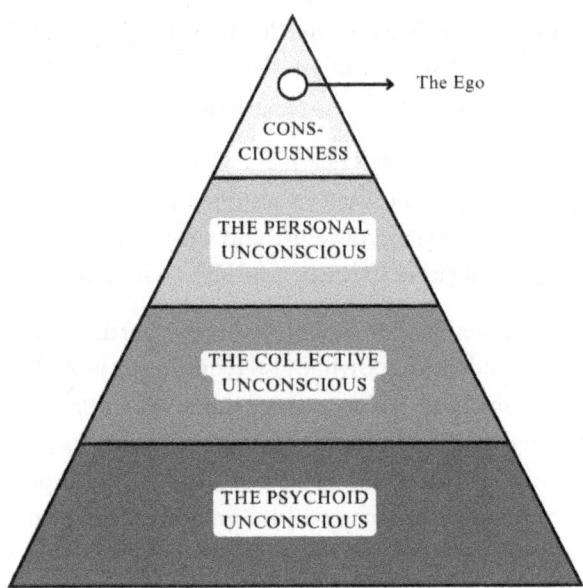

Figure 3. Diagram of the Psyche

This diagram demonstrates Jung's four strata of the psyche. At the very top we see consciousness, which is, very simply, everything we are aware of and experience firsthand. Here we might imagine ourselves standing in Jung's nineteenth-century salon, surrounded by all that is familiar to us (or would have been in Jung's era, at least). At the center of the field of consciousness is the ego (Latin for "I"), the seat of self-identity. Though there's a pervasive negative connotation attached to the word today, in depth psychology ego is an essential part of the psyche. The ego is you as you know it, with all of your particular desires, skills, anxieties, likes and dislikes, and everything else unique to you.

We descend now into the first realm of the unconscious, finding ourselves in that musty medieval manor. This stratum, which Jung called the personal unconscious, holds our repressed, forgotten, and subliminal material. It contains only what is unique to us, such as our suppressed traumas, lost memories, and rejected flaws, as well as our individual complexes and shadows.

While Freudian psychology generally tells us this is the limit of the unconscious space, Jungian psychology delves deeper. Now we go down into those Roman ruins, into the stratum of unconsciousness that is ancient and universal to all. Jung calls this the collective unconscious, which he describes as containing "the whole spiritual heritage of mankind's evolution, born anew in the brain structure of every individual."[2] The concept of the collective unconscious was inspired by Jung's observation of images, motifs, and symbols which repeat around the globe, regardless of geography, time, or culture. This content is collective because it appears as abundantly in mythology and iconography as it does in our individual dreams. The collective unconscious is the container of transpersonal human experience, the realm in which archetypes reside.

Jung may have been the first to formally define the collective unconscious, but it has always been an innate human fascination. As far back as our oldest attempts at storytelling, we have been enchanted with tales of the hero going off into the forest or the cave or the sea, symbolically plumbing the depths of unconscious mystery. And as tarotists, belief in the reality of the collective unconscious is not only undeniable; it's essential. If the seventy-eight cards express the range of human experience, then our experience must have shared foundations. Each card we pull speaks to our individual lives, but does so by communicating some core elemental or archetypal truth.

Still, there is another layer to go. Now we open the trapdoor and slip down into the primordial cave filled with bones and lost fragments, entering the stratum Jung called psychoid unconsciousness. Though a somewhat obscure concept even among Jungian theorists, the idea of the psychoid is Jung's attempt to explain the relationship between psychology and physics—the interplay between psyche and matter. Jung believed that there was a layer of unconsciousness we never access consciously, but nonetheless presents material spontaneously and autonomously. For example, maybe you dream that your friend is having a baby, only to get the call with the very same news the next day, or you are overwhelmed with tension when you walk into a coffee shop and then suddenly an altercation breaks out. The psychoid is more of a metaphysical than psychological theory, but as tarotists we are no strangers to a little magical abstraction.

It is this psychoid space that facilitates divination, for, as von Franz suggests, at this depth "the unconscious *knows* things; it knows the past and future, it knows things about other people ... and this knowledge of the unconscious Jung calls absolute knowledge."[3] Here we have the mystery that we cannot (and probably should not) try to explain. As Jung himself would argue, it is the activation of the psychoid unconscious that chooses the cards we draw. And it is our receptivity to the psychoid that allows us to occasionally brush against this "absolute knowledge" presented via the cards, likely appearing as senses and flashes that seem to come from nowhere.

The tarot works through the cooperation of all the strata of the psyche at once. We begin in the psychoid space, drawing a card chosen from the root of that vast unconscious mystery, then connect to it in the realm of collective archetypal wisdom, then make sense of it through our personal hidden truths, and finally feel it settle into our conscious awareness and the clarity of the ego-mind.

Demystifying Archetypes

The theory of archetypes is both Jung's most well-known and most widely misunderstood concept. For those with only a peripheral grasp—whether shaped by perusing internet lists or getting lost in the tangled rhetoric of post-Jungian discourse—archetypes are often mistaken for personality types, reduced to twelve or sixteen clickable labels. In reality, an archetype is not a fixed identity but a container for a fundamental expression of human experience. As Jung himself emphasized, archetypes are something we can identify within ourselves, but not something we can identify *as*. We cannot be an archetype any more than we can be an idea, a feeling, or a god.

To understand the concept of archetypes, we must look back to Plato's *eidos* or Forms. According to Plato, all that we experience in the physical world is an imitation of the timeless, immutable essences that exist in a higher spiritual reality. These Forms are imprinted in the soul before birth, containing the inherent knowledge of their individual perfection. There is a divine Form of an elm tree, a Form of a father, a Form of friendship, a Form of individual will. These Forms act as blueprints, shaping our intuitive understanding of what things are and what they can become. An elm tree does not need to be told how tall it can grow to bloom into its fullest expression, just as we do not need an explanation of what true friendship means to know that we have it.

Plato's Forms provide the foundation for Jung's archetypes, though Jung conceptualized them not as perfected ideals but as primordial images, the universal thought-forms residing in the collective unconscious. Archetypes are not static. They are fluid and dynamic, adapting to different cultures and historical periods while their fundamental essences remain unchanged. They are not fixed objects, figures, or principles but rather living patterns of meaning that shape human experience. The Great Mother is an archetype, as is the Hero, the Maiden, Hope, Apocalypse, and Love. Regardless of whether one is born on the Eurasian Steppe ten thousand years ago or in twenty-first-century urban America, these deep structures of the psyche persist, shaping the way we experience the world.

Where people often become stuck in understanding archetypes is how, with their various names and presentations, we find the thread that connects them. The key is to remember that because of their mutability, they do not always appear in the same shapes (think of the difference between the Wise Old Man archetype in Yoda versus Gandalf) and are rarely experienced in isolation without other symbols or images (what is the damsel without her savior?). Therefore, to determine the core of an archetype, we must examine its innate characteristics. Von Franz explains:

> Every archetype is a relatively closed energetic system, the energetic stream of which runs through all aspects of the collective unconscious. . . . Therefore, although we have to recognize the indefinable vagueness of an archetypal image, we must discipline ourselves to chisel sharp outlines which throw the different aspects into bold relief. We must get as close as possible to the specific, determinate, "just so" character of each image and try to express the very specific character of the psychic situation which is contained in it.[4]

When exploring an archetype, our task is to discover its "just-so" qualities—what makes it unique and specific without limiting it to a fixed package. Archetypes are ineffable, but not indiscernible. Though we cannot categorize an archetype with a clipboard and a checklist, we can, as von Franz continues, "circumscribe it on the basis of our own psychological experience and from comparative studies, bringing up in to light, as it were, the whole net of associations in which the archetypal images are enmeshed."[5]

The tarot gives us a collection of seventy-eight images illuminating the core archetypal experiences of living. When we pull a card and feel that prickling of the skin, that swelling of the heart, we know we're encountering something archetypal in nature, something that exists both within and beyond us. We are plugged into a constellated archetype within our psyche, and our task is to consciously explore it.

I'll offer a personal example to concretize this. As a child I had enormous reverence for my grandfather, whom I like to describe as an armchair theologian. Over the years, this reverence extended to other white-haired men who possessed great wisdom, one of whom was Carl Jung. When I read Jung's work or browsed my grandfather's trove of books, I felt not only appreciation but *awe*. All my intellectual or spiritual pursuits were, to some degree, efforts to prove my worth to these masters. Though I did not know it yet, they reflected an active archetype within me, one I came to know vaguely as the Old Knowledge-Keeper.

After years of meeting this Old Knowledge-Keeper archetype in books and teachers, I at last decided to seek my own knowledge and get my master's degree. A few days before the semester began, the archetype appeared in the following dream:

> I am brought to the Jung Institute by a classmate. I am a bit embarrassed, shy, and feeling that I am an imposter who does not belong here. A woman sits behind a desk, and as she checks my name on the list, she says, "Finally I can put a face to the name! I've enjoyed seeing what you've been studying." I feel relieved that perhaps I am welcome after all. Then I hear male voices coming from upstairs. I walk up the stairs (which look just like the stairs to my grandfather's attic library) and see Jung sitting in a chair with two analysts perched on the step below him. They do not see me because they are swept up in a passionate psychological discussion. Again, I feel unworthy and don't dare to approach. I watch Jung, who looks off in contemplation.

By entering Jung's institute in the dream, I metaphorically entered the archetype's domain. My dream-ego's nervousness highlighted the real-world discomfort I'd felt (unconsciously, of course) in integrating the archetype and developing my own intellectual authority. Enthroned at the top of the stairs, the archetype of the Old Knowledge-Keeper still sat "on high" and I did not believe myself worthy to approach.

Barely a month after this dream, I opened my first Rider-Waite-Smith tarot deck and drew the Hierophant card, which I recognized as a near exact replica of my dream image. I realized then that by projecting this archetypal Old Knowledge-Keeper onto my idols, I had trapped myself as a supplicant who could never become the source of knowledge herself. Through a slow, effortful process, I worked to form a new relationship with the archetype, learning to embody his wisdom for myself. It was several years later and a month before welcoming the first class of students into my *Archetypal Tarot School* that I stood in Jung's home library in Zurich and realized the change in me. Rather than being overcome by awe and that old belief that I'd never be worthy to earn his knowledge, I felt sincerely grounded and confident in all I had learned from him.

Though I first encountered this archetype years before I had any knowledge of the Hierophant card, they were nonetheless one and the same. Just as von Franz suggests, I realized this through personal psychological experience and the comparative study of both my own dream imagery and the imagery of the card. I have called it by many names, visualizing a priest in a temple, a psychoanalyst in an office, and my grandfather in his brown Lay-Z-Boy, but the archetype at the center remained unchanged. It was still the same Form—the old, masterful sage with a holy knowledge only he can teach—and with the tarot's guidance I was at last able to consciously explore and integrate it.

Before we move on, it's important to establish definitions for the five main archetypes that we'll be discussing throughout this book. These are the most fundamental thought-forms in our psyche, the core parts of how we experience ourselves. These are ego, shadow, persona, anima/animus, and Self.

1. The Ego

Though Eastern spirituality encourages us to transcend the ego, in Western depth psychology we must preserve the ego in order to have an individual experience of living. As we already mentioned, the ego is not our self-centeredness but our self-identity—the I that seeks self-realization, clarity, and self-knowledge. The ego is the archetype of the conscious dreamer who navigates the unconscious dream of the psyche, or as Jung described it, it is the candle flame against the vast, subsuming dark. It is akin to the archetypal hero within us, the center of the personality who believes itself to be the center of its universe. Thus, while it is the seat of our consciousness, its view is limited to only what it knows, and it is resistant to all it does not.

2. The Shadow

The shadow is often misunderstood as the "bad" or negative within us, but in reality it encompasses everything that has been split off from the ego and relegated to the unconscious. While it does contain traits the ego deems intolerable—such as envy, rage, or selfishness—it also holds suppressed strengths, forgotten talents, and unlived potential that, for whatever reason, we've refused. Buried within the shadow are forgotten memories, suppressed traumas, and abandoned desires—all that has been cast into the dark.

Yet the shadow is never truly lost. It reveals itself constantly, through fits of denial or stubborn projections and a host of other furtive ways. The ego, needing to maintain its self-image, instinctively wards off any insight from the shadow. To confront it is to dismantle our illusions of perfection, forcing us into the difficult but necessary work of self-reconciliation.

3. The Persona

The persona is the outward-facing expression of our identity. While it is sometimes condemned as a "mask" or a fake representation of self we present, it is an important barrier between the judgments of the outer world and the vulnerability of the inner soul.

The persona only becomes problematic when we overidentify with it and prevent the flexibility to present our true nature. For example, we might believe ourselves to be the business rather than its creator and thus suffer its failures personally, or we might insist we are a "good friend," boiling with the many grievances we refuse to voice. We must remember that we are not *what* we do or the role we play, we are the doer and the player behind it.

4. The Anima/Animus

Jung identifies the anima and animus as the "soul-image" who ferries us to deeper communication with the unconscious. As the "contrasexual" archetypes, the anima exists in the male psyche, appearing perhaps as a sort of mother or muse—a figure that imbues the man with feeling and love—while the animus exists in the female psyche, possibly as a spiritual guide, inspiring her to agency and enterprise.[*]

This is one of Jung's most controversial theories, and it's important to remember that Jung and his colleagues were naturally indoctrinated into the patriarchal conditioning of the mid-twentieth century. Some contemporary depth psychologists believe the anima and animus should not be limited to gender and exist in us all to various degrees. (We'll touch back in on this idea in our discussion of the first six cards of the Major Arcana.) Despite the criticism, there is something undeniably powerful to be drawn from these archetypes, as they are the foundation of our concepts of Divine Masculine and Divine Feminine, which are essential to our modern archetypal language.[†]

---

[*] There are many ways that the anima and animus can manifest in the psyche, and these are only common examples.

[†] Here and throughout the book, the capitalization of *Masculine* and *Feminine* points to these concepts as archetypal energies. The lowercase *masculine* and *feminine* are used as regular adjectives to describe social constructs.

5. The Self

The Self is by far the most ineffable of Jung's archetypes. Jung describes it both as the totality of the individual and as a sort of *imago dei* or God image alive within each human being. The Self points to both what we might call our individual "higher Self" and the experience of a transpersonal source of being that exists within us all. Ultimately, the Self transcends the ego and is the goal of individuation—the thing we are trying to discover within us. It is the archetype of wholeness, encapsulating, in the psychological sense, the unification of our conscious and unconscious halves, and in the spiritual sense, a meeting of our human and divine natures.

We will be discussing the Self often throughout this book (sometimes calling it *soul*), but we do not need to overintellectualize it. It's the sacred seed of *youness* that is both entirely personal and extends beyond you. It is, to put it in Platonic terms, the great Form of you that you both already are and can become.

Synchronicity and the Oracle

The greatest mystery of the tarot is how it works. How do we manage to pull the cards that reveal the exact wisdom or truth we most need? The answer, simply, is through the principle of synchronicity. Another Jungian idea that has been distorted in mainstream terminology, Jung's theory of synchronicity was inspired by decades of observing how seemingly random external events have profound resonance in psychological development. Indeed, more than these things having resonance, they seem to speak directly to the individual's psyche and have a deep impact on their individuation.

Synchronicity can be defined simply as "meaningful coincidence" of inner and outer happenings without causal connection (that is, related by direct cause). Today we often use the term to describe striking repetitions or special signs that catch our eye, but the most important part of these meaningful coincidences is the *meaning*. In order for something to qualify as a synchronicity, it must have real meaning or psychological significance for us.

Jung studied this phenomenon seriously, even enlisting the collaboration of Nobel Prize–winning physicist Wolfgang Pauli in his quest to discover its scientific foundations. He proposed that the inner world of the psyche and the outer world of matter are intrinsically linked and used the alchemical concept of the *unus mundus* as the cornerstone of his theory. Latin for "one world," the unus mundus suggests that the world is woven with an underlying metaphysical fabric that unifies all existence. Again this idea dates as far back as Plato and suggests that all things are interconnected and directed by that greater "absolute knowledge." This is both a spiritual idea and a practical one. While the true nature of this greater knowledge can never be known, the universal experience of seemingly disparate elements interacting in meaningful ways is undeniable. In essence, if both our psyches and the material world originate from the same source, they may indeed reflect and inform each other.

Most of us understand synchronicities as those repeating symbolic glimmers (such as seeing butterflies for weeks) and electrifying coincidences (such as thinking of an old friend just as they text), but I would like to again offer a personal example to demonstrate the *meaning* within this phenomenon.

I have a friend who is known by all as a profoundly dependable, competent person. Though typically laid-back and optimistic, when an issue arises he has a superhuman ability to rush in, take control, and save the day. This tremendous power developed in childhood when, as the son of immigrant parents, he learned how to support and manage every need of the family. As he grew into adulthood, his family continued to rely on his competency, and as the years passed, it was clear that his tremendous strength was beginning to exhaust him.

Though warned by many to slow down and be attentive to his own needs, when yet another crisis arose my friend again ran to his family's aid. When he was pulled over for speeding and asked to do a sobriety test, he was surprised and confused but did not lose his composure. However, as he stepped forward, he was dismayed to find his legs wobbling and trembling as if they'd lost all strength. No matter how hard he tried to force his muscles to respond, he had lost all control over his body. Though the Breathalyzer proved his sobriety, my friend was left deeply rattled.

As he recounted this story to me, I joked that it seemed he was finally stopped in his rush to save the day, and the comment clearly struck him. I asked if perhaps his sudden affliction of physical powerlessness mirrored his powerlessness to control everything for his family. Instantly that strange, electric pulse that often heralds the culmination of a synchronicity filled the room. It was suddenly evident how directly this outer event reflected his inner one and the profound meaning it had for him.

We could of course label this event a coincidence (which it is), but we cannot deny the mystery and significance of its *meaning*. My friend needed the symbol of being "pulled over," being forced to stop in his rush to fix and save in order to finally feel what he'd been suppressing. Below his competency was a frightened little boy whose legs literally shook with the weight of the world on top of him. In finally being halted, that inner child's fear manifested both physically and symbolically, and a door was opened between this unconscious experience and his conscious orientation. Now, at last, understanding and change were possible.

Synchronicities can be large and potent or small and muted. Sometimes the meaning breaks through suddenly, as it did with my friend, or it might be subtle and slow, unfolding over weeks or months. Synchronicities can arise at any time, but they tend to intensify when we are at a pivotal stage of our individuation process, which, of course, is also when we tend to reach for our decks.

Divination is a form of synchronicity. When we consult the cards—the physical matter of the outer world—we are presented with a reflection of our own inner psychic experience. The images, numbers, colors, gestures—though conceived by another's imagination and pulled entirely at random—take on *personal meaning*. Cynics argue that divination cannot reliably reflect our psychological condition, but as von Franz says, the only difference between scientific analysis and divination is that "the experiment eliminates chance, the oracle makes chance the center."[6]

Placing the principle of synchronicity at the center of our divination transforms this element of chance from utter randomness to mysterious intentionality. The card that comes is drawn by the cooperation of our individual psyche and physical matter via the unus mundus, the one united world. And though we cannot explain this phenomenon (not yet at least), remember that von Franz suggests that divination contacts the "dynamic load" of an activated archetype within us. In other words, when we use the tarot, we are not necessarily reaching for some divine intelligence to tell us what we're meant to do, nor are we simply manufacturing meaning from pictures on cardstock; we're submerging into the living potency of our own archetypal experiences in order to truly understand them.

Keep in mind that reading the cards as inner realities does not exclude their application for outer ones. In fact, the tarot often points toward both at once. This is because, as the principle of synchronicity shows, what happens outside of us is not at all unrelated to what's happening within us. This is the heart of the hermetical maxim "As above, so below," which is often completed with "as within, so without." What is "above," metaphorically outside of ourselves, is in harmony with what is "below," within ourselves. The tarot works through the undetectable, ineffable, mystical connection between psyche and matter—the human soul and the molecular machinations of the universe.

As tarotists, or any manner of diviner, we must have faith in the principle of synchronicity. We must trust the oracle—the divinatory device—to be the medium through which synchronicities can emerge. We must remember that the outer and the inner are one. The cards that come are true.

— CHAPTER 2 —

ARCHETYPAL METHODS AND TECHNIQUES

The true Tarot is symbolism; it speaks no other language and offers no other signs. Given the inward meaning of its emblems, they do become a kind of alphabet which is capable of indefinite combinations and makes true sense in all.

—A. E. WAITE

The tarot speaks the language of symbol, the cipher for which is redefined in each individual consulting the cards. We can learn from our gurus and growing stack of tarot books, but the meaning of the cards and how they apply to our lives are ultimately ours to decode. It is in both learning the depth and breadth of the cards *and* practicing sincere self-contemplation that we develop the skills to effectively translate the tarot's messages of wisdom.

This practice of self-contemplation is generally what we mean when we discuss inner "work." In any practice dedicated to inner work, our goal is to manifest the true depth and potency of our individual selves, which requires the concentrated effort of transposing the potentials of our personality from unconscious dormancy into conscious actualization. This is accomplished by self-excavation—diving into what is wounded, uncomfortable, hidden, or ignored so that we might heal or move closer to a state of wholeness. That is a reason why we call it work: it requires commitment, intentionality, and a methodology.

In this chapter, we will explore frameworks for this methodology, introducing approaches to working with the cards psycho-spiritually.

Whether through our discussions in this book or the cards you pull, when something is sparked in you, be it curiosity or frustration, take it as an invitation. Allow yourself to pause, consider, investigate. What resonates with something in your own life? Where do you feel the surge of emotion, confusion, or connection? Where is that swirl of energy rising out of and what is it drawing you toward? Though the following techniques are designed to help you enhance your work with the cards, they are also methods to help you meet yourself.

Finally, remember that rather than a formulaic approach to the cards, we should develop a philosophical one. We generally go to our decks looking for solutions or answers, hoping that they will solve our crises and secure our future, but the function of tarot is not to relieve us from the tension of living. In fact, we might say that the tarot's purpose is to help us *hold* that tension. It offers us the momentary insight to discern our desires, feel our complexity, and locate the source of our conflicts. As a philosophical tool, the tarot teaches us how to exist in the both/and, where we are poised between the little story and the big story, the everyday self and the higher Self.*

Building Relationship with the Cards

Too often the sole focus for beginner readers is memorization, believing that if they can mentally store seventy-eight keywords (or 156 with reversals) they will be able to interpret any card in any reading. But as with learning a new language, all the vocabulary we drill gets lost when we're shoved into a conversation. This is because forced memorization, while effective for a short time, is devoid of *meaning*. We might successfully list off keywords by rote, but we are not able to comprehend the card with any real depth.

The trick to learning the cards and retaining their meaning is not forcing mastery but cultivating relationship. Applying an assigned definition from a guidebook is far less effective in determining meaning

---

* Throughout this book, whenever the word *self* is lowercased, it refers to a personal experience of selfhood at the ego level, the small self, and when it is capitalized as *Self*, it refers to the bigger, archetypal and divine Self.

than contemplating how the cards appear as the real archetypes, figures, or experiences within our psyche. Each time we draw a card we must see it as the initiation of a new conversation, inspired and guided by our references and keywords but not defined by them. When we actually listen to the card, it speaks. When we *relate* to the image, it comes alive.

In order to forge relationships with our cards, we must interact with them. This requires a more intentional, slow-moving practice in which we can actually listen, reflect, and probe their many layers of wisdom. Pulling fewer cards less often affords us this time and space to explore their dimensions with greater reverence. You may also want to start a tarot journal in which you record your reflections. You might begin your entries by referencing a guidebook or jotting down some meanings, but the purpose of a tarot journal is to process and record your personal, intuitive reactions. Engaging the card at this level will automatically encourage greater intimacy with it.

For example, journaling with the Ten of Wands might look something like:

> *The Ten of Wands shows a man struggling with a heavy load. My guidebook tells me I should consider how much I can actually "cope with," and I sense this has something to do with carrying the emotional load in my relationship. I can see that I'm overburdened right now and need to put some of that down. However, I worry that if I do, no one else will pick it up. I'm pushing against a weight I can't manage alone, but at the same time I'm afraid that if I ask for it no help will come. What else can I do but keep holding it up and try to move forward? This is the Weight of the World that Cannot Be Dropped.*

By moving beyond the traditional keywords and connecting to the deeper feelings and responses, the card becomes a symbol. It activates a metaphor conveying an individual experience that brings the card to life while also highlighting the wisdom needed to potentially resolve the inner conflict. Rather than "know" what the card means, we have initiated a relationship with it via personal meaning.*

Strengthening Intuitive Clarity

In the spiritual sense of the word, intuition is spontaneous information received from an unknown internal source; in the psychological sense, it is the mode of perception that draws directly from the unconscious. We often expect intuition to occur as that sudden burst of clairvoyant insight, but more often it comes as a creeping, spreading unconscious awareness that mixes with our preexisting desires and anxieties. Therefore, intuitions rarely feel clear, and so we can't help but want confirmation.

This is typically when we pull those "clarifier cards," and though they can sometimes bring illumination, more often than not they muddle rather than sharpen our readings. Adding clarifiers (or any other extra divined bits of information) contributes yet another layer of complexity, which we will likely struggle to make sense of. When we place the emphasis on *connection* rather than clarity, we make room for intuition to rise fully and organically (though more slowly). Then our task is to learn how to strengthen our trust in it.

If a spark of meaning comes through with a card, even if it feels brittle and unsure, sit with that token of wisdom and investigate it. Release the demand to know with your intellect and center your attention on what *feels* true. It is important to be willing to be wrong. In fact, being wrong is excellent information for evaluating the way you uniquely sense your intuition. Notice the subtle differences you experience when you are wrong versus when you are right. Keep in mind as well that not all intuitions will lead to positive insights, so when intuiting things that may feel disappointing or scary, hold them lightly as a question rather than a judgment.

---

* Of course, working with the cards in this more intimate way, it's inevitable that we will come up with an interpretation that contradicts our guidebooks. While there is undeniable value in having a standardized set of keywords for the seventy-eight cards, remember the tarot does not speak in definitives. When your readings are both flexible and personal, you will bond with the cards much more quickly.

Intuition is generally not experienced intellectually but somatically. The unconscious—the source of intuition—does not exist only in the dark corners of the mind, but in the blood, the muscle of the heart, our very cells. We can connect with it as deeply within the wisdom of the body as within the wilderness of our dreams. When we feel something—a tingle, a throb, a shiver—believe it. Always follow the energy. Trust what the body knows rather than pressuring the mind to make it all make sense.

The Power of the Question

As Ursula K. Le Guin writes, "There's no right answer to the wrong question."[1] We generally come to our decks with a specific question seeking a specific answer. But rather than give such answers, the tarot's real gift is to point us toward the *better question*. There is always a truer question that might reveal the blind spots, motivations, and denials behind our uncertainty. In our archetypal approach, we want to be guided toward these better questions that prompt deeper self-inquiry and exploration.

Finding this better question requires that our inquiries be open-ended, leaving as much room for interpretation as possible. (There is nothing more frustrating for a beginner tarotist than squeezing a card to fit an overly narrow question while rigidly trying to preserve its guidebook-assigned meaning.) To make your questions more open-ended, first **consider the feeling or thought behind it**. Next, **reflect on what answer you most need or hope to receive**. When you blend these together, you should arrive at something both broader and more precise. For example:

INITIAL QUESTION	THE QUESTION BEHIND IT
"Should I take that job?"	*"Why am I so nervous about moving on?"*
"Does she really love me?"	*"What is the source of my insecurity in this relationship?"*
"Should I move out of my parents' house?"	*"How do I know I'm ready to take control of my life?"*

With this level of openness, pulling the Two of Cups when asking about a new job won't stump us or get us speculating about office romances, but instead allow us to explore our inner struggle—maybe our need for greater reciprocity at work. The aim is not to "get it" and move on, but to investigate our relationship to our inner experience so that we may better understand its influence on the outer one.

If broadening your questions is a challenge, setting an intention may be more beneficial. With questions, we're looking for answers; with intentions, we're seeking conscientious change. The subtle shift from *What will happen?* to *Help me prepare myself for what's to come* can make an enormous difference in the direction of a reading. In setting intentions, we are attuning to our immediate experience and drawing out the tension hidden within our need to know.

For example, if you seek guidance in an important decision, before asking what's the right choice, again consider both what feelings or thoughts motivated that question and what you hope to learn from the cards. Perhaps you feel deadlocked and need to understand why, or maybe you've already intuited what's right but are reluctant to commit without validation. Gathering up these insights, your intention may be: *I feel pulled in two different directions and can't sense which one I really want*, or *I need to understand my hesitation in accepting this decision*. The specificity of such intentions will bring much more clarity and nuance to your interpretations of the cards.

Of course, this broadening of the question or intention makes it difficult to run to our decks seeking solace after situations such as a breakup or a loss. We don't want to inquire about the deeper meaning of our heartbreak when all we really want to know is if this is really happening. As von Franz recommends, divination is most effective when there is no immediate emergency at hand, and there is a valid reason for this. Because divination works by responding to "the dynamic load of an archetypal constellation," when an archetype is evoked in our psyche, the resulting intensification of psycho-dynamic energy is generally what the cards reflect back. When we come to our deck in an emotional storm, it is those emotions—denial, rage, despair—that become the constellated archetype that the cards mirror. It is best to allow the storm to settle before engaging with the cards or recenter your intention on the state you are in. Then you will be freer to tap into the true question you need to bring to the reading.

The Active Imagination Technique

During his own period of "confrontation with the unconscious," Jung formulated the active imagination technique to directly communicate and engage with it. This method sits somewhere between meditation and lucid dreaming, using symbols or images drawn from our dreams, synchronicities, or spontaneous fantasies to consciously initiate an episode of imaginative fantasy guided by the unconscious. In our archetypal tarot practice, we draw these symbols or images from the cards we pull.

It is an excellent technique to use when we pull the same card repeatedly, or when a card seriously confuses us, or when we simply feel that there's something *more* we're meant to uncover. Just keep in mind that, as Jung often warned, engaging the unconscious does not come without risk. This work can sometimes feel overwhelming and disorienting when big things arise. It's always recommended to check in with someone before and after, and make sure you feel supported.

Step 1: Lower the Mental Level

Because our goal is to facilitate communication between our unconscious and conscious minds, it is important to be psychologically primed and receptive. Jung described a state of suppressed consciousness called the *abaissement du niveau mental*—the lowered mental level—in which we can soften our concentration and loosen our inhibition. There is no set way to access this state, but we know we've achieved it when we are open and somewhat detached from the ego. My personal technique of mental lowering is to visualize the sun slowly sinking through the sky until I find myself in the darkness of the soul-space. You might also spend a few minutes in traditional meditation or initiate a breathwork sequence. Whatever you choose, the purpose is to bring yourself to a state of presence and receptivity without mental focus.

Step 2: Move through the Imaginal Realm

Recall the image of the card you're working with or open your eyes to take it in. When ready, let go of the illustration on the card and conjure the image within your own imagination. Perhaps you see the Hermit, or feel the King of Cups watching you, or find yourself in the wide meadow of the Four of Wands. Now the unconscious speaks. Allow whatever you encounter to guide you or reveal something to you, but do not let the ego interrupt and direct. Let yourself be transported into the archetypal world, however it comes. Everything within this space has meaning, so be attentive.

If you do sense the ego trying to push the plot forward, gently remind yourself to let go. And if nothing happens when you begin (which can be common at first), try initiating a dialogue or drawing your attention to a specific element of the scene. Of course if anything becomes too intense during the process, you always have permission to exit. It may also be helpful to set a timer to bring yourself back in case you do get a little lost in the inner wilds.

Step 3: Record and Express

Once you feel the episode has come to its natural conclusion, immediately record your experience. This is not an intellectual exercise, but a time to engage your sense of creativity and play, paying close attention to what you felt and sensed. Expression is the key to this stage, as you want to preserve your connection to imagination. Use any art form you enjoy, such as painting, movement, or writing to capture the depth and significance of the experience, and don't get bogged down with perfection or precision. If this feels challenging for you, you may want to try one of the following prompts:

> *Draw the emotions you felt.*
>
> *Write a stream-of-consciousness description of what you saw, tasted, smelled, felt, and heard.*
>
> *Move your body in a way that reflects what you wanted or feared in the scene.*
>
> *Speak aloud whatever words encapsulate the core of the experience.*

Step 4: Amplify and Analyze

Amplification is the word Jung used to describe the work of exploring and developing the significance of symbols within both the personal and collective unconscious. If, perhaps, you met the Hermit in your active imagination and he led you to a peak under the crescent moon, you might explore your personal associations with the crescent moon (such as a memory it brings up or subjective feeling it engenders), and then move on to researching its symbolic significance in myth and art.

After amplifying whatever symbols seemed significant, you can now analyze the experience. Keep in mind this is not about psychoanalyzing ourselves, but about opening a line of communication with the unconscious. For example, if your work of amplification leads you to connect the crescent moon to ancient fertility rites, you may wonder if the scene is showing that the path of solitude will bring you to a place of new spiritual fertility and growth. Or you may consider your personal association of dread with the crescent moon and investigate what you fear the Hermit is guiding you toward. Be curious, not critical. Your analysis should come fluidly, but not necessarily immediately, so do not force it.

The Alchemical Shadow Work Technique

Shadow work is an extremely popular method of self-deepening, but we must be careful how we approach it. Shadow work is not what we would consider self-care. It is not simply an exercise in confronting your bad behaviors or working through your inhibitions. The shadow is all that is pushed away and foreign to the ego, and so shadow work is the lifetime process of slow, intentional integration—meeting the shadow, embracing it, and discovering its creative potential within us. As depth psychologists Connie Zweig and Steve Wolf put it:

> To live with shadow awareness is to turn away from the peaks toward the valleys, away from the heights and the rarified air, toward the depths and the dark and the dense. It is to turn toward the

unpleasant thoughts, hidden fantasies, marginal feelings that are so taboo. To live with shadow awareness is to move our eyes from up to down, to relinquish the clarity of blue-sky thinking for the uncertain murkiness of a foggy morning.[2]

To seek knowledge of the shadow is a heroic pursuit. The ego naturally fears the shadow because in confronting it—particularly that which tells us we're equally villain and hero—we inevitably face a crack-up and a reckoning. We question the very nature of who we believe ourselves to be, and we must be unfailingly honest. As intense as it is, this is work that actually changes us. It holds the key to unlocking our creativity and potential, empowering us to live as the Fool—authentically, boldly, wholly.

However, we must be wary of trying to heal or transcend our shadows. Shadow work is a process of acceptance and integration, not repair. To work with the shadow, we must in a way befriend it, viewing it as a mystery to be unfolded rather than a curse to be rectified. For the shadow lives in the same depths as the soul, and the soul does not discriminate between dark and light. It is faithful only to what is true.

We regularly encounter cards that connect us to some aspect of shadow. Cards that confuse us, agitate us, or contradict us generally reveal exactly what it is that the ego is refusing to see. If we believe we may have identified a shadow card—whether by its placement in a spread, its inversion, or simply the discomfort it creates—we can mindfully bring it into an alchemical shadow work practice. Remember that our task here is to temporarily abandon ego-certainty and be willing to ask questions we've never before considered and entertain what we're most afraid to be true. Also keep in mind that the delicacy of this work requires us to be tenderly scientific in our approach. We must do our best to mute our biases and judgments and be both objective and compassionate.

To begin identifying a shadow card, **pay attention to what it initially brings up within you**. Our instinct is to reach for the guidebook, but first check in with your unfiltered reactions. It's important that you are as honest as you can manage. We often resist surrendering to this level of honesty because it reveals tension, which the ego wants to immediately reconcile or escape. Instead try to hold the tension, considering questions like:

What was my first thought when I saw the card?
What was my initial feeling or emotion?
How does my body feel right now? If there's tension, where is it located?
What does the card make me think of?

Once you've established some awareness around your reactions, **consider what it is you are resisting about the card**. This provides insight into what the ego is threatened by—what it's trying to ward itself against. For example, you might notice that you resist looking at things with a new perspective, or you resist accepting that this is the hand you've been dealt. Now, gently **ask yourself** *why*. Perhaps the answer is that you resist the card because it encourages optimism and that annoys you or you are afraid it's saying that your circumstances are your own fault, which upsets you. Follow whatever comes up without judgment, rationalization, or analysis. We are still in the phase of gathering information, so do not worry over arriving at conclusions.

Now that you have a sense of what aspect of shadow the card represents, engage the alchemical shadow work process outlined below.

The Alchemical Stages of Shadow Work

Perhaps the best explanation of what shadow work actually looks like can be drawn from alchemy in its fourfold operation of disintegration, purification, illumination, and then transformation. This was a major inspiration for Jung in his understanding of individuation, recognizing that just as the alchemists believed that the prima materia could be transfigured into the philosopher's stone through this four-step process, our character could be similarly transformed via a four-stage psychological arc.*

---

* There is no definitive number of stages in alchemy, however these are the four Jung outlined in his discussions of alchemy as a metaphorical process of individuation.

The first stage is the ***nigredo***, Latin for "blackening," which Jung described as the stage of confession or catharsis. To begin with shadow work, we must first identify the shadow (or whatever piece of it comes into view), which often feels like a confession. This is a dark moment for the ego, who, by questioning what it once held as impermeable truth, begins to question itself and deteriorate. The tarot can be a powerful tool in initiating this first step, which we will demonstrate shortly.

The second stage is the ***albedo***, the "whitening," and what Jung titled the stage of elucidation. After our confession, we are available to real insight. We experience a sort of purification, a softening and cleansing of the ego that allows us to reconnect to soul. There is a sense of illumination and awakening to truth which brings a state of grace. Light is shed where before there was only darkness.

The third stage is the ***citrinitas***, the "yellowing," the dawning of consciousness. Jung identifies this as the stage of education because this is the point in which we seek understanding. Now that we can see the shadow material, we can investigate the impulses and neuroses beneath it and begin to discover its origins. The task is not to solve but to learn the deeper truth of who we are underneath.

Finally, the last stage is the ***rubedo***, the "reddening," the transformation. With a strong understanding of the shadow material, we can forge a new relationship to the seed of truth it formed around. This is a moment of reunification, a redemption of what had been lost in unconsciousness. We overcome the previous blindness of the ego to expand our scope of self-knowledge. In essence, we feel like we've ascended ourselves and are much changed.

After confessing our shadowy tendencies and behaviors, elucidating the deeper experience within them, educating ourselves on the core wounds that activated them, we can now step out of the loop of darkness and choose another path. We can achieve atonement with shadow and move closer toward the whole Self.

Allow me to offer an example from my own experience. There was a period of time in which I was awaiting an answer for a project I was extremely eager to move forward. In my readings I kept pulling the Eight of Wands inverted, which generally signals delays and stagnation.

I knew this was a shadow card for me, both because of its inversion and my ego's intense resistance, which very much itched for the Band-Aid of a clarifier to give a more palatable answer.

To understand what aspect of shadow it represented, I first noticed my initial reaction, which was obvious frustration and disappointment. I tapped into my resistance around this card and felt that it was not a delay that worried me, but the impression that I would never receive the answer at all. When I then probed the *why* beneath it, the response came quickly: *I know that the universe does not conspire to help me, but to thwart me.* Here was the shadow belief I was called to better understand and integrate. I was holding on to an anger and pessimism that could not be assuaged rationally.

I brought this belief into the nigredo stage, confessing my anger as well as the underlying narrative I'd created that the universe wished me to struggle. This stage brought up many uncomfortable feelings: sorrow, bitterness, self-pity, abandonment. I sat with these feelings over the course of a week, holding their discomfort and tension, and eventually I felt the albedo illuminating the deeper truth behind them. My self-pity softened and a deeper sense of exhaustion came to light, a feeling that I must always fight for the good in my life when for once I'd wanted to simply receive it. I returned to the Eight of Wands and saw how perfectly the card depicted this. While I had been waiting to receive the wands thrown down to me from the heavens, on a deeper level I feared once again having to muster the godlike strength to throw them up myself.

With this new understanding of what the card revealed, I embarked on the citrinitas phase, learning more about this inner experience. I examined how this pattern developed in my childhood and how it intensified in my young adulthood. I explored the part of me that always expected a challenge and how it kept me tight and resentful. I recognized the ways it had helped me make great progress in the past and where it sabotaged me now. Seeing all of this clearly, I understood this shadow-belief's role in my psyche and the path to making peace with it.

Again, this process took time. From the moment I first drew the Eight of Wands until I felt the warm inhale of the rubedo settling in was no less than six weeks (and that was with committed, intentional work). We all share the same dream of sudden transformation—and it can indeed happen in those precious, shocking moments—but most of the work we do is slow, labored, and meandering. Rather than a lightning bolt streaking across the midday sky, transformation moves like the clouds, gradually curtaining away to unveil the radiant sun of change.

In the end, I saw that it was my own relentless grip on those wands that prevented me from having arms open to grab them when they finally came. My task was to learn how to put down my fists and receive. The transformation—the change—would be difficult and slow, but I knew it would shift the path of my life deeply.

PART 2

THE MINOR ARCANA

— CHAPTER 3 —

THE MULTIFACETED POWER OF THE PIPS

This is not a psychological or spiritual discipline for self-improvement. It is simply being aware of this present experience, and realizing that you can neither define it nor divide yourself from it. There is no rule but "Look!"

—ALAN WATTS

Philosopher Alan Watts famously described Zen Buddhism not as ruminating on God while one peeled potatoes, but by simply peeling the potatoes. In essence, the act of reaching God—metaphorically, reaching Self—comes not through solemn philosophizing but present living. The Minor Arcana are the potatoes. They are the lived realities we experience daily. While the Major Arcana guide us through the quest of individuation, the Minor Arcana show us the dynamics of our psyches, revealing its inner conflicts, strengths, processes, and neuroses. Put directly, they are the archetypal experiences not of sublimity but mundanity. This is the tarot's essential nature, and possibly its most profound lesson—that all life sits between the divine and the ordinary, what philosopher Mircea Eliade called the sacred and profane. We cannot encounter the greater secrets without living through the lesser.

We venture now into those lesser secrets, and in this chapter we will illuminate the three key ways to understand the Minor Arcana with an archetypal perspective: through the cognitive function of the suit, archetypal numerology, and the monomythic arc. Keep in mind these are only *possibilities* for interpreting a card. We can focus on only one of these elements while reading, all of them, or none of them. The purpose of this chapter is to add layers of meaning from which you can draw to bring more variability and depth to your relationships with the cards.

The Four Functions and the Four Suits

One of Jung's most influential contributions is his theory of personality types. Jung suggests that the personality is composed of four modes of cognitive functioning—thinking, feeling, sensation, and intuition—and that a person's type is determined by the degrees of superiority and inferiority of each of these functions. This theory was eventually adapted into the widely popular Myers-Briggs Type Indicator or the MBTI, which assigns individuals to one of sixteen personality types (the four functions arranged in four variations). However, the aim of understanding these functions is not strictly typological categorization, but to highlight the particular powers and pitfalls within our individual psyches, which in turn can help us live with greater self-awareness.

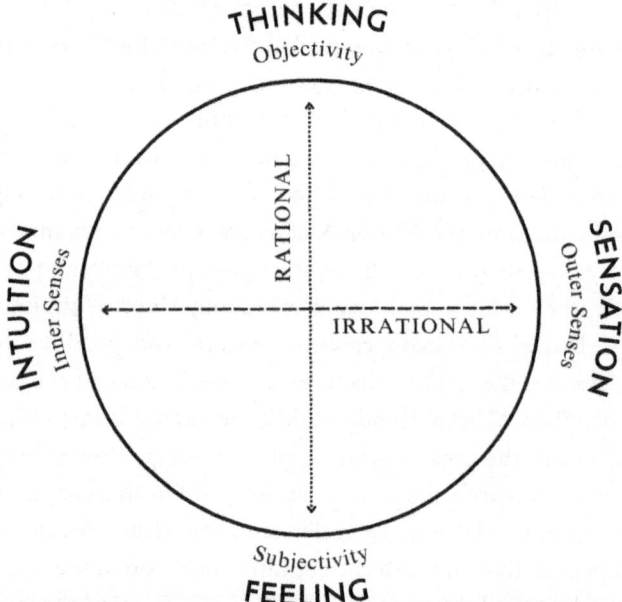

Figure 4. Diagram of the Four Cognitive Functions

Jung broke down the four functions into two categories, rational and irrational, which contain pairs of natural opposites. The rational functions (thinking and feeling) are based in judgment and evaluation coming from what we might identify as the mind and the heart respectively, whereas the irrational functions (sensation and intuition) are not without reason but beyond it, relying on perception and direct experience. Here is how we can understand these functions:

- The **thinking function** is generally objective and uses reason and rationality to comprehend things and what significance they hold. In this mode we are *discerning and analyzing* things as true/false or right/wrong.
- The **feeling function** doesn't engage logical analysis, but subjective value, connection, and relationship. In this mode we are feeling our way through, *relating to and evaluating* things as pleasant/unpleasant or good/bad.
- The **sensation function** perceives through our physical senses. It focuses on facts, details, and practical solutions, always interested in the what over the why. In this mode we are observing and interacting with *concrete reality*.
- The **intuition function** perceives via the invisible senses, tapping into inherent possibility or the greater meaning in things. It ignores the what and chases the why. In this mode we perceive information *instinctively and unconsciously*.

Though we possess all four functions, they naturally form a personal hierarchy in our psyches. There is always one function that is superior (meaning that it is conscious and familiar) and one that is inferior (meaning that it is mostly unconscious and foreign to us), while the remaining two straddle that liminal line between consciousness and unconsciousness. This hierarchy establishes our unique personality types, but it also reveals to us where we are comfortable and where we struggle. For example, being easily stressed by the rational rigor of thinking function, feeling types may thrive at planning a thrilling vacation but become hopelessly overwhelmed when figuring out the schedule. Or intuitive types, who are always delighted by the spark of possibility, may feel bewildered when their sensation-type friends can't come up with something to add to the vision board. When we cannot consciously engage the parts of us that are somewhat unnatural or mindfully lean on the parts that have always been a source of strength, we often feel deadlocked, powerless, or incapable of growth and change.

The tarot is an excellent tool to illuminate these functions in our psyche. Most tarotists are familiar with the traditional correspondences between the tarot suits and the elements, but through these pairings we can easily add the layer of the cognitive functions:

Suit	Element	Function
Cups	*Water*	*Feeling*
Swords	*Air*	*Thinking*
Pentacles	*Earth*	*Sensation*
Wands	*Fire*	*Intuition*

The rationality of the thinking function needs pure air and the sharp edge of the discerning Swords; the emotionality of the feeling function ebbs and flows with the waters held deep in the Cups; the exuberance of the intuition function shines like flame as it follows the possibilities the Wands pursue; and the sensation function is grounded as the earth, embracing our reality as the Pentacles we hold. Just as the tarot might offer all of these suits in a single spread, we are engaging all of these functions in varying degrees at any given point. Therefore, we don't need to think of them exclusively as typologies, but rather as the four faculties through which we meet the world.

Furthermore, considering these natural oppositional pairings (Cups and Swords, Pentacles and Wands) can add a powerful layer in our understanding of the Minor Arcana and ourselves. The deep feeling of the Cups needs the balance of the Swords' discernment in order to live with clarity, just as the intellectual vigor of the Swords needs the empathetic tenderness of the Cups to temper their rigidity. The deep roots of the Pentacles require the intuitive passion of the Wands to draw them toward their potential, just as the expansive energy of the Wands needs the material focus of the Pentacles to make their visions manifest.

Cups and the Feeling Function

Although we use the word *feeling* synonymously with emotion, in depth psychology feelings and emotions are distinct. Emotion, what depth psychologists call "affect," is a response to a psychological trigger which causes states of anger, guilt, excitement, etc. Feeling, however, is about personal relationship to things. The feeling function is about evaluation, not through the logic of the mind but through the values of the heart. It determines what we most want and whether things feel good or bad or somewhere in between. Rather than objectively analyze and judge, it subjectively connects and relates.

The Cups represent the very personal experience of what we love, value, and find meaningful. They relate to both the inner and outer world through sensitivity and reciprocity. This deep knowledge and appreciation of our personal values require a fluid connection to the soul, the seat of unconsciousness, which also highlights the Cups' relationship to our desires, our empathy, and our imagination. This suit binds us to that yearning for intimacy with the world and self that flows through us all.

Swords and the Thinking Function

Across from the subjective feeling function is the objective thinking function, which is informed exclusively by its rationality and intellect. Our thinking function allows us to differentiate right and wrong and make deliberate choices. The discernment of the thinking function helps us supersede our personal biases, confusing emotions, and conflicting desires to make clear judgments. Without the entanglement of feeling, the thinking function can easily cut away what hinders us or bring sharp clarity to the chaos of our complexity.

The Swords act as our tool of mental lucidity, directing both how we take conscious action in our lives and how we sort through our thoughts. It is true that the Swords are sometimes considered the suit of strife, but this is a reflection of the ruthless rationalism that the thinking function can take when it feels weak or unclear. When the Swords fail us, we become trapped in our own self-critical judgments; the narratives we tell ourselves about who we are keep us bound to our pain and powerlessness. We should not forget that incredible power of the Swords to protect our deeper needs, to create boundaries, to make the hard decisions, to cut through the swamp of emotion. It is the Swords, when wielded correctly, that can lift the fog of anxiety and give us the agency to live intentionally.

Pentacles and the Sensation Function

The irrational functions of sensation and intuition are perceptive, meaning that they are centered around how we take in the world around us rather than what judgments we make about it. With the sensation function, perception is focused on immediate reality—an awareness of body, environment, and concrete experience.

Sensation is not just the information gathered by our five senses, but how we experience that information. It is attentive, and the perceptions it draws become our reality, coloring our thoughts, emotions, and choices. Sensation grounds us in what is right in front of us. In contrast to intuition, sensation is not so much interested in what's *behind* its observations as what's *present* in them. Put another way, the intuitive type paints a garden because it is a metaphor for beauty; the sensation type paints it because it is beautiful.

In our capitalistic world, we tend to associate the Pentacles of the tarot with money and work projects, but that is a gross reduction of their significance. For the last several thousand years, matter has been associated with sinful Eve or the devil and placed in direct opposition to the perfection of the spiritual realm. What the Pentacles open us to (and what society is starving for) is the healing of this split. They bring us back to the center of immediate experience, embracing presence and concrete reality. The pentacle is the work of the hands, be it a coin, brick, fruit, or the functions of the body. When we are in correct relationship with this suit, we may thrive financially, but we also may thrive through stability, wellness, or emotional growth.

Wands and the Intuition Function

The intuition function is arguably the most mysterious and intriguing in Jung's typology. Like sensation, intuition perceives things around us, but while sensation does so with observed data, intuition just *knows*.

In this usage, intuition doesn't mean psychic insight, but rather something much more routine and instinctual. The intuitive function is attuned to the ever-flowing unconscious currents, which often sweep us away with ideas, inspirations, and spontaneous innovations. It expands beyond the concrete to explore the unseen, fixing its attention, always, to possibility rather than reality. The intuition function is energetic and quick to ignite—getting things or seeing things instantaneously. Gazing either inwardly or outwardly, its primary interest is always in the *why*.

Driven by a sense of purpose and creativity, the Wands follow the pull of our intuitive insights. They inseminate life with new meaning, perpetually enlarging the vision of life. They represent our life force—what Jung identified as the *libido*, which is distinct from Freud's idea of sexual energy—the energy of the psyche which carries its flow of inspiration, passion, and progress.

Archetypal Numerology

A card's number is equally as significant as its suit. Numbers carry an undeniable allure, pointing to both quantity (real discernible amounts) and quality (symbolic significance). There is an innate identity in 1 that is distinguishable from 10, and there is a reason why fairy tales love 3s and 7s. Numbers hold power, and so considering the card number can offer a deeper and more nuanced interpretation of the cards.

In our following discussion we will not apply any specific numerological tradition. Instead we are considering the number in its archetypal context, drawing from its significance in myth and culture. Keep in mind that there are countless ways to study numbers, and so, as with everything else, you should continue to explore your own associations and connections.

1: Unity and Purity

Unlike any other integer, 1 is singular and indivisible. $1^2 = 1$, meaning it is whole in itself and cannot be grown or enhanced. What this represents archetypally is the monad, the Pythagorean idea of the oneness of all things. It is the purity of a homogeneous essence. It is undifferentiated consciousness and the singularity of being.

As the Ace, the tarot 1 represents the total, pure energy of the suit. In the Rider-Waite-Smith deck, each Ace is shown as a divine hand draped in greenery, emerging from the clouds to bring its gift to earth. This gift is the fullness of the suit, bursting with its individual potential.

2: The Tension of Opposition

Though 1 does not grow when multiplied by itself, it does change when added to itself. When we combine one totality with another, we get duality. There's now a subject and object, a thesis and antithesis, an I and a Thou. And this is necessary for our development, for if we are to become aware of our nature, we must both be the observer of ourselves and the observed.

As both conscious and unconscious beings, we are constantly in a state of duality. One part of us clings to hope and another to fear; one loves while another loathes; one acts while another avoids. In the tarot, the 2 shows the need to hold this tension, negotiate duality, seek balance, and discern choice.

3: Synthesis and Dynamism

A central theory in philosophy is the Hegelian dialectic, which states that philosophical progress begins with a thesis, then moves to the negation of that thesis called the antithesis, and then achieves resolution via synthesis. 3 is indeed the number of this synthesis, which both reconciles the tension of opposites in thesis and antithesis and allows for a *both/and* perspective. It is a symbol for new possibilities and broadened horizons. In the tarot, 3 is the number of dynamic energy or growth, emerging from the previous struggle with renewed intensity, motivation, and a conscious orientation toward expansion.

4: Stasis and Containment

There's a natural sense of order and permanence to 4, demonstrated in the four directions, the four elements, the four humors, the four phases of the moon, the four mathematical operations, the four seasons, and on and on. 4 sets up the corners of discernible reality and grounds us in it, containing and systematizing the chaos of life.

While in Jungian psychology 4 is seen as the number of wholeness, the tarot 4 is more attuned to the static passivity that follows the dynamic activity of 3. It represents stabilization and safety in the status quo, but when left too long to linger, it can become petrifaction.

5: Humanity and Conflict

5 holds a wide range of symbolic meanings, appearing in various traditions as a number of luck, spirituality, and sacred femininity. In the tarot, it appears both as a number of humanness and conflict. Connecting to the five senses, the five appendages, the five digits on each limb, even the five wounds of Christ, with 5 we are pointed toward the microcosm and the mortal side of our being. But also with 5, we meet the baser aspects of our being—the human weaknesses of self-pity, despair, volatility, and callousness. The conflict caused by these encounters can bring tremendous struggle, but also tremendous opportunity for growth.

6: Harmony and Evolution

The Pythagoreans considered 6 to be the first perfect number, as it is both the sum and product of its factors. While this sense of order was a stabilizing force with 4, it is expansive with 6, bringing forth a new harmony and rapid evolution. The world was formed and arranged in six days according to the Judeo-Christian story and over the course of six periods according to the Zoroastrian tradition. The tarot 6 often indicates dynamic development or an evolved perspective or approach.

7: Mystique and Paradox

7 is a magical number. We connect it to the seven planets of antiquity, the seven notes in a diatonic scale, the seven days of the week, the seven

deadly sins and seven heavenly virtues, the seven chakras, the seven colors of the rainbow, etc. But we also find it in countless myths and tales, such as Snow White's seven dwarves, the seven horses of the Hindu sun-god, ancient Egypt's seven paths to heaven and seven halls of the underworld.

7 is a number that holds an undeniable mystique and is somewhat paradoxical. In Western culture today, 7 is both a lucky number for gamblers and an unlucky one for mirror-breakers. Indeed, 7 has a trickster-like nature, simultaneously pointing to divine blessings and human fallibility. As St. Augustine puts it, it is at once the number of Sabbath and sin.

In the Minor Arcana, 7 shows us caught between activity and passivity, honesty and deception, possibility and fantasy, righteousness and foolishness. There is a theme of promised reward, but also a sense of missing perspective, as if we are seeing things from the wrong side (if we can even be sure of which side we're on).

8: Auspice and Action

Jung identified 8, the doubled quaternity, as the number exploring the intricacies of 4's wholeness: the four cognitive functions become eight in their extraverted or introverted natures, the four phases of the moon now add on their waxing and waning, and the four directions each have a midpoint between them.

8 is an auspicious number, one that's connected with movement and focus. It is abundant and directed toward a higher state: the Noble Eightfold Path guides souls to liberation in Buddhism, and there are eight gates to paradise in Islam. And as a numeral, 8 is a rotated lemniscate, the infinity symbol, which reminds us of the perpetuity of the created universe (which is much bigger than our mortal workings). The tarot 8s propel us forward and though they are not without responsibility they always yield reward.

9: Arrival at the Threshold

9 leans toward the coming 10, and thus holds subtle tension. Troy was besieged for nine years; Demeter searched for Persephone for nine days; a baby is gestated for nine months. There's a sense of longing and

anticipation in 9, a sense that the final moment must (and will) come, but the journey to get there can be—even in its final stages—disorienting. The tarot 9 portends the close of a cycle, presenting the opportunity to hover at the threshold, whether our intention is to learn a final lesson, appreciate our achievements, or delay the inevitable end.

10: Totality and Completion

As the sum of its parts up to 4 (1 + 2 + 3 + 4) and as a variation of the 1 (1 + 0 = 1), 10 is the number of totality. There are ten sephirot or divine emanations on the Kabbalistic Tree of Life, ten Heavenly Stems that reveal the cycles of time in ancient China, and Ten Commandments for worshipping the Abrahamic God.* With 10 we have come to the final expression of what was possible, arrived at the highest state of being, and there is nothing more to be achieved.

What is interesting in the tarot is that this state of completion and finality does not always end well. And this, perhaps, is because completion is not equivalent to perfection. This is an essential lesson in the tarot and in life. Whether happily or tragically, every story ends.

The Monomyth of the Pips

Drawing upon Jung's collective unconscious, mythologist Joseph Campbell formulated his theory of the monomyth (more commonly known as the hero's journey). According to this theory, virtually all myths, regardless of time, place, or people, are variations of a universal template. He describes the monomyth as:

> an archetypal story that springs from the collective unconscious. Its motifs can appear not only in myth and literature, but, if you are sensitive to it, in the working out of the plot of your own life. The basic story of the hero journey involves giving up where you

---

* There are several variations on the spelling of Kabbalah. In Christian mysticism it is generally spelled Cabala, and in hermetic esotericism it's Qabalah. Because the most widely accepted spelling by actual practitioners is Kabbalah, that is what I have chosen to use.

are, going into the realm of adventure, coming to some kind of symbolically rendered realization, and then returning to the field of normal life.[1]

This archetypal story is the same we find in the pips as we pass through this threefold process of seeking, development, and actualization. The pips are not telling the story of our individuation journey as a whole (that is the purpose of the Major Arcana), but the journey we make within each of the four suits.*

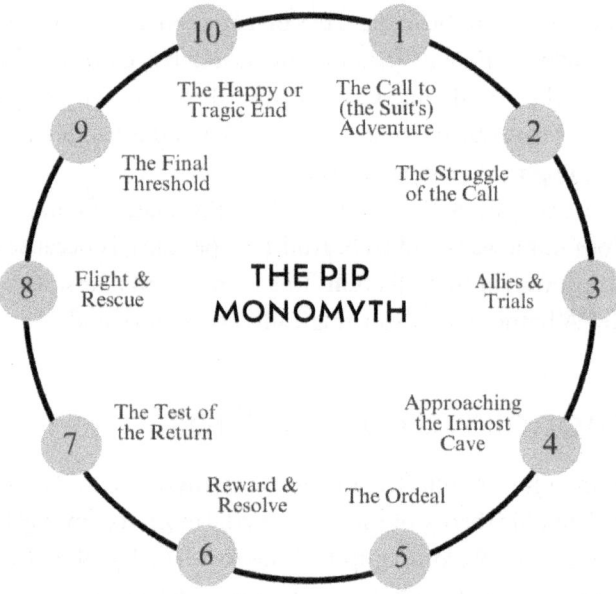

Figure 5. Diagram of the Pip Monomyth

---

* I have adapted Campbell's formula to reflect the cards' number and particular nuances. I like to remind my students that though we love it when such correspondences line up like an overlay on a projector, mystical knowledge is not a one-to-one system. Adaptation is allowed, and, in fact, important as we develop. Exact symmetry is not the point; meaning is.

Ace: Call to the Suit's Adventure

Just as Campbell's hero is called by an outside force to start their journey, the Ace is presented as a divine initiation, offering us the promise of growth. However we experience it, whether by way of a life-changing opportunity or a bit of shrewd advice, once we feel that we have been handed that precious token, the journey is ready to start. Here's how we might experience this within each suit:

- The Ace of Cups asks us to embark on the grail quest and learn what we most love and value.
- The Ace of Swords places the sharp blade of discernment and intellect in our hand and asks that we learn how to wield it.
- The Ace of Pentacles gives us a seed of potential, asking us to plant it, name it, and attentively nourish it.
- The Ace of Wands sparks a sudden flame of passion in the spirit, asking that we follow its mysterious pull.

Two: The Struggle of the Call

The boon of the Ace is intoxicating, but when we begin to follow that call into our external reality, we are quickly overwhelmed by the task. If we fail here, we can become stuck, regressing back to the wonder of the Ace where we can be comforted by its promise while unwittingly refusing to manifest it. (If you've ever pulled an Ace inverted multiple times in a row, this may be exactly the reason.)

- The love of the Cups flows easily when it is ours alone, but when it is given and hoped to be reciprocated, we must balance how much we offer of ourselves and how much we expect to receive.
- When the Swords are confronted with two equal paths, there is a crisis. Before we had unified clarity, but now we must discover our powers of differentiation and choice.

- As the singular Pentacle multiplies, we must spread our resources among them, learning to "juggle" all that we cultivate and care for.
- The Wands' flame of passion draws us forth, but when we bring it out into the golden sunlight, suddenly it doesn't seem so bright. We must hold our small, emerging vision against the vastness of the open world.

Three: Allies and Trials

At this stage of the hero's journey, the hero encounters monsters and mishaps, as well as new sidekicks and mentors. Similarly in this third stage of the pip journey, we move beyond our struggle and accept the help of allies and pass through trials of development. The hero moves beyond what Campbell calls the zone of deliberation and engages in the action.

- The deep, dense feeling nature of the Cups learns the necessity of joy and frivolity by connecting to community.
- The hyperrationality of the Swords recognizes the force of emotional vulnerability with the trial of heartbreak.
- The self-sufficiency of the Pentacles learns the value of support and accountability by leaning on others' skills.
- The sense of passion and purpose is rekindled in the Wands as the hero faces the trials of patience and perseverance.

Four: Approaching the Inmost Cave

In Campbell's hero's journey, there is always a period of preparation before the darkest point of the story—the Ordeal. Campbell calls this stage the "Belly of the Whale," in which forward motion is interrupted by a deathlike moment of inward reflection. For some of the suits, this stage brings paralysis and panic, and for others it brings renewal and release. But the task at heart is to contemplate the inner quality of the suit, which may come to be either the hero's greatest downfall or greatest weapon.

- The Cups are suddenly drained of their previous vibrance and struggle to connect to their deeper values, resulting in apathy and numbness.
- The Swords prepare for future challenges by restoring their mental energy and clarity in the total silence of retreat.
- The Pentacles submit to their stifling need to control reality and their resources, which keeps them bound and stagnant.
- The Wands detour into the open fields of their inner nature, finding a moment of peace and harmony in the domain of simple presence.

Five: The Ordeal

Now we come to the Ordeal, in which the hero faces the harshest challenges of their journey. Here at the midpoint of the tarot arc, before we begin to reascend and approach renewal, we must confront the remnants of our old attachments and previously failed lessons. This is the point of the great conflict, not with outer enemies but with the shadowy qualities of the suit itself.

- The Cups are overcome with the depths of feeling, contending with sorrow, grief, and emptiness.
- With their unempathetic rationality, the Swords turn callous and brutal in their crusade to be infallible and always right.
- The promised bounty of the Pentacles is lost to the fear of poverty, both material and spiritual.
- The Wands' fire ignites into combativeness, turning all their vibrant passions against each other.

The task of the Ordeal is not to defeat the experience, but to see the other side, the other way. Because, of course, we are both the victim and the villain, and if we were to realize this fact and survive this conflict, we might indeed experience real change. We might turn our eyes to the cups that are full and drink; we might recognize our ruthlessness and make amends; we might enter the sanctuary of the church to be warmed; we might realize the futility of fighting and instead choose allyship.

Six: Reward and Resolve

Campbell tells us that once we've survived these trials, the hero's hard-won knowledge of the self and the world results in his apotheosis—a sudden deified stature. With this transformed perspective, the hero has what it takes to complete the quest. This is the moment in myth when the hero drinks the magical elixir or seizes the god's sword, and in the tarot it is the moment when the suit achieves a level of resolve and reward. A new light has entered the hero—a compensating tenderness, humility, equilibrium, or resoluteness.

- The Cups remember the beauty of their innate sense of love and inner values and look to the treasures of the past to restore their depth.
- The Swords realize that their old means of living no longer function and make the radical decision to move to a new shore and new perspective.
- The Pentacles finally understand the balance between ownership and stewardship, releasing control over resources to develop a more generous nature.
- The Wands at last focus themselves on a singular champion or drive who can successfully channel and guide their energy.

Seven: The Test of the Return

With this strengthened understanding, we can now initiate our return to establish a new way of being. However, the road back requires that we implement what we've learned, and so sometimes the hero languishes and flails, failing this endeavor. In the tarot, we see this in the sudden bifurcation of the path: one way leading us to rise above and the other to fall behind. We must solidify our connection to the essential power of the suit, and from that place choose the path forward. As we will see, from this point on two of the suits master this challenge, while two struggle.

- The Cups return to the present and are shown the many possibilities of how to live, but rather than listen to the feeling wisdom that tells them what is most valuable and true, they are overcome by the intoxication of fantasy and imagination.
- The Swords have forgone their natural integrity for the quick success of manipulation and cunning. As they tiptoe away, they must wonder if what they've "gotten away with" holds any real achievement.
- Though the fruit is ripe, the Pentacles hesitate. They oscillate between readiness and uncertainty, doubting the instincts and skills they've developed throughout the journey, and thus become paralyzed.
- At the first hint of a threat the Wands jump eagerly back into battle without knowing what opponent they face. Deafened to their intuitive instincts, they may not even sense what it is they're truly defending.

Eight: Flight and Rescue

In order to return, the hero must now flee or be rescued. After the hero's failure to initiate the process naturally and thoughtfully, life must force the way forward. This is the point in the monomythic arc where the stories begin to diverge. The Wands and Pentacles experience what Campbell calls the "Magic Flight," the inspired rush to freedom. The Cups and Swords, however, remain wary and fearful, and so they must be pulled through in what Campbell calls the "Rescue from Without."

- The Cups wake up from their illusion and at last grasp both the value in what they have and clarity of what they don't. The unknown beckons, and they mournfully leave what they have known for what could be.
- The Swords find themselves bound, blindfolded, and seemingly helpless. Be it by the help of a stranger, the wind, or a sudden swell of courage, they require aid to be freed from their mental knots.

- The Pentacles, with the materials now harvested and at hand, unhesitantly begin hammering away at the final labor of manifestation and growth.
- The Wands relinquish their futile fight and soar down from the hilltop, swelling with the blessing of inspiration, vitality, and intuitive insight.

Nine: The Final Threshold

The final step before the completion of the journey is the Crossing of the Return Threshold, but here there is yet another opportunity for defeat. On our hero's journey we hear the call, enter the cave, survive the ordeal, and realize the great treasure, but the last and perhaps greatest of these challenges is taking responsibility for how we actually live these lessons we've won. This is an intimate and isolated task (which is why I believe each figure of the 9s is alone). At this stage only two suits (Cups and Pentacles) will make it across the threshold, while the other two (Swords and Wands) resist and ultimately end their journey in defeat. This may be disappointing, but it is remarkably honest. Not all journeys are successful, and as the tarot depicts the full spectrum of our experience, the failures, too, must be included.

- Seated at a table of plenty, the Cups enjoy the bounty of feeling satisfaction and sincere gratitude for what they've earned throughout the journey.
- Tormented by anxiety, the Swords doubt their mental strength and turn into weapons that threaten doom rather than defend clarity.
- The Pentacles luxuriate in their garden of ease, independence, and abundance, balancing effort and pleasure to fully enjoy the fruits of their labor.
- Crippled by their fall, the Wands barricade themselves from the threshold of change, keeping them safe though stagnant and resentful.

Ten: The Happy or Tragic End

The last leg of Campbell's hero's journey is titled the "Freedom to Live." The hero is confident in the wisdom they have learned and knows it will prepare them for whatever comes to pass. In the tarot we have a slightly different sort of conclusion. The cards present us with two possibilities—the happy or tragic end. The story might end blissfully or calamitously, but neither is a promise or a prison.

What this last stage of the pip monomyth reminds us is that the end is fleeting and always leads us right back to the beginning. Our journey through the suits is perpetually cyclical, and whether we may make it to this place of freedom or remain trapped at the threshold's gate, the journey is soon to reinitiate itself.

- The Cups make it to the happy end of feeling bliss, but there is a whisper of impermanence here. The rainbow will slowly dissipate and we are back to the beginning.
- The Swords are murdered by their own looming terrors. The image is one of total defeat, and we know the only solution is the clean breakthrough of the Ace in hand.
- The Pentacles earn their desired wealth and prestige, but there is also a pervasive emptiness. Bounty brings celebration, but not always meaning, and so what's missing draws us back to the start.
- The Wands gather up the energy spent building their barricade and try to reapproach the threshold, but the weight is too much to bear. They must all be dropped so the singular Ace can reemerge.

Imagining a New Ending

Each of the suits experiences their unique struggles and is offered their unique lessons, but of course, the cards will never show us how the suits' stories might change if we actually learned from them. That is the task of our own imaginations, and taking the time to rewrite their end can be keenly illuminating. What would happen if the Wands actually made it across the threshold? Or what if the Cups refused the rescue of the moon's call into the unknown? What if the Pentacles never harvested their bounty? What if the Swords finally managed to cut themselves free?

We are not, like the tarot pips, doomed to play out the same story into infinity, so by imagining how they might get a new close to their stories, we might similarly be able to imagine a new end for ourselves.

CHAPTER 4

THE PIPS

In the previous chapter we explored alternate lenses we can apply when reading the Minor Arcana. In this chapter we will move through the pips card by card, discussing their traditional meanings with a depth psychology perspective. As always, these meanings are not definitive. Use them only to stimulate your own interpretations and reflections.

Keep in mind that while I've included some brief possibilities for the cards' inversions, reversals are usually wholly dependent on the context of the reading. In my archetypal tarot approach I teach several ways to approach reversals and warn students against narrowing their rich possibilities by simply thinking of them as the opposite. In general, I like to think of reversals as a way of indicating something is not in its right state. That might mean they point to a blind spot in the ego or a pattern of behavior we're ignoring or a place where the psychic energy is stuck and stagnant. The best way to discover a reversal's significance is to stop worrying over what it *means* and be curious about *why* the card choose to come up that way. How does the card upside down flip your own perspective? What might it be trying to reveal?

CUPS

Feelings are for the soul what food is for the body.
—RUDOLF STEINER

Ace of Cups

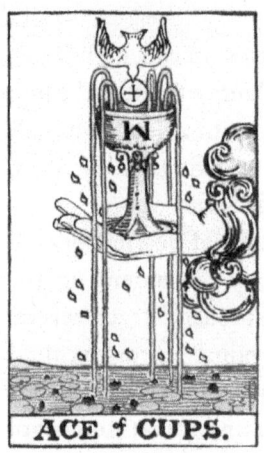

With the Ace of Cups we have the holy grail itself in hand. Bearing the sacred waters of archetypal love, it is, as A. E. Waite puts it, the "house of the true heart."

The holy grail is the elusive relic that drew numerous noble-hearted heroes to its quest. Though known as the cup Jesus used at the Last Supper, its origins extend beyond the Christian tradition and connect back to the cauldron of the Celtic great goddess. There are a host of concepts ascribed to the grail: healing, rebirth, love, soul, the unconscious, the cosmic womb, and, psychologically, the lost feeling function. As depth psychologist Robert Johnson suggests, Western culture's prioritization of the thinking function has advanced society toward tremendous heights, but at the cost of its feeling depths. Like the grail, our feeling hearts have become something we must seek and retrieve.

The Ace of Cups is this font of feeling. When we pull it, we are indeed called to consider love, but the great love of being, the love of sincere relationship with our souls. Focused inwardly, the Ace of Cups may herald a period of spiritual renewal, rekindling our devotion to our deep desires and essential truths. Outwardly, we may connect more fluidly to our gifts of compassion and empathy. With this Ace at hand, we might feel as if we are succeeding in our own grail quest, at last finding and cherishing that precious treasure of great value, whether it be the realization of a dream, healing of a wound, cultivating a loving relationship, or any other longing.

Reversed, we may cling to the idealistic quest for that evasive treasure, feeling as if life cannot begin until we have it. However, just as the grail appeared when least expected, the Ace cannot be forced to appear nor prevented from vanishing. Life is not initiated by winning the prize, but simply by embarking on the quest. Another possibility is that we find ourselves with the grail in hand, and yet still doubt ourselves worthy of it. As the legend of Perceval tells us, when we do find it, we must ask, "Whom does the grail serve?" While the author Chrétien de Troyes died before penning the answer, we can guess it. The grail serves the soul within us all. We are all worthy to drink from the holy cup. When we are given the opportunity to return to love and our feeling depth, we must take it.

Two of Cups

The Two of Cups brings the inner grail of the Ace of Cups into the real world, finding an other to share it with. We associate this card with partnership and romance, but we should not forget the deeper secret of the 2s—the duality between I and Thou. With the lover's hand reaching beyond his own cup and toward his beloved's, we know that the Two of Cups is about how we attune to both our personal experience of love and the experience of the other's love. There is freedom and fluidity in the bond when the feeling function is deeply engaged. We offer our cup freely and are vulnerable enough to drink from the cup we're given. In this state of true reciprocity, we see and are seen wholly and honestly, and something deeply healing is shared.

Reversed, we may resist the openhearted sharing of our cup or reject what is shared with us. If we do not succeed in holding the tension of the exchange and protecting its integrity, relationships and connections may turn distrustful, selfish, or generally disharmonious.

Three of Cups

The Three of Cups shows a scene of unbridled mirth. The inwardly facing feeling function can become weighed down with its own dense self-plundering and forget the necessity of felicity. Here we are encouraged to actually enjoy this life we find so precious. Sometimes we must simply go out and drink, laugh, dance.

The dynamic energy of 3 points toward growth, and so this card can also suggest expanding our connections and source of joy in community. With this card, love and support are given openly and friendship forged easily. The fruit is ripe, and we are free to take in the richness of life.

Reversed, we may turn too indulgent in the pleasures of our feeling side and get lost in revelry. While fun and play are essential, they, too, must be balanced. Alternatively, we may be too introverted in our feeling function and neglect the cultivation of connection via community that is so important to our growth.

Four of Cups

As we leave the state of extraverted joyfulness and return to introverted solitude, our cups once filled with rich wine now carry tasteless water. Whatever the cause, with this sudden loss of vigor our vibrant psychic energy dries up and everything feels pointless, empty, lifeless.

Like the element of water, the feeling function flows through us, acting as a font of vitality that gives life meaning. As long as we are connected to what holds value for us, we feel alive. However, if that stream of feeling goes suddenly still and we lose that connection, our longing for life also flatlines. The resulting experience is one of apathy and inertia. Whether this leads us to distance ourselves from our emotions in favor of numbed stability or alienate ourselves from deep, sustaining relationships, the Four of Cups loses connection to soul.

We must not neglect to notice that the Ace of Cups has returned to the frame. Reversed, this card may come to remind us of the gift of the Ace, the holy grail. If we could lift our attention from the neurotic, anxious, or apathetic focus, we would see it right in front of our eyes.

Five of Cups

We arrive at the darkest expression of our feeling side and find ourselves engulfed by sadness and loneliness. As Jung suggests, our feeling function is the basis for our fight-or-flight responses, and so when encountering sincere emotional pain, we often deny it or run, thus preventing ourselves from developing the strength to hold it. (Even many traditional interpretations insist that we focus on the two remaining cups, shooing us away from pain to fix our sight only on the good.) Of course, we should not forget the love and healing available in those remaining cups, but we must also grieve what has been spilled.

Feeling embraces grief and joy alike. There is meaning in our suffering equal to the meaning in our love. Grief and sorrow are not failures but rich with life force, and it is an essential trial for our psycho-spiritual growth to be with our pain. Then, when enough tears have been shed, we can return to the fullness of life awaiting us.

Reversed, we may be trying to suppress our distress. However, if we do not appropriately face our pain, sorrow can become symptom. We might suffer a host of psychosomatic ailments in an attempt to fight or fly from the pain. Another possibility is that we are indeed wallowing in the self-pity the image presents, and thus need a more forceful turn back toward the good we have been ignoring.

Six of Cups

The children in the image tell us this card is about youth, memory, and mentorship, but more deeply it indicates a return to the past experiences that formed our subjective sense of self and innate value system. There are points in our individuation when to move forward we must turn back and examine those formative experiences that defined what matters, what we love, and who we are. Often this retrospection points us toward childhood, but it can focus on any phase of life. We are asked to revisit the memories of what has supported us and what has hurt us, what we've supported and what we've hurt, meeting both with appreciation and curiosity. What is won from any such effort of reflection is an open and vital companionship with our deeper feelings and needs. We may very well become a tender mentor to a past version of self still alive within.

Reversed, we may be trapped in nostalgia, looking back with rose-colored glasses or idealizing a past that never was. Sometimes we feel too severed from our past to return or can't seem to remember who we once were. This is an opportunity for dedicated inner child work, connecting to our purest origins.

Seven of Cups

In the Seven of Cups, we struggle to differentiate between possibility and fantasy. Through the Cups' power of imagination, we feel everything we long for and everything that terrifies us with equal intensity, and thus we drift out of concrete reality and into the archetypal realm. Things may appear to be either glorious or horrific, making it impossible to choose a direction or even know what it is we really want. While we may be greatly inspired or appropriately cautioned by the glimpses of gold and dragons—those hopes and fears—the task here is to come down from the world of illusion and place ourselves back at the center of the heart with its unique values and desires.

Inverted, we can become addicted to the fantasies of our dreams and thus paralyzed, too afraid to risk losing the vision by attempting to make it real. Alternatively, being so overwhelmed by the archetypal gloss over reality, we may become either inflated or deflated (meaning that our egos have either expanded beyond their proper limits or collapsed). Then we might watch our dreams balloon out until we lose ourselves to delusions of grandeur or cower from them feeling tragically small and unworthy.

Eight of Cups

Known as the card of "moving on," there's a nuanced quality of both sadness and resolve that is important for understanding the Eight of Cups. We are presented with the choice of abandoning what we once valued so that we might seek a new path in an unknown landscape. We are caught in a tension of the opposites: it is both crushing to leave and crushing to stay. However, there is a rare and precious opportunity. Rather than decide our path by way of the Swords' logic of mind, we can choose according to the Cups' wisdom of heart. If we can develop faith in our ability to withstand the tension, holding to our most valued truths through the chaos of complexity, we may indeed trust our feeling instinct to guide us toward the more worthy destiny.

The risk in this card, when inverted, is that rather than moving on, we are running away. Instead of trying to understand our inner tension, we are simply escaping it. On the other end, we may resist the call altogether and instead cling to that which we know must be left behind. This resistance is strongest when we feel unduly pressured. The choice can only be made when we are ready to make it, but it must be made.

Nine of Cups

A man sits at his table of plenty, smiling with placid satisfaction. This card is often associated with wish fulfillment, and we can see that he is indeed rich with all he desires. But remember, the feeling nature of the Cups connects us not to material abundance but a wealth of worth. The cups on his table are filled not with material achievement, but with the experiences of meaning in his life. His satisfaction comes not from attainment but genuine contentment with himself and his circumstances.

The essential keyword for the Nine of Cups is *gratitude*. Although we will continue to reach for growth, we have an opportunity to feel sated with what we have already poured into our cups. Here we can see the value in what we have cultivated in our lives and feel appreciation and pride. We feel at peace knowing it is enough.

Inverted, there is often a pervasive dissatisfaction that blinds us to gratitude. We may be so eager for the coming Ten of Cups' rainbow that we miss the simple serenity of contentment now available. Or we may have become smug and prideful, counting up our cups while turning numb to their deeper meaning.

Ten of Cups

This card is one we often wish to appear in our readings, believing it promises the happy ending we all desire. However, the symbol of the rainbow over the dancing family suggests that though it is a beautiful moment, it is also a transient one.

True happiness is indeed possible, but only if we accept that it is also temporary. As Jung says, "No matter how ideal your situation may be, it does not necessarily guarantee happiness. A relatively slight disturbance of your biological or psychological equilibrium may suffice to destroy your happiness."[1] Happiness is a condition of life only reached in those moments we are deeply connected to our feeling center, when the heart space has yawned open and we can feel the potency of our contentment and gladness, no matter how fleeting they may be.

But we must remember happiness is not the goal: wholeness is. Inverted, we may be clinging to an image of the perfect life that prevents presence with the satiety of our feeling side. Or, possibly, we are caught in a projection in which the fairy-tale image of perfect love and happiness has become the expectation for our real, human relationships and experiences. In these cases the Ten of Cups fosters continual disappointment and becomes a burden and block to genuine love.

SWORDS

Obscurity is dispelled by augmenting the light of discernment, not by attacking the darkness.
—SOCRATES

Ace of Swords

While the Ace of Cups drew us to seek the holy grail, the Ace of Swords invites us to consider another magical totem of Arthurian myth—Excalibur, the sword of triumphant sovereignty.

For a thousand years Excalibur has been an emblem of valor and dignity, and it is by winning this sword that Arthur transforms from boy to king. Most know the version of the tale in which Arthur pulls Excalibur from an anvil, but in another it is the mysterious Lady of the Lake who offers it from her magical waters. Metaphorically, she draws the sword of sovereign power out of the murky depths of unconsciousness, displaying it as the symbolic breakthrough of conscious clarity. It is Arthur's unique ability to courageously and judiciously wield this gift that makes him worthy of his kingship.

Like Arthur, we may wield our magical Ace of Swords as the talisman of honed judgment and intellectual strength. It is a tool of both differentiation and purification, its sharp, steeled edge cutting through confusion and defending us from harmful vulnerabilities. We earn this sword when we are ruled not by impulse, but by reason, directing our lives with integrity and clarity of will.

The Ace of Swords is the illumination of truth and justice. When we pull it, it is time to focus on what feels clear and true. It may herald a sudden breakthrough, discovering a resolution to a problem, or understanding some previously puzzling aspect of ourselves. It encourages sharp action, whether that is establishing boundaries, making solid decisions, or displaying our authority. With this Ace, it is time to trust our agency and sovereignty in ruling our lives. This is not a moment of serene contemplation, but rather one in which we must engage the objective thinking function and make the choices we know must be made.

Reversed, the Ace of Swords may show the disengagement of our thinking function, causing us to refuse necessary action or suffer cloudy judgments. When pointed upward the sword shows the mind rising to higher insight; downward it shows its self-fixation and lack of vision. In order to enjoy the profound clarity and power this Ace can inspire, we must allow ourselves to transcend our established beliefs and mental limitations and be willing to take action.

Two of Swords

When we split the brilliant clarity of the Ace into two—thesis and antithesis—we get the crisis of dilemma in the Two of Swords. With the mental sharpness of the thinking function deadlocked between equal possibilities or conflicting truths, the power of the sword to differentiate and decide is thwarted.

In this tension we experience uncomfortable mental paralysis, but as Jung reminds, the oscillation of opposites eventually leads to equalization and a new perspective. The task now is to listen carefully and objectively to the argument of each side without demanding resolution. Then we might eventually strip away the blindfold and let in new insight, loosing the heart from its crossed cage so that a new perspective can illuminate the way to synthesis.

Reversed, we may have convinced ourselves that the dilemma is a deadlock, and thus give up on our responsibility of discernment and choice. We might also tend to inundate ourselves with unnecessary options or concerns, debilitating our thinking process and dooming us to indecision.

Three of Swords

It is surprising to see such anguish in the realm of the analytical thinking function, but emotion—what depth psychology calls "affect"—is not relegated to the feeling function alone. The dynamic energy of 3 sweeps up the rational swords in a storm of emotional torment. When our pain becomes evidence, proving that we're unlovable, too much, too broken, bound to be alone (or whatever story we've talked ourselves into), the Swords' clarity of reason offers no balm.

When we are heartbroken, our thinking minds tend to interrupt the natural period of emotional processing to "make sense" of our hurt and rationalize our way through. But sorrow is often senseless, and our urge to analyze and fix only keeps the swords stuck where they are. We narrativize our suffering, telling ourselves stories that are often painfully self-critical, further wounding our bleeding hearts.

Now may be the time to consciously remove the swords and use them as weapons of self-defense rather than self-assault. Upside down, this card tends to reveal toxic patterns of blame, both on ourselves and others. We may have become attached to our wound, recognizing that to let it close up means letting go of the stories we've clung to. Now is the time to defend the soft spots and prioritize healing.

Four of Swords

After the torrential misery of the Three of Swords, the thinking function finds itself much more at home in the contained space of 4 and surrenders to mental stillness. Though we are in a tomb, there is no sense of loss here. Instead, as A. E. Waite describes it, we are in a willing state of retreat. Rather than continue to mentally exhaust ourselves, we can use our powers of differentiation to recognize what we can and cannot manage. This is the time to hang up those rigid rationalizations and daunting decisions and welcome a moment of restoration, whether by withdrawing from the mental loads of life or cloistering ourselves somewhere to rest and renew.

There is, however, a real warning in the Four of Swords reversed. We may have hidden away in the tomb in a sort of dissociative "playing dead," refusing to take up the work of sorting through our thoughts, actions, and choices. In this inverted state, we feel "turned off" from life, powerless, and even apathetic.

Five of Swords

In the Five of Swords we arrive at the greatest flaw of our thinking side—its denial of empathy. This card is clearly one of conflict, and in its traditional interpretations we are often asked whether we identify with the embittered loser or the ruthless winner. In other words, either we fall victim to self-pitying dejection at being proved wrong or turn callous in savage defense of our "rightness." Whichever side we find ourselves on, this card challenges our assumptions of mental or moral superiority. Whether we are in conflict with a real person or an aspect of ourselves, we must be curious about where we fall on this spectrum and persevere to return to a state of empathy and understanding, both for our enemy and ourselves.

Reversed, the Five of Swords often demands that we take a sober look at how our thinking function may have sharpened our tongues and hardened our hearts. Although the ego's instinct is to deny it, we all sometimes devolve into the bully or the victim. Our fury and self-righteousness can blind us to the true nature of our actions and beliefs.

Six of Swords

Hooded and bent, as if tears are still being shed, a family journeys in a small boat laden with swords. The Six of Swords is a card of transition, but not an eager one. The old way cannot continue. A new shore must be sought.

Though this card is grim, it is arguably one of the most successful of the Swords suit. A decision has at last been made. With steadfast resolve the boat crosses the churning tides of unconscious emotion, stilling the waters as it moves. What is won in this transition is a new, resolute perspective. The far shore is a symbol of the new, clearer way we understand our lives and the direction we wish to take them. This is the point of the transition: to see ourselves from a fresh vantage point and rid ourselves of what we no longer need to carry with us.

Of course, we will not arrive and instantly be freed of our past patterns or old ways of thinking. The inversion of this card may point to an unwillingness to seek change or let go of the baggage which, though heavy, is all we have known. Rather than welcome a new orientation or mindset, we resist it and thus miss the opportunity for renewed clarity.

Seven of Swords

Here is a scene of deception, and when we consider the paradoxical nature of the tarot 7, we might wonder who exactly is the deceiver and who is the deceived.

The man on the card is an archetypal trickster whose job is to fool and sabotage using his mischievous cunning. We may feel targeted by such a trickster in an outer situation, but often it is ourselves we deceive. It is easy to mentally undermine ourselves, talking ourselves out of our convictions or buying into negative thought patterns that interfere with our growth. Many of us suffer from that infamous imposter syndrome, in which we believe ourselves incapable of meeting standards that we are absolutely equipped to handle.

Inverted, this is an opportunity to take an honest look at our more shadowy patterns of manipulative behavior. As shameful as it feels, we all have underhanded tendencies. We might deflect blame or negativity onto others by ways of gaslighting, guilt, or corrupt logic. These behaviors mentally distance ourselves from the discomfort of our own faults, but in the end we are only deluding ourselves and remaining unconscious.

Eight of Swords

The Eight of Swords is the card of entrapment and imprisonment. Our thinking has become too rigid, our narratives and beliefs too binding. As in the Two of Swords, the blindfold suggests a lack of greater insight, but the woman's tied arms suggest she also lacks the powers of choice and action (though they are only a stretch away). Though 8 is the number of movement and freedom, we are bound up in stories of our helplessness, blinded to any possible way free.

This is not to say that we aren't genuinely trapped, or that our feelings of helplessness are invalid. Instead, this card suggests that we should not focus on the conditions of our powerlessness, but where power remains. With a developed sense of discernment and a little determination, we can challenge our constrictive narratives and beliefs and take responsibility for our liberation.

Inverted, we may indulge in our victimhood. Though an uncomfortable truth, it is human nature to find pleasure in pity. When we insist that we are victimized by the conditions of our lives, we both enjoy the comfort of others' sympathy and the relief of being pardoned from developing the mental fortitude to free ourselves.

Nine of Swords

In the dead of night we are tormented by imagined dangers we mistake for objective reality. The clear dichotomies of sense and nonsense, right and wrong, true and false that once were the core strength of the Swords have become indistinguishable, and the rational mind is overcome by the anguish of its anxious thoughts.

The woman cannot sleep because when we sleep, we dream, and when we dream, the ego-mind surrenders to the irrational wisdom of the unconscious. To the rigidly rational thinking function, this release seems a greater threat than relief. However, the thinking mind already suffers waking nightmares, which it can no longer eliminate with reasons and solutions. The only answer is to "go to sleep," giving up our obsessive fixations and seeking unconscious illumination.

Upside down, anguish becomes haunting. Now is the time to tear down our worries from the wall. Anxieties tarnish the Swords' natural sense of reason and make it unreliable, and now more than ever we need the clarity of the swords to defend us from terror. It is easy to give in to panic and a sign of mental resilience to refuse it and radically channel our efforts toward resolutions and peace.

Ten of Swords

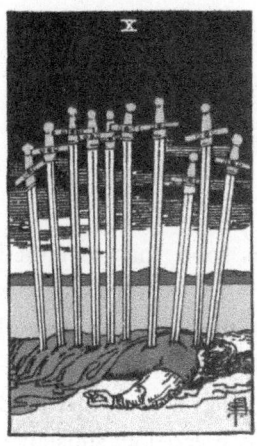

This is one of the most feared cards in the deck, with traditional interpretations containing terms like backstabbing and ruin. From a psycho-spiritual perspective, however, it represents a sudden (though avoidable) collapse of the balanced ego.

We know well that the Swords' power is discernment, and we employ it daily in our tasks of recognizing our limitations, analyzing our behaviors, and challenging our destructive thoughts. However, when we avoid or refuse these tasks, we fail to thoughtfully examine ourselves and what is slowly "stabbing away" at us. We may make excuses or avoid responsibility, unwittingly moving dangerously close to depression or burnout. Over time these swords thwart our sense of strength, clarity, and control within our lives, and eventually (often all at once) we collapse beneath them as our resolve gives out.

Inverted, we have hit an utter mental dead end. The Ten of Swords upside down depicts the mess of the muddled mind that has failed to become self-aware. We may experience a period of disorientation or despair, and our best recourse now is a radical pause and gentle self-analysis, seeking the breakthrough of the Ace.

PENTACLES

All credibility, all good conscience, all evidence of truth come only from the senses.
—FRIEDRICH NIETZSCHE

Ace of Pentacles

Manna, the mysterious food that sustained the Israelites in their forty-year trek across the desert, is a powerful mythological symbol for exploring the depth of the Ace of Pentacles. Though no bigger than a coriander seed and as light as dew, this bread-like substance fell from heaven, the Book of Exodus tells us, to feed the starving Israelites, replenishing both their bodies and their faith. Manna's essence as the food of supernatural nourishment has been reproduced in many myths and stories (think Christ's eucharist or Tolkien's elvish lembas bread), and signifies the parallel of physical and spiritual restoration.

This is the same mystery and miracle of the Ace of Pentacles. With this Ace we are offered the nutriment of the external world, which in turn enriches the internal world of soul. Like the Israelites, we might consider each flake of material blessing that falls on us as the sustenance for both our embodied living and our psycho-spiritual growth. Our task is always to harvest it with care, acknowledging the sacredness in the gifts we are given to manifest.

Drawing the Ace of Pentacles, we often receive the gift of something new, cocreated by our mortal effort and the benevolence of the universe. This may be a job opportunity, the development of a skill, an artistic project, a blooming relationship, an acceptance to a program—anything that is full of potential. Whatever the Ace brings, it is tangible and actionable, but at the same time engages our creativity and sparks our enthusiasm for life and what we might cultivate within it. The Ace of Pentacles encourages us to drive our hands into the earth and concretize the new energy into something potent and real.

Upside down, this Ace can signify our neglect of a vital opportunity. It may be that we are frozen waiting for the benevolent gifts of the universe to appear or that we are ignoring those gifts because we doubt the quality of our efforts to develop them. The sensation function in particular has the tendency to delay itself and excuse its hesitations, but the Ace of Pentacles is a rare and special offering that must be received and nourished.

Two of Pentacles

The Two of Pentacles shows us the struggle of balancing the multiplying realities of life. With each new pentacle (our various needs, responsibilities, and activities), our task is to mindfully fold it into the flow. The libido energy must be reallocated and adjusted to support the new thing without sacrificing what we are already holding up. If we are sensitive to the cues of our bodies, minds, and hearts, we can find an intuitive rhythm in our juggling that relieves us from frantically trying to control it all or dropping our balls entirely. Then, no matter how the sands shift beneath us or the waters rage around us, we will maintain the perpetual, natural cycle of this effort.

When the weight of our burdens exceeds our pleasures, or vice versa, life becomes lopsided and things will inevitably fall. Externally and internally, it becomes exhausting to maintain. Pulling the Two of Pentacles reversed may encourage us to reevaluate the many aspects of life we are managing. The psyche seeks balance, and we don't want to suffer a crash in order to be motivated to find a more sustainable flow.

Three of Pentacles

An architect, mason, and monk work together to complete the construction of a monastery. Because of their collaboration, this card is often interpreted as an invitation to teamwork or shared goals. However, what these three figures exemplify more deeply are the key virtues of the sensation function: the architect possesses skill and artistry; the mason embodies practical finesse; and the monk appreciates how stone and mortar assemble into something holy.

The Three of Pentacles is about building something real and lasting. It is not a house or place of commerce they construct but a religious dwelling, reminding us that the mundane efforts of life ultimately serve something sacred. The structures we create and the plans we labor to make real must be fortified by both substance and meaning. We must consciously enlist those necessary parts of ourselves to build lives that are carefully crafted, sturdy, and attuned to the higher goal.

However, none of us can accomplish this work in isolation. Reversed, we might be pushing ourselves to act as architect, mason, and monk without seeking outside support. Alternatively, we may find ourselves trapped in projects in which we feel like a cog in the machine and lack that essence of meaning, in which case we may need to mindfully shift the perspective for ourselves or the group.

Four of Pentacles

The stasis of 4 becomes stagnancy as the man's fixation with the "stuff" of life subverts potential development. The pentacle over his crown wards off higher insight; the one across his heart blocks deeper feeling; and the two under his feet prevent true grounding.

This is a card we associate with hoarding, be it things, money, memories, or any other resource. We clutch these materials of life in order to bring a sense of security to the ego determined to maintain its control. While this does win us the illusion of stability, our fixation on our immediate resources stalls our growth. Our perspective becomes tight and small, and we can only see what we grasp in our hands, which is usually only a fraction of what we actually have.

Reversed, the Four of Pentacles creates a false reality of scarcity and our tightfisted attitude becomes neurotic obsession. This card can point to complexes in which resources become tied to our sense of power in life. Whether we grew up with little or were taught that value is determined by financial or professional success, in these cases we tighten our grip to contradict beliefs that we're worthless, vulnerable, or lacking—be it money, attention, or love.

Five of Pentacles

When the fear of scarcity becomes our reality, we quickly lose our grounding in the sensate strengths of the psyche. Untethered from our previous comforts, talents, and plans, we believe ourselves lost. While clearly pointing to poverty and adversity, the Five of Pentacles also presents us as victims to our own bitterness and panic, alienated from the sanctuary that waits just beside us.

Here we see the consequences of our total dependence on the material world. Wounded and wandering in the snow, the Five of Pentacles depicts our alienation from the inner foundations of the Self. Without this perpetual support, when the external world inevitably lets us down, we suffer feelings of abandonment or being "left out in the cold." The beggars do not enter the monastery built in the Three of Pentacles, either because their turmoil has blinded them to it or because they do not trust that they can be helped. We cannot avoid suffering, but we can allow ourselves to seek sanctuary.

Reversed, the Five of Pentacles suggests that our poverty is spiritual rather than material. The emphasis on material life may indeed be preventing greater relationship with our depth. Alternatively, we must ask ourselves if we are too ashamed or bitter to open ourselves to aid. We alone can choose to enter the church, seek support, and reconnect to the sacred.

Six of Pentacles

What was unthinkable to the miserly figure of the Four of Pentacles is natural for the benefactor in the Six; with less attachment to what we control comes greater generosity, reciprocity, flexibility, and trust that our resources will not be depleted. Here we find the evolved perspective of 6, bringing a new agency and confidence in engaging the material side of life, particularly in finances, work roles, or family dynamics. There is both the freedom to give and the humility to receive.

Inverted, the give-and-take can become toxic. Perhaps we become too attached to the persona of the generous one or the needy one and get locked in dysfunctional patterns with others. In these cases we often suffer a pervasive burden or guilt, which indicates that we must either acknowledge that we've hit our limit of generosity or reconcile our shame and take responsibility for our own needs.

Seven of Pentacles

For the first time the Pentacles are not represented as money or a material to manage or manipulate but as fruit, nourishment, something to grow. The Seven of Pentacles encourages patience and thoughtful planning, challenging us to trust what we have planted. All things have their season, and rather than try to control, the ego can simply be ready when the fruit of our labors has ripened.

As with the other 7s, again we face paradox. We must wait, and we must act. As the suit of earth, the Pentacles thrive when we take a slower pace, but the great challenge in this card is the hovering question of *when*. The sensation function often overthinks and struggles to attune to its instincts, and if we hesitate too long, we may become paralyzed and possibly waste the opportunity before us. This is the test of the Seven of Pentacles: can we use our skills to sense whether it's best to be patient a while longer or finally begin the harvest?

Inverted, the anxiety of this problem has succeeded in thwarting our growth. We may be either spurred too early by impatience or hopelessly halted by uncertainty. Rather than panic over the problem of *when*, we should turn our attention back to sensation's strength—the *what*. Here we can rehone the skills and clear facts that we've relied on thus far to help us take right actions.

Eight of Pentacles

Here we have the impressive focus of the sensation function hard at work, producing at incredible speed. The man is dedicated not simply to the completion of the work but the craftsmanship, showing how great things can be accomplished if we give great attention to the task. When we submit ourselves entirely to this libidinal concentration, we may be shocked at what comes out of us. Simply, now is the time to engage in the work, focusing on the output of our talents.

However, in our society fixated on constant growth, we can be pressured into a perpetual state of productivity that is ultimately unsustainable. Reversed, we may be warned against the drudgery of working without the motivation of meaning or the danger of toiling away to meet unappeasable expectations. Another possibility is that our somewhat inferior or suppressed sensation function has become preoccupied with the particulars and insignificant details, sabotaging ourselves with a relentless perfectionism. In this case, the work truly never stops.

Nine of Pentacles

Perhaps the most natural (and underserved) aspect of the sensation function is the recognition of what is pleasurable to us. The woman of the Nine of Pentacles luxuriates in a host of sensory pleasures: the touch of her silk dress, the warmth of a beautiful day, the companionship of a parrot familiar, the sweet smell of grapes ripe on the vine. We have passed the point of effort and striving. The task now is merely to enjoy.

Pleasure compensates for the exhaustion of labor, which can come not only through sensory enjoyment but also by others enjoying the fruits that labor produced. Though she stands alone in her garden, the woman has clearly cultivated a bounty meant to be shared and appreciated. We are encouraged to celebrate our powers of independence and self-sufficiency, while also honoring the great gift we return to the world.

Inverted, we may be stuck in the hustle mindset that tells us we must do more, making things ever bigger and better. As with all the 9s, there's a sense of isolation in this card that, when reversed, seems less about self-sufficiency than the "I can do it all by myself" mindset. With this exhaustive attitude, the precious simplicity of gratification is lost to us.

Ten of Pentacles

Traditionally, the Ten of Pentacles is the card of material success. A family dances in their manor, the grapes of the Nine adorning their fine clothes. Ostensibly, it is a sign of achievement and abundance, an invitation to revel in the wealth we have worked hard to earn.

However, there is again a secret in this card pointing us to an entirely different dimension of life. Rather than being implanted into the scene as in the previous nine cards, the pentacles are laid atop the image and arranged in the pattern of the Kabbalistic Tree of Life.

Our attention is brought again to the realm of spirituality and the mystical path of individuation. We can relish these material successes we've won, but we must not forget the greater purpose of our journey.

Reversed, we may find ourselves like the old man, jaded, bored, and wondering what it was all for. We may also be in the opposite position, becoming far too possessed by either the riches we have or are seeking. We all know the moral here, that even the richest people in the world can feel unfulfilled. Abundance can give us security, pleasure, and even peace, but it cannot give us wholeness.

WANDS

There will come a point in everyone's life, however, where only intuition can make the leap ahead, without ever knowing precisely how. One can never know why but one must accept intuition as a fact.

—ALBERT EINSTEIN

Ace of Wands

We return to the Book of Exodus to explore a mythology of the wand, locating it in the hand of the prophet Moses. Chosen by God to liberate the enslaved Jews from Egypt, Moses receives his call through a voice within a burning bush that tells him of this great destiny. He is initially hesitant to accept the vision, and God orders him to cast his staff on the ground where it instantly transforms into a snake. As Moses picks it up by the tail, stunned, it changes back into a staff, and God says, "This... is so that they may believe."

These are the same words the intuitive function speaks to us. When the fire of imagination is lit and the vision of possibility sparked alive, we must believe. We do not know the source of these mysterious perceptions that reveal hidden realities and potentials, but they are nonetheless real. It is not by reason or evidence but by intuitive faith that Moses knows his magical staff can draw water from rocks, produce plagues, turn rivers to blood, and part the sea. Similarly for us, when we engage the power of the intuitive function, it is not logic but instinct that guides us to the true potentials of our lives.

The Ace of Wands is the spark of life. Although it's typically described as mental stimulation—a flash of insight or a light-bulb moment—the Ace of Wands is often experienced somatically—an electric tingle snaking along our spine and limbs. When we draw this Ace, it may signal a time of bursting ideas and rapid innovation. We may suddenly have a new sense of purpose, a vision of enterprise, an awakening of potential. This is not a moment to worry over hows and whens, but a time to get lost in the whys. The only task is to believe in the spark and follow where it leads.

As easy as it is to strike the match of the Ace of Wands, it is easier to snuff it out. When inverted, the Ace of Wands indicates a time of uninspired listlessness. We may become creatively numbed and drained of passion; or turn nostalgic for a past phase when the spark was bright, fretting it will never be rekindled. It is important to remember that this is not a permanent lethargy and we must have faith that the unconscious will once again appear with a blazing vision calling us to follow.

Two of Wands

The Two of Wands is a card of tension and ambiguity. A man stands on a parapet, poised between the world "out there" and the world in his hand. Often we interpret the globe as a symbol of his grip on his fate, but as with all the 2s, it also reveals a conflict of opposites.

After the invigorating spark of the Ace, we must marry our great vision with the conditions of the world and suddenly there is a crisis. As A. E. Waite puts it, "Between the alternative readings there is no marriage possible; on the one hand, riches, fortune, magnificence; on the other . . . chagrin, sadness, mortification."[2] Our intuitive imagination tells us we can make the impossible happen, initiating our visions and conquering the world, but when we look out at the overgrown fields and uncrossable rivers, we despair at the probability of failure. The result is hesitation and dread—a "mortification" of the psychic energy. We are challenged with holding both faith in the viability of our ideas *and* awareness of their possible futility.

Inverted, we may fall victim to this fear that it's all for nothing and thus toss the gift of the Ace away, giving up before we even started. Or we may have fully indulged the fantasy that we can take on the world and set our goals inhumanly high. The task is to protect the inspiration without becoming immobilized or delusional.

Three of Wands

While the man in the Two of Wands was stiff with uncertainty, the man of the Three of Wands is confident and clear-sighted. He is reserved but engaged, having sent out his ships (metaphorically initiated his ideas) without disillusionment. The challenge for us now is to distinguish the brilliance of our plans from the promise of their success, which allows us to take chances that feel natural and effortless. We must be hopeful, but not desperate. Our rewards may be far off, but still we should be proud of what we have already accomplished and eager for what will come next.

The Three of Wands is a card of anticipation, and so if it is inverted, we may feel exhausted by the waiting, and that easy, libidinal flow of intuitive energy becomes anxious and impatient. When it loses its receptive faith in the visions and instincts rising from the unconscious, the intuitive function can also turn paranoid and devolve into doubt. We may go back and obsess over all that we didn't prepare for or tailspin with stories of what may be going wrong. The challenge is to take the risk, let the ships sail, and trust the course we've plotted.

Four of Wands

In the Four of Wands our extraverted libidinal orientation shifts suddenly inward, focusing on the realm of hearth, home, and simple harmony. The two women move away from the rigidity of societal order and into the wild fields, choosing to be contained by the order of their own inner nature. There will be more opportunities to follow the pull of our passions, but for now we can frolic in the ease of a life lived by daily intuition, by what *just feels right*, finding the thrill of the Wands not in progress but contentment. It is in this harmonious tranquility that we find the tender gladness of togetherness and celebration.

Inverted, the Four of Wands is often negated into ideas such as "disharmony" and "arguments," but instead, we might consider how we're languishing in the stage of energetic stagnancy of the 4s. In this state, we suffocate our libidinal flow and turn ill-tempered or ill at ease. Another possibility is that we may need a conscious cleansing or refreshing of our energy, making both the inner and outer domain a space conducive to feeling at peace.

Five of Wands

As Jung tells us, conflict engenders fire, "and like every other fire it has two aspects, that of combustion and that of creating light."[3] Here five boys are engaged in such intense conflict that it has devolved into impassioned chaos, and combustion seems imminent.

We often find ourselves involved in a battle between our contrary drives, perspectives, and complexes. One part of us fights to focus on career, while another demands we face our self-doubt, while yet another begs for relaxation.

Rather than be riled to the point of explosive frustration, we must make room for each of the voices within us to speak and release its energy. Investigating or interviewing each of these drives will allow them to feel seen and heard, and then the intuitive function can more easily light the right way through.

Inverted, we are indeed headed toward combustion. The fiery nature of the Wands is reluctant to surrender its passion in favor of more diplomatic paths to resolution. We may also be projecting this internal conflict outward, finding ourselves combative and embroiled in unnecessary disputes. Perhaps these situations are unconscious attempts to distract us from more pressing internal battles.

Six of Wands

The ego rises above the inner conflict of the Five of Wands, and we have successfully aligned ourselves with a singular drive or focus. There is a sense of pride and victory in this hero, as all the other aspects of self that were once engaged in the conflict now rally behind a clarified purpose. Our intuitive vision is clear, and our libidinal energy unimpeded as we make confident progress in life. Something impressive has been achieved, whether in our outer lives or inner ones.

The Six of Wands has a clear shadow side, however, when the hero's success is not personal but performative. The audience signifies the need for external approval and recognition to validate our success. This is a struggle between deciphering the victories of the ego and the persona—what we truly desire versus what would satisfy others' expectations (be they real or imagined). Now is the time to use our intuition to tap into our most authentic sense of purpose and offer ourselves the validation needed to confidently follow it.

Seven of Wands

As this hero passionately fights for something important, it seems as if the flame of the intuition function is engaged with something meaningful. However, as with all the 7s, there is a paradox: do we see a hero defending his righteous position, or is he an overambitious hothead eager for combat?

The Seven of Wands calls us to defend our position, but we must be prudent in how we manage this task. We should remain resolute, but we should not assume that all battles must be won, nor that all threats mean failure. We must bring our imagined foes into the frame so that we see the true face of our challenges. Armed with this knowledge and the wisdom of our instincts, we may indeed intuit when we must leap up in forceful defense of our passions and when we must conserve our energy and find a more docile path.

The Seven of Wands reversed warns that while we should protect our positions, we should be wary of believing ourselves invincible or anticipating the attack. We can find a powerful sense of enthusiasm for life when we fight for "what's right," but without a bit of mediating discretion telling us we may be up against more than we can handle or that we're battling someone already waving the flag of surrender, we can be overcome with anger or aggression. With such a retaliatory attitude, we may eventually begin to make enemies out of passing shadows or even our best allies.

Eight of Wands

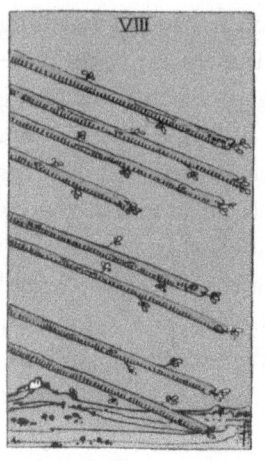

The Eight of Wands is the only card of the Rider-Waite-Smith tarot that does not display any anthropomorphized element, be it a shadow, hand, heart, or face. With the exception of a lone house on a distant hill, humanity is conspicuously missing, exemplifying the card's absence of ego. Here, the focus is not on how we direct or struggle with our intuitive powers, but on the force of unconsciously driven intuition itself.

The Wands simply fly, whether cast down from an invisible god or up from an intrepid hero out of frame. The intuition function sweeps in with that remarkable potency, inspiring us to explore new innovations, make astonishing connections, accomplish what yesterday seemed impossible. With this power out of the hands of our grasping egos, we are led by the libidinal energy itself. And truly, it is when we remove ourselves from the picture that the lines explode into art, the words flow onto the page, or the solutions just click into place.

Reversed, it seems as if that breakthrough might never come. We feel stalled out, delayed, or dried up. However, we must remember that the inspiring state of the Eight of Wands is not something we can make happen, nor is it something we get to keep. The energy of intuitive flow is intoxicating, but also fickle and fleeting. We must simply be receptive to its arrival and yield to its departure.

Nine of Wands

We typically equate the Nine of Wands with sympathy, acknowledging the man's resilience despite his wounding. However, his bitter expression and bandaged head shows that the injury is not to his body or heart, but to his ego. His wall of wands are set up not only to protect him from further harm, but to barricade him from the open world that threatens his diminished ego-control.

Sometimes we need the barricade. Sometimes we need to pull back and remove ourselves from the threats of living. But when our efforts fail, when we feel ourselves rejected, insulted, or dismissed, we might misdirect our energy into resentful isolation. Our brittle egos nurse our outrage, and thus rechannel our libido energy into building fences rather than transcending boundaries. With such a one-sided attitude, we block the intuitive inspiration that might draw us across the threshold into greater possibility and strength.

Inverted, this card is much the same as upright, but now we have the added question of whether some part of us feels safer hurt and stuck than healed and free. At this final stage before we end our Wands journey, now more than ever adaptability and self-reflection are essential. We should reengage the intuitive function to imagine our liberated futures and free ourselves from festering wounds.

Ten of Wands

The Ten of Wands shows how our energy is driven into enduring the struggle rather than accomplishing the task. Like Sisyphus who was cursed to roll a boulder up a hill for eternity, we continue to strive to clear ourselves of a weight we will never be able to shed. The endeavor of managing all the energetic burdens of life quickly exhausts us, but rather than reorganize the weight or put some of our wands down, we simply push through until we crumple under the effort.

In the Ten of Wands we neglect to use the intuition function to do what it does best: innovating new, more enlivening ways of being. Rather than wearily labor on, this is an opportunity to pause our futile efforts and reengage the intuitive, creative faculty that can imagine a lighter path forward. In order to make any progress, we must ask how the energy must be redistributed and what must be let go.

Inverted, the invitation is to drop the load. We must take stock of all that we're carrying, and though it is undeniably difficult, choose to put it down. Even at the risk of disappointing others, facing genuine failure, or suffering real loss, we must put it down. The psyche needs release from the impossible pressure and room for the Ace to return.

— CHAPTER 5 —

THE MANY FACES OF THE TAROT COURT

*You, my own deep soul,
trust me. I will not betray you.
My blood is alive with many voices
telling me I am made of longing.*
—RAINER MARIA RILKE

For many, court cards are the most intimidating of the deck. In traditional reading they represent the people around us, but often identifying these characters and their purpose in the spread is challenging. A card might seem to point to our father, friend, and boss all at once, or we might not be able to connect it to anyone at all. A psycho-spiritual orientation makes the courts not only more approachable, but often the most illuminating cards in a spread. Rather than representing who we're encountering *out there*, they represent who's speaking *in here*. They show us the array of subpersonalities that are alive and active within us all. Our goal is to get to know these unique sides of ourselves, learning how they support or sabotage our individuation. By offering us a face to focus on, they help us acquaint ourselves with the many voices within telling us how we should live.

To build relationship with the tarot court, we must get to know and befriend them. Each possesses a unique personality and set of traits that come more into focus each time they arrive on the table. We do not need to overanalyze or demystify their symbols; we simply need to join them in conversation. The more we engage with them as real, living entities, the clearer their individual characters and roles in our psyches become. And though these are not the only ways, there are four key lenses through which we might relate to the court cards in our psyches: as projection, persona, typological maturity, and complex.

Projection

Projection is as spontaneous, natural, and involuntary as any bodily function. As defined by Freud, projection is the unconscious process of refracting inner content—what Jung calls our shadows—onto outer others in order to keep it at a distance and protect the fragile ego. Projections can be both personal and archetypal. On the personal level we might spot our own unconscious selfishness mirrored by a friend, and at the archetypal level we may find the invincible tyrant incarnated in our boss. Though we typically project away what is shadowy in our personalities, we can just as easily project out the good, such as revering a strength in our partners that we are blind to in ourselves or idolizing a neighbor as the perfect archetypal Mother we long for. Whether "bad" or "good," the essential rule of projections is that whatever we cannot identify in ourselves is made other, and so it is *in* others that we encounter these aspects. As Jung wrote, "Projections change the world into the replica of one's own unknown face."[1]

Any tarot card can reveal a part of us we've projected, but because they are human figures with distinct faces, voices, and personalities, it is especially common with court cards. For instance, we might see the charging Knight of Swords as our friend who is tragically impulsive, thus unconsciously distancing ourselves from our own reckless attitude, or we might project the beautiful Queen of Cups onto a new girlfriend, becoming enraptured by her love which we don't realize we deny ourselves. If we connect a court card to someone we know, we do not need to immediately diagnose a projection, but simply question which characteristics within them are also—maybe—within ourselves.

Persona

When a court card appears as a representation of our persona, it generally refers to how we present ourselves to the world or the roles we try to fill. Like projection, the persona is not inherently negative and is not only normal, but also necessary in the psyche. It is the public face of our personality, the proverbial mask we wear that both allows us to feel socially adapted and shields the more vulnerable "true" personality. The persona only becomes problematic when we misidentify it as the sum of who we are, binding ourselves to it and abandoning our authenticity to maintain the mask.

This is something to which we all fall victim occasionally. The King of Pentacles may highlight an attachment to our persona as the successful business owner, which drives us to overwork ourselves to uphold it, or the Queen of Wands may show our persona as the perpetual life of the party whose charisma and sociability exhaust our more introverted side. When a court card feels instantly recognizable as a facet of ourselves, it may be an opportunity to consider how much we genuinely identify with this aspect of our personality versus how much we feel we must perform it.

Typological Maturity

Considering their rank and suit, we can also read court cards in a more systematic way as the stages of development of our cognitive functions. As we discussed in chapter 3, though we all have our individual formula of superiority and inferiority with these personality functions, all of the functions exist in us to varying degrees. We may at any point be in a phase of growth or regression with a function.

The traditional structure of the deck shows the court cards in a hierarchy of social rank, but we can also think of them as a hierarchy of *developmental* rank. The Pages are immature; the Knights are developing in maturity; and the Queens and Kings share full maturity.* Drawing the

---

* We are not speaking of maturity in a positive or negative behavioral sense, but simply as an evolution of competency or authority in the suit.

Page of Pentacles, for instance, may indicate we currently have a more inferior or immature expression of our sensation function, while the King of Wands may show a strong and matured intuitive function. In this reading of the court cards we can see where we can more consciously focus our development or rely on our natural strengths.

Complexes

The final and most psychologically potent way of reading court cards is as complexes. Though they sound intimidating, we can think of psychological complexes simply as pockets of personality that are distinct from the central ego. We are all made up of a web of complexes rising up and falling away in perpetual flow. As depth psychologist Robert Johnson explains:

> We can see [complexes] as independent energy systems that combine in us, for they are autonomous: Each has its own consciousness, its own values, desires, and points of view. Each leads us in a different direction; each has a different strength or quality to contribute to our lives; and each has its own role in our total character.[2]

We might imagine it this way: just as a pearl is shaped around a single irritating grain of sand, each complex within us is formed around a nucleus, be it an archetype, trauma, or some other psychological disruption. Over time it hardens and becomes "autonomous" in that it forms its own personality, behaving in unique and independent ways, launching up out of the shadow to speak or act when its nuclear irritant is triggered.

Let's take the example of the inferiority complex as first outlined by depth psychologist Alfred Adler. If a child is consistently told they are inferior in some way, they will inevitably develop a psychological wound around this perceived lack of worth. This is the nucleus of the complex. As they grow up, they may push themselves to become highly successful, unaware that their striving for superiority is an unconscious effort to compensate for that old wound of inferiority. Every time that wound is triggered—perhaps when they are passed up for a promotion or disciplined for an error in a report—this compensating complex will rise up and momentarily take over, acting autonomously and possibly

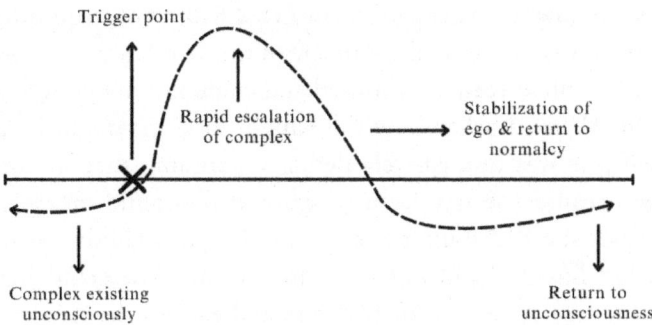

Figure 6. Diagram of a Complex

antagonistically to the true ego-self. It may push them to work endless hours, sabotage coworkers, or overexaggerate achievements, all to protect that original wound of inferiority and worthlessness. Essentially, there are two personalities coexisting: the child made to feel inferior who simply wants to be valued and the complex intent on being superior in order to eliminate the original wound. If the person cannot identify this complex when it appears, they will be ruled by it, acting in ways that may betray who they really are.

Complexes present themselves in our patterns of behavior and thought, but after years of living with them they can be hard to identify. We tend to be taken over by a complex when its originating wound or archetype is triggered, and then later, when the complex has receded and the ego is again in control, we think: *Why do I do that? What's wrong with me?* The tarot can be a powerful tool in recognizing our complexes, examining their influences on our psyches, and identifying their origins.*

---

* It's important to note that complexes are not always bad. We may develop complexes that help us in many ways, as with the inferior child who pushes themselves to become successful. However, as we grow and change, previously supportive complexes may interrupt our growth or overtake other aspects of our personality, driving us to act in damaging ways.

Let me offer an example. I once had a client tell me that she'd been working hard to heal the emotional neglect of her youth and wanted guidance on how to go deeper. The inverted Knight of Cups caught my attention, and as I described the image of this petulant, overly sensitive teenager, my client seemed confused and could not match it to anyone in her life. When I asked how the Knight of Cups might be present in herself, she was immediately defensive, arguing that she was only sensitive because she had been so ignored as a child. She explained that though she had fought hard to validate this childhood pain for herself, her husband did not seem to care or understand her emotional suffering. As we spoke, her calm and earnest demeanor became increasingly agitated and even a touch histrionic, as if acting out this wounded hero-knight. When this energy receded a few minutes later, I asked what had triggered that response. She admitted that she acted the same way with her husband whenever he seemed more skeptical than supportive. It seemed that his lukewarm attitude pressed into that wound of not feeling emotionally validated, and her instinctive reaction was to become this moody Knight rushing in to protect herself from those old feelings of rejection. Exploring it together, we saw that this Knight of Cups complex crusaded to defend the validity of her feelings, but his intensity and impatience was actually pushing her loved ones farther away.

Court cards give a face to these energies within us, allowing us to speak to them, learn from them, and eventually integrate them—if we know how to work with them.

Working with Court Card Complexes

When we pull a court card and sense that it represents a side of our personality, this is a prime moment to consider the card as a complex. When we examine our complexes, we are ultimately confronting our shadows, facing our deepest wounds, and taking accountability for our most challenging behaviors and beliefs. It is hard psychoanalytic work, and so it goes without saying that it is best done in the containment of a therapeutic setting. However, we can still, carefully, begin this sort of inner work on our own.

Over my years of study and practice, I have adapted a five-step technique to carefully investigate these complexes with the court cards and integrate them back into the personality. We'll walk through this process now using the example of the Queen of Swords.

1. Identify the Card in You.

After you've pulled the court card and identified it as an aspect of your personality, begin by getting a sense of who the card is to you. With the Queen of Swords, for example, you might think of her as someone critical and emotionless or maybe feel she is a woman of fierce rationality and strong problem-solving skills. Whether you first refer to a guidebook or connect to the card more intuitively, the goal is to explore the energy and personality that *you* find in the card.

Once you have a clear image of who the person is and their particular qualities—in our example perhaps a critical mother who is loving but stern—consider the behaviors, thoughts, feelings, and reactions they demonstrate within your psyche. With this critical and maternal Queen of Swords, perhaps you know that you tend to scorn your friends' foolish plans or ruthlessly bite back when someone says something less than thoughtful. Remember that this is not a moment of blame but simple identification.

2. Notice When It Comes and Goes.

In this stage we are investigating the particular triggers of the complex so that we may eventually understand its origin. This is an exercise in mindfulness, noticing the microinteractions and subtle behaviors that activate it. With the Queen of Swords, maybe you notice that your critical attitude with friends gets triggered when they ignore your advice; or maybe you sense it receding as you become suddenly embarrassed by your callous comments.

Most of what we observe in this stage might feel trivial, but beware of defensiveness or denial already interrupting the process. We can think of complexes as we would real people, and no one is comfortable when their actions are placed under a microscope. Simply begin to watch with curiosity and nonjudgment.

3. Give It a Name.

Naming a card is a crucial part of the process. In order to fully understand and eventually attempt to integrate this complex, we must differentiate it from our ego. When we begin to examine our complexes more critically, their previously unconscious machinations and manipulations are now plain to see, and we may be overcome with shame, anger, or self-loathing. If we have not successfully separated the ego from the complex, when we begin pulling it apart—as we see in the Tower—we will simultaneously tear ourselves down. Yes, we will eventually need to take responsibility for its actions, but first we must see the complex as an inner other who is distinct from our true self.

There is no need to overthink the naming process. Often the complex already possesses a name we've given it naturally. In our example, you might call the complex simply "The Queen of Swords," or you might label it something more specific such as "The Ice Queen" or "The Heartless Mother"—whatever feels most personal and accurate.

Once it is titled, anytime the complex is activated in your psyche, name its presence. This will help you to both distinguish its unique identity and form an intimacy with it. With the Queen of Swords, then, when a coworker shoots you a backhanded compliment and you feel yourself turn steely and mean, remind yourself that "The Ice Queen" has entered the room. This should give you pause and create distance to properly analyze what you think, feel, and do next.

4. Ask Why It's Here.

Now that we have an understanding of the complex's behaviors, triggers, and core identity, we can try to uncover the original wound that formed it. Because complexes are living sides of our personality, they may resist analysis or the reopening of our wounds to protect themselves, but this is the point in the process where real change may be possible.

We can begin by asking the complex why it's here. Entering into active imagination or internal dialogue, we can speak to it directly. Sometimes there is an immediate answer, and sometimes we must be patient in this interrogation. Perhaps the Queen of Swords admits that she believes she's impervious to mistakes or that she gets upset when others' don't acknowledge that she's always right. This information may lead you to inquire *why* she is this way, and with continued investigation and time, it may become clear that she's defending a part of you that feels deeply vulnerable and terrified of getting life "wrong."

Another option is to consider the early experiences that may be attached to the complex. For example, perhaps the Queen of Swords reminds you of your mother who tended to alienate herself from others when she was emotionally suffering. This may lead you to see that you learned to turn away from rather than toward people when life is challenging, which in turn causes a deep-rooted distrust of others that makes you seem cold.

Keep in mind that this work is slow and deliberate and will take time. Complexes rise and fall naturally within the psyche, but some are formed from deep-seated wounds that absolutely do require a conscientious approach or a dedicated therapeutic setting. Always use your best judgment and seek help when things feel overwhelming.

5. Forgive and Integrate.

Facing our complexes is a form of shadow work, and as with all shadow work, forgiveness and acceptance are a vital part of the process. When we address these complexes, we uncover some of our most shameful and sinister parts, and though we also discover the wounds behind them, we are no less responsible for them.

In my own early analysis, I quickly discovered a potent complex that was causing harm in many of my closest relationships. At first the complex raged with denial, blaming everyone around me, but slowly I was able to notice its patterns, identify its triggers, and name it when it appeared. Over the course of several months, I located the wound it was protecting within me, and then at last I was able to start the healing work.

As difficult as this process had been, it was not nearly as challenging as dealing with the shame that came from it. I had empathy for it and the wounded child underneath, but acknowledging that it had caused my loved ones any amount of pain or frustration was unbearable. However, it was only by doing this work that I was able to slowly begin healing and integrating it. Once I accepted accountability for the complex when it was triggered, I was not overcome by it. I began to see the choice in my response, allowing me to sidestep its negative behaviors and attend to the deeper wound it wanted to defend.

Something that can bolster this process is imagining the court card in its benevolence. The Queen of Swords complex may be critical and cruel, but all aspects of our psyches inherently contain their opposite, and so we can also locate her strength and protective love. By reaching for the more positive aspects of the card, we may rediscover the natural wisdom the complex had originally formed to teach us. Then we might step into that part of ourselves with greater consciousness and self-forgiveness.

— CHAPTER 6 —

THE COURT CARDS

As we move through the court cards, we will explore them on three levels: first, through their intrinsic personalities; second, in their potential meanings both upright and inverted; and lastly in the possible ways they might present as an intrapsychic figure. This third level of exploration is in no way definitive and only a suggestion among countless possibilities. For some cards we will examine their mythic correlations and for others the possible complexes or inner experiences they depict, but for all of them we should remember that their significance is wholly personal. You might instantly connect with one of these suggestions, but be wary not to take it as a diagnosis. Or you might not relate to any of these reflections, in which case you should pursue other possibilities guided by your own intuition or unique relationships to the card.

Additionally, with the courts we can bring in another layer of Jungian wisdom: the concepts of extraversion and introversion. Most think of extraverts as outgoing, boisterous people who love a party, and introverts as solitary bookworms who love quiet rainy mornings. However, Jung used these terms to point to our *orientation* of psychic energy, whether it tends to turn outwardly or inwardly. The extraverted personality derives meaning and seeks development from its external experiences, where the introvert does so via internal experience.* Therefore, we might think of the Pages and Kings as introverted

---

* There is no such thing as a pure introvert or extravert. Many introverted people love parties, just as many extraverts prefer quiet mornings. Rather we should think of them as ends of a spectrum, and each of our four cognitive functions can be expressed at different points on it.

because they draw meaning from their personal discoveries and self-sovereign laws, while the Knights and Queens are more extraverted because they seek meaningful connection and engagement with the world at large.*

THE PAGES

Knowing yourself is the beginning of all wisdom.
—ARISTOTLE

The Pages are the most immature and inexperienced rank of the tarot court, but this immaturity is not a lack of sophistication as much as it is innocence. The Pages have a childlike energy, which makes them inquisitive and eager for growth; but like a child, they can also be easily overwhelmed, insecure, and naive.

Being more introverted, at their core the Pages are about self-exploration—learning their individual gifts, flaws, desires, and fears. They can focus our attention on the inner child we once were, or they might point to emerging parts of ourselves that are new and undeveloped. The mission of the Pages is to learn as much as they can about their own innate qualities. Their curiosity is not yet about what they can do out there in the world, but about what they inherently possess that makes them special—what potential they hold. They signal new beginnings, encouraging us to once again allow ourselves to arrive at a start.

---

* Other tarot scholars may view the Queens as introverted and Kings as extraverted, but in my opinion this stems from the inherited bias that the masculine principle is purely active and thus outward-facing and the feminine is passive and inward-facing. However, we have moved beyond this bias in archetypal theory, and know that the Masculine and Feminine are much more complex than the images of the virile husband and docile wife.

Page of Cups

The Page of Cups is sensitive, imaginative, and dreamy. She is sometimes scorned for her idealism, but this Page is deeply connected to her innate values and principles, believing in the goodness in herself and the world. As the most immature stage of the feeling function, the Page of Cups is learning how she *relates* to both the inner and outer universe. Though naive and even gullible, she loves truly and follows her heart.

With the Page of Cups, we should contemplate how we permit ourselves to indulge in our inner worlds. It may be a time to luxuriate in imagination or the whimsy of inner fantasy. Tapping into the Page of Cups, we should feel more deeply and freely without worrying over worldly responsibility. Like Narcissus, we might allow ourselves to gaze into our depths, falling in love with our own beauty, longing, and capacity to love.

Reversed, we may behave too much like Narcissus, perseverating on our own subjective experience. Alternatively, our naive openheartedness may be making us vulnerable to others' cruelties, which can quickly wound the defenseless inner Page. A final possibility—and perhaps the most common—is that we have sacrificed our feeling for a more rational orientation to life. Then we must quest to recover that childlike longing to reattune to our hearts.

We might imagine the internalized Page of Cups as a sort of Sleeping Beauty complex. When our active feeling center is rejected or we feel pressured to subdue it, we may feel "put to sleep," unconsciously barricading ourselves in the protective thorns of our negative emotional impulses. These may present as sensitive outbursts, fits of sullenness, or even a thorough dissociation from the feeling center altogether.

During a flare of her chronic illness, a past student pulled the Page of Cups to reflect on her emotional turmoil and brought it into active imagination. At first it wouldn't speak, and she found that it was trapped in a locked box at the bottom of a lake. My student went diving in several active imagination sessions until finally the box opened and the Page spoke, explaining that it was my student herself who had locked her away. Shocked, my student realized that by trying so hard to remain positive in her illness she had unconsciously suppressed her openhearted feeling nature. In consciously embracing it, she quickly improved both emotionally and physically.

Page of Swords

The Page of Swords is a youth of sparkling intellectual curiosity and quick-witted cunning. She is energetic, inquisitive, mentally agile, and thrives on her independence. As the most immature stage of the thinking function, the Page of Swords processes information instantaneously though incompletely. She is clear on what is right and wrong, though she may not yet be able to express why or recognize shades of gray.

Pulling the Page of Swords, we may be facing a period of decision-making that requires us to become clear on our rationales or navigating new responsibilities that demand a sharper mental acumen. Now is the time to hone the faculty of discernment and really question what we feel clear about. How might we better communicate our needs, establish stronger boundaries, or discern shrewder solutions?

Reversed, the Page of Swords struggles with detachment, either by becoming too aloof or failing to accept when her ideas are naive or unsophisticated. In the former case, we may turn impassive and unfeeling, relying on our rationality to escape uncomfortable emotions and challenging discussions. In the latter, our unrefined judgments can become vindictive or outright malicious, cutting out positive attachments the moment they require a more amenable side of us to emerge.

The Page of Swords can appear as the disciplined inner child denied the right to free, unbridled self-expression. She becomes dependent on her inherited dichotomies of right and wrong, unable to mature with flexibility and confidence in how *she* chooses to live. When caught in this sort of complex, we may be stuck as the perpetual "good student" waiting for instructions. We may feel hopelessly indecisive or suffer intense emotional fits when the "rules" change or we must learn to adapt to the shifting conditions of life. We may rebel with self-isolation or project our frustration outward by attacking others with blunt, callous critiques. In these cases the best medicine may be exactly what the Page of Swords fears—abandoning our rigid rationales and indulging in our hearts' desire.

Page of Pentacles

The Page of Pentacles' unique power is her focus. As the immature, introverted stage of sensation, her entire world is what she can touch, see, learn, and do. She's attuned to her body, although she doesn't yet know exactly how to interpret its signals; she can observe complex details, though may not see the larger pattern they create. Her world is vibrant with discovery, curiosity, and wonder, and she is still very much its student.

The Page of Pentacles invites us to focus on what is right in front of us. We should draw our attention to the rhythms of our bodies or the real, humble work of our hands. She loves to learn and try, but does not worry over mastery or artistry. Our intention now should be simply to cherish the pentacle itself—our special project, talent, or fascination—and approach it with openhearted devotion.

Inverted, the Page of Pentacles' focus may become obsessive and excessive. Our fixation on getting things "right" can overshadow the enjoyment of our growth, and we might even suffer from symptoms such as brain fog, listlessness, or acute insecurity. Another tendency with this reversed Page is to overindulge in our pleasures, languishing as the hedonist, the loafer, or the perpetual student. It is time to reengage in the here and now with the pen, the paint, the body.

We might identify the gifted, perfectionistic Page of Pentacles as the miller's daughter in the story of Rumpelstiltskin. When the miller brags that his daughter is skilled enough to spin straw into gold, the king locks her away, demanding she perform the task or be executed. Though masterful at her craft, the miller's daughter knows that her talents are only human. Therefore, when the magical imp Rumpelstiltskin offers to complete the task for her, she eagerly accepts, not realizing that the cost will eventually be her firstborn child. What Rumpelstiltskin represents is the complex of perfectionism and superior skill that the Page of Pentacles discovers in herself, but the cost of this perfection is the sacrifice of her authenticity and true potential symbolized by the child. When the Page of Pentacles pressures herself to accomplish the impossible, she loses the blissful effort in cultivating and loving her gifts.

Page of Wands

The Page of Wands is the bright, passionate, and impatient youth eager to burst into the world. In its introverted form, the intuitive function perceives its intuitions in the moment, questioning the immediate *why* of things. This Page is spontaneous and enthusiastic, following the draw of wonder even if it leads directly into the tiger's den. She seeks to know the world as fully as she knows herself, driven always by the unconscious tides of inspiration.

The Page of Wands invites us to have faith in our intuitions without yet making meaning of them. It may be a time to develop trust in our intuitive instincts, allowing ourselves to be daring, confident, and fervent in our widening passions. We may meander here, but that is well and good. The Page does not know to what horizon she journeys, but she faithfully follows the energy. Perhaps an adventure is exactly what we most need.

Reversed, the Page of Wands can be chaotic. We may abruptly change course or drop initiatives. Our behavior can become increasingly erratic and temperamental; our frantic impulses can make us hasty, gullible, and prone to trouble. Intuition is a powerful force that can easily overwhelm an undeveloped ego, and so we must follow it from a centered place.

The Page of Wands is a sort of Icarus, the notorious boy of Greek myth who flew too close to the sun. When Icarus's father crafts wings of wax and feathers so that Icarus might escape their prison, he is instructed not to fly too near the burning sun nor the raging waters (metaphorically, to avoid the common pitfalls of intuition: inflation or inundation by the unconscious). Of course, as Icarus soars across the sky, his mortal limitations are forgotten and his wings melt, sending him crashing into the sea.

The inner complex of the Page of Wands is intoxicated with being alive, but struggles both with tempering her passions and heeding more prudent wisdom. Fearing restriction, the inner Page of Wands can quickly rebel and fly into territories she is not equipped to manage. The task is to preserve our intuitive seeking while also recognizing how we've retaliated against its suppression by becoming reckless, inflated, and deaf to caution.

THE KNIGHTS

Remember that there is nothing noble in being superior to some other man. The true nobility is in being superior to your previous self.

—W. L. SHELDON

The Pages, now strengthened in their experience of selfhood, step up in maturity and become the Knights—the burgeoning heroes of the tarot.

Where the Pages were introverted and mostly passive, the Knights are extraverted and active, focused entirely on how they interact with the world at large. This development mirrors our real-world growth. Like adolescents, the Pages explore themselves simply to figure out who they are, while the Knights are like young adults fresh out of high school, convinced they are ready to take on the world. The libidinal energy of the Knight shifts from self-probing to self-actualizing, making real progress in life.

The Knights' primary focus is motion and development. We make great strides in this phase, but with such momentum we are also prone to overestimating our abilities and tripping ourselves up. Therefore, with the Knights we find ourselves accomplishing the most forward progress, but we also hit the most frustrating pockets of stagnancy and error.

Knight of Cups

The Knight of Cups is the epitome of poise, representing the feeling function finding its grace. The sometimes self-centered introverted feeling turns generous and warm in its extraverted state when it has an object to seek—something or someone to love. Like his younger form as the Page, the Knight of Cups is dreamy and idealistic, but rather than prove his naivete, these qualities add to his charm. He loves without inhibition, offering all of himself to the object of his affections. However, this openheartedness is also often his downfall, making him particularly susceptible to possessiveness, melodrama, and the agony of heartache.

Right side up, we often associate this card with romance, but it can just as easily point to our feeling development in work, family life, or community. We draw the cup from our own hearts and hold it before us—symbolically, we take our own precious values and offer them back to the world, hoping it will value them in return. What this Knight models is genuine vulnerability, cherishing the beauty of what we've cultivated within our cup while also seeking someone to drink from it.

What the Knight of Cups fails to understand, however, is that not all the world feels what he feels or loves as he loves. This oversight makes him tragically sensitive, and when slighted, he has neither the humility nor the maturity to understand that difference is not rejection and rejection is not annihilation. When reversed, the Knight of Cups can act out this emotional insecurity in toxic ways: throwing tantrums, cheating, seducing, abusing substances. His inversion may indeed invite us to contemplate our own emotionally puerile behaviors.

As an inner figure, this Knight of Cups is the quintessential Knight in Shining Armor. He shows us an expression of the animus as the inner lover who comes to save us, dressed in virtue and drunk with adoration. We may project this noble hero onto another, have it projected onto us, or find this faultless champion crusading in our own psyches as a complex. Though a compelling image, when we idealize this Knight we sabotage his honorable desire to be seen as he truly is and loved for it.

Knight of Swords

The Knight of Swords is the fastest of his brothers, spurring his horse into a frenzied gallop. His earlier incarnation as the introverted Page was somewhat detached and distracted, but here we see the extraverted thinking function focused in its rush to take action. There's an assertive sureness in the Knight of Swords, a sense that he's off to seize the moment or save the day. He relies entirely on the infallibility of his logic, which enables him to act quickly and decisively. At the same time there's something unnerving about his speed, and we instinctively guess things are going to end badly. The thinking function judges by reason, which is blind to its faults and biases. The Knight's reckless speed is propelled by his brazen faith in his own determinations. He has literally thrown caution to the wind.

When pulling the Knight of Swords, we may need to tap into that bold self-sureness and push our plans forward. As our thinking develops, we will need to test its discernment, which we can only do by charging ahead and putting it to use. That being said, there is a fine line between assurance and arrogance, and when we are moving at a breakneck pace, we can easily overestimate our judgments and overlook the finer points in our decision-making. This is the doom of the reversed Knight of Swords, whose reckless confidence rebuffs outside insight as he rushes into something he may have tragically misjudged.

Many struggle with the hubristic Knight of Swords complex, a pattern we see reflected time and again in myth and literature. Shakespeare's Macbeth blindly trusts the prophecy of his kingship, only to secure his downfall through murder and ambition. In Greek mythology, Arachne's boastful confidence in her superior weaving provokes Athena's wrath, and the goddess curses her to weave forever as a spider. Even *Star Wars'* Anakin Skywalker, so convinced of his own power, succumbs to the Dark Side, leading to his ultimate ruin.

Certainty is the gift of the thinking function inflated with its own sense of judgment, but its cost is connection to instinct and humility. Often, the overdevelopment of this hubris arises as a defense against the discomfort of feeling fallible, mediocre, or weak. Yet, in striving to prove our superiority, we risk overestimating our rational powers and unwittingly setting ourselves up for failure.

Knight of Pentacles

While the Knight of Swords rushes to victory, the Knight of Pentacles seems frozen in place, examining his pentacle as if he's not sure what to do with it. The Page of Pentacles thrived in the inward experience of investigating her reality and potential, but the Knight's outward focus becomes mired in the detail, nearly inert in the effort to observe, assess, and plan. It may be weeks or months, but this Knight will take the necessary time to understand the complexity of his tasks, patiently and deliberately persisting until they are accomplished.

When pulling the Knight of Pentacles, we may need to develop a more steadfast intentionality in our labors. We may desire those big leaps forward, but this Knight teaches us the truth of that classic adage: "Slow and steady wins the race." When we allow our sensation function to carefully examine all the elements of our experience before taking action, we may craft securer foundations and arrive at more solid solutions.

Of course there is a downside to these laborious methods. Reversed, the Knight of Pentacles warns that if we indulge in this meticulousness, we may go from slow to stagnant. We worry over pointless details, inundate ourselves with unresolved to-do lists, or repeat the same task, hoping this time for perfection. Then we are simply plodding along, allowing ourselves to hem and haw between beige or gray paint, and after months the walls are still left bare.

The Knight of Pentacles' idleness may be a symptom of a complex around the fear of taking ownership over his life. For some—especially sensation types—the energetic effort to consciously direct our lives is daunting and even paralyzing, resulting in a sense of failure that intensifies our lack of initiative rather than correcting it. With so many choices, details, and ways we might go wrong, we become overwhelmed and turn avoidant, couching ourselves in the comfort of stasis. There is no urgency for change, because change is the great threat. If we dug a little deeper, we might even locate that original gifted child in the Page, once so talented and productive, now crippled by the enormous task of growth.

Knight of Wands

The Knight of Wands is at once spontaneous and impatient, charming and volatile. Although he can be capricious with his extraverted intuition, this Knight is ruled by his swells of inspiration and lust for meaning. His ambition is not for achievement, but purpose, seeking always to innovate, motivate, make a difference, change the world.

Pulling the Knight of Wands, we might be moved toward an enthusiastic goal, whether that be in career, love, artistry, or self-mastery. We may be called to break out of our interior fantasy world of what-ifs and pursue external actualization. This is not a card of plans and practices but of following vital energy. Aflame with excitement and thrilled for the boundless future, we should let nothing deflate our emergent quest for meaning.

Being still in development, the Knight of Wands will at some point attempt a feat he cannot master. He will inevitably face his energetic limits and be disappointed to learn that not everything holds the promise he projects onto it. Because of his brashness, this stubborn Knight often ignores the essential lessons, rebelling against self-reflection and refusing self-discipline. Thus, when pulling this card reversed, it may be a signal to temper our intensity. If we do not do it willingly, fate may force the definition of "learning our limits" upon us.

The Knight of Wands is the inner crusading hero. He revels in saving the day, and because his intuitive instincts are almost always right, he becomes easily inflated with overconfidence. We might imagine him as a sort of Indiana Jones: the morally mutable hero who always has a little dirt on his face, always trusts his gut, and whose arrogance is the source of his undeniable charisma. We sometimes need this relentless faith in our intuitions, but this brazen courage may stem from an inability to face our fallibility. When we pause to consider the true risk of being wrong and missing our mark, we're vulnerable to doubt. And this, for the valiant hero, is the ultimate defeat.

THE QUEENS

Give your hands to serve and your hearts to love.

—ST. TERESA OF AVILA

Now that the Pages have developed their unique skills and the Knights have tested and honed their limits, the suits progress to full maturity in the Queens and Kings.

While the medieval mind may have believed Queens came below Kings in the natural hierarchy, in our twenty-first-century archetypal lens, the Queens and Kings are a pair whose powers are distinct but equally essential. The Queens represent the mature *eros* orientation of the suit, which expresses the relating, Feminine principle; the Kings represent the mature *logos* orientation, or the governing Masculine principle.* The Queens connect and care, and the Kings compose and control. When we meet these figures within ourselves, we often find them as mother and father, possibly representing the internalization of our real parents or supplying images of inner parental complexes.

The Queen is the mother who nurtures, serves, and guides us to connection with others and our lives. She is independent but also deeply protective, whether it be of those around her or the work she births into being. Like the Pages and Knights, the Queens possess both positive and negative qualities. They can be at once tender and fierce, supportive and overbearing, encouraging and smothering. The Queens nourish our maturation with love, but can also overwhelm us with their intensity.

---

* We'll be discussing these terms in the next chapter, but simply we can think of eros as the Feminine principle of connection and logos as the Masculine principle of reason.

Queen of Cups

The Queen of Cups sits comfortably in the liquid depths of the soul, her focus firmly fixed on the precious cup she nurtures. We connect the Queen of Cups to intuition, but this particular gift comes from her profound empathy and feeling wisdom. She is creative and compassionate, attuning to the deepest feelings of those she loves without a word of explanation needing to be uttered.

The Queen of Cups shows us embracing ourselves and others with unconditional love and understanding. Right side up, she is the warm, soothing inner maternal voice telling us everything will be alright as long as we follow our hearts. She might represent our own need for her gifts of self-tending and love, or she may exemplify the mature side of the extraverted feeling function, manifesting in the selfless support we offer those around us.

Inverted, the Queen of Cups loses her mediating empathy. She can become self-obsessed and embittered, prioritizing her own fickle emotions. Because she feels deeply and is sensitive to the unconscious, she may believe that only *she* intuits the right paths for her loved ones, which may lead to an oscillation between her ability to smother and spite.

The Queen of Cups can appear in us as the mother figure who is profoundly loving or profoundly selfish. In her positive aspect, we may see her as the internalization of that perfect mother, possibly projecting her onto our partners, friends, or feminine role models. In her negative aspect, we may indeed suffer the emotionally abusive mother complex which employs shame and manipulation to stagnate our individuation.

Another possibility is that we feel we must embody this Queen ourselves, particularly if we are in a role of emotional tending or support for others. I once pulled the Queen of Cups for a client who was a newly licensed therapist, and she related that she strived to embody this devoted, soulful caretaker for her patients. However, the more they needed her, the more resentful she became. She was suffering the exhausting pressure of always needing her cup to be full. The Queen of Cups inspires us to offer our cup to others, but we must remember that the cup we hold is also ours to protect and cherish.

Queen of Swords

We perceive the Queen of Swords as somewhat disconnected from the natural nurturing tendencies of her rank. The Swords require objectivity, which necessitates distance and conveys a sense of being cold or aloof. However, it's empathy that guides this Queen's sword. With it she protects our vulnerabilities and defends our growth.

As mediator of the thinking function, the Queen of Swords is gifted at differentiating right and wrong in personal relationships and moral dilemmas. When we draw her, she may demand that we put away our emotions to make more discerning choices or uphold sturdier boundaries. She may encourage us to listen to the "tough love" wisdom within that tells us to wipe away our tears and do what must be done.

Right side up, the Queen of Swords can be a powerful ally in steadying us when we are gripped by our emotions, but inverted, she may berate us for feeling anything at all. She may turn woefully dismissive of any displays of sensitivity or compassion, which she sees only as weakness. In this state, the Queen of Swords becomes the stony and critical mother, stripped of her feminine relatedness (which is why we tend to associate her with widowhood or childlessness). Being so rigidly rational, there is no place for love.

We might turn to Aeschylus's *Oresteia* for a mythological depiction of the Queen of Swords. When Orestes is put on trial for murdering his mother to avenge his father, it is the goddess Athena who casts the decisive vote for his acquittal. Athena argues that life comes solely from the father's seed and the mother serves only as a vessel—ergo with no legitimate bond to the child, matricide cannot exist. In her pursuit of pure reason, Athena severs herself from the Feminine principles of love, care, and protection for the cold logic of Masculine intellect. This is the same failing in the Queen of Swords, and when consumed by this complex we may find ourselves becoming overly rational, dismissive, and ruthless, especially with those we love the most.

Queen of Pentacles

As the mistress of the matured sensation function, the Queen of Pentacles is the embodied matriarch. She is the true caretaker of the tarot, concerned not with finances or career security but her own natural rhythms, pleasures, and satisfaction in helping things grow and flourish.

The Queen of Pentacles calls us to "self-care," the tending to soma and psyche. She reminds us that growth does not come only from what we've earned or achieved, but is inherent in our cells and the simple yet sublime task of daily living. She initiates us into the present moment, asking us to connect to our environment and feel into what we truly need, insisting that we let the body answer, not the brain.

Inverted, this Queen easily gets lost in her sensation side, becoming overly preoccupied with the conditions of outer life. She may become obsessive about routines, cleanliness, or etiquette. Any minor inconvenience or physical discomfort may turn into scornful fixation and endless complaints. Her selfless caring can corrupt into begrudging self-sacrifice, leading her to become resentful and force guilt upon those she loves.

When we encounter the Queen of Pentacles as an inner figure, we may either feel pressured to be the "perfect mother" or become too focused on pleasing and caretaking. In the first case, we strive to adopt the persona of the devoted nurturer, and when we inevitably struggle against this endless caregiving, we are wracked with shame. In the second case, we truly *are* the perfect mother, giving all of ourselves all the time until we no longer can.

I had a client who was an elementary school teacher and adored her job. However, after her mother passed away she began to feel repulsed by her students' need of her. When the Queen of Pentacles showed up as the first card in her reading, she quickly identified it as her late mother who had cared for her well-being but was also overbearing and controlling. The deeper we explored, the clearer it became that my client had compensated for the influence of this negative side of the Queen by unconsciously adopting her positive, selfless side. Now liberated from her mother's imposed guilt, my client's lifetime of repressed anger broke through. For decades she had dutifully sacrificed her individual needs for her mother's, and at last her inner Queen of Pentacles refused to give any more of herself, even to her students.

Queen of Wands

The Queen of Wands lights up a room. Her connection to the intuitive function excites her passion and enamors the world with her flame. Her fire makes her enthusiastic, magnetic, and confident, but it can just as easily make her overwhelming, distrustful, and self-righteous. As quickly as she can ignite our dreams, she can sear them to ash.

The Queen of Wands' intuitive gift sees the hidden truth in things. When we pull her, she lends us not only this gift of vision, but also her aura of confidence, urging us to step into our spotlight. She is by far the most encouraging of the Queens, telling us to boldly go for whatever it is we desire and take up space. With such confidence in her powers, she inspires our own vivacious claims on our passions and potential.

As encouraging as the Queen of Wands is right side up, she can be equally belligerent inverted. When ignored, she becomes combative and paranoid, her flame of charisma darkening into vanity. She can turn brutally impatient and intolerant of introspection. The Queen of Wands fears not being believed and trusted, especially when she invests so much of herself into what she cares for, but unfortunately her strategies to earn that trust can be manipulative and even conniving.

As an inner archetypal figure, the Queen of Wands may appear on either side of a spectrum of enchantment between witch and muse. As the witch, she is the cunning sorceress, binding us to her will. She may trick and delude us, making us feel powerless. We might project her outward, finding her in our enemies, or feel her hissing chastisements in our own ears. As the muse, she becomes the *femme-inspiratrice*, mesmerizing us with her mystical inspirations. We may experience her as the alluring anima, stimulating us to surpass conventional boundaries, or we may be glamoured into believing that we own her superhuman charm. Either way, we must be wary of putting our faith entirely in her intuitive power.

THE KINGS

He who controls others may be powerful,
but he who has mastered himself
is mightier still.

—LAO TZU

We arrive now at the final stage of our court progression with the sovereignty of the Kings. Where the Queens develop the wisdom to relate and serve, the Kings' authority is internally defined. They are the mature, masculine expression of their suit—the father focused on their faculties of order, authority, and reason. As a more introverted standpoint in comparison to their mates, the Kings are less interested in the world and people around them than they are in their own personal judgments and successes.

However, this level of control can also make their negative side intensely domineering, turning them exacting and cruel. They are intent on self-mastery, which urges them toward an attitude of dominance that can be either steadying or controlling. The Kings, therefore, can both present us with a model of personal power and bombard us with impossible standards and tyrannical criticisms.

King of Cups

Where the Queen of Cups luxuriates in the sea of feeling, the King of Cups brings structure to these watery depths. He is not threatened by his emotions or his natural desire for relationship and love. He errs toward the spiritual and the creative, but resists floating away with imagination. At his best, he is strong yet tender, well-versed in his own feelings and attentive to the feelings of others.

The King of Cups encourages emotional responsibility. The subjectivity of the feeling function can easily drift into self-centeredness, which makes us emotionally indulgent and weakens our ability to compromise. The King of Cups helps us claim accountability for our feelings without losing control over how we express them or how much libidinal energy we divert toward them. We can feel what we feel and still be resolute and respectful.

Inverted, the King of Cups may fall victim to emotional egotism. He tends to sabotage opportunities of connection, whether by arguing that no one could satisfactorily "understand" him or abandoning his thoughtful nature when he feels slighted. His watery feeling side can overwhelm his kingly solidity, making him easily stressed and disorganized. When the King of Cups feels as though he's losing his grip, he may even turn hedonistic, forgetting the hearts of others and thinking only of what would please or soothe him in the moment.

In his positive aspect, the inner King of Cups might appear as a grounded father figure, holding the complexity of our feelings without dismissing or rationalizing them. As a more negative figure, he might appear as one who is emotionally avoidant or easily agitated by "bad" feelings.

A client came to me after secretly betraying her husband. Though she felt shame for her actions, she was clearly resistant to reflecting on the damage she'd caused herself and the relationship. With the King of Cups, she was challenged to confront this resistance, and she arrived at the realization that to examine her choices meant confronting her enormous guilt, which would strip the inner King of Cups of his brittle control over her emotional stability. Discussing this complex together, we saw that it was time for her to find the positive, emotionally competent side of the King of Cups and finally face what she had done.

King of Swords

While the Queen of Swords used her blade to protect and deliberate, the King of Swords wields his to determine his laws of right and wrong. His superior intellect and rigorous ethics make the King of Swords' judgment so strict that he cannot tolerate the messiness of complexity. His powers of reason can indeed be fortifying, but, being so rigid, they can also be demoralizing.

When he appears for us, the King of Swords lends us his unshakable integrity and rationality. He makes swift order out of uncertainty and chaos, helping us develop discipline and certitude, raising our own swords to strike with clear action. With such sure foundations, the King of Swords always trusts his internal compass of justice, and he teaches us to cultivate the same clarity. He provides us with the mental strength to make solid plans, cut through emotional overwhelm, and take up the mantle of authoritative living.

Upside down, the King of Swords may be a tyrant or a doormat. On one side, his austere impartiality turns cruel and critical, believing only in the validity of his own logic. On the other side, his grip on his sword falters and he is alienated from his powers of choice, finding himself crippled by doubt. If we do not find the innate strength of our own sovereign discernment, we are doomed to compensate one way or the other.

Very often the King of Swords appears within us as a censorious inner father complex who berates our every effort. Devoid of empathy, he becomes the hyperrational lawgiver, furious and unsympathetic, demanding that we do better, be smarter. We might conjure the story of King

Solomon, who, when two women came claiming to be the mother of the same child, ordered the baby be split in two so each could get half. Though the true mother immediately surrendered her claim to save the baby, it was through sheer brutality that his righteous judgment was achieved. We must be wary of the King of Swords' armored fidelity to "law" that obstructs compassion and compromise.

King of Pentacles

When passed to the King, the Queen's pentacle transforms from a blessing to a product. To him, value is decided not by appreciation but accumulation; his motto truly is "bigger is better." The King of Pentacles is the most ambitious of the four Kings, but his need for progress and expansion unfortunately strips the pentacle of its sacred, embodied nature. He toils to achieve the mastery that earns his rewards (which are many), but meaning is often forgotten in the process.

The King of Pentacles teaches us the discipline of real work. With his extraordinary grasp over the structures of growth, he inspires our mastery over procedures, techniques, and business acumen. In a reading the King of Pentacles may offer himself as a support to both establish these skills and embrace our ownership of whatever we are building in our lives. When inverted, however, this King's focus on materiality can quickly corrupt into materialism. He may turn greedy, stingy, and domineering. He may also go idle, pushing the labor onto others, or force his goals recklessly and thoughtlessly, producing disappointing results.

In Johann Wolfgang von Goethe's *Faust*, the titular hero (who has sold his soul to the devil to live like a god) decides the last thing left for him is to become emperor, which means he must build an empire. With no available land, he decides to reclaim land from the sea. Faust builds massive dams and destroys long-standing homes with no care for the consequences. When at last the personified Care blinds and cripples him, Faust rapidly plummets toward his demise. Though he built an empire, he never has the chance to rule it.

What we learn from *Faust* is that when we are unconsciously motivated by the King of Pentacles' avarice, we lose our own capacity for care, and then all our efforts will ultimately be for naught. He acts as the unforgiving father who is interested only in the result of our efforts, disregarding how it drains or demeans us. When we are trapped trying to satisfy this King within ourselves, we will inevitably withdraw our spiritual investment in the fruits of our labors. We are simply trying to prove our value (be it via income, likes, or votes) at the cost of our sense of higher meaning.

King of Wands

The intuitive drive toward meaning and purpose finds its greatest realization in the King of Wands. This King is quick, optimistic, and inspired by his innovative vision. He uses his intuition to glimpse the bigger picture, which he emboldens himself to claim. With his confidence and noble presence, he can easily inspire followers, persuade investors, or lead the masses.

The King of Wands motivates us to take control and follow our instincts. When we draw him, we are encouraged to step into positions of leadership. His entrepreneurial spirit aids in our efforts to envision new futures, and his unquenchable energy keeps us motivated. The King of Wands offers us the opportunity to consciously choose a life of meaning, vitality, and power, if, like him, we refuse to fear it.

Inverted, the King of Wands can either turn aggressive or impotent. He loves to "fight the good fight," but when his sense of what the right path is becomes murky, he can be viciously impatient. Alternatively, he may deny his power, especially when we are initiating a new enterprise or stepping up into a superior role. When met with an opportunity to embrace a sense of mission and authority in life, the fear of discovering our true weakness leads us to hide away and refuse rather than challenge ourselves to grow.

As an inner figure, the King of Wands' ingenuity and potency make him a useful ally, but also a ruthless taskmaster. He might appear alternately as the inner leader who bolsters our strength or the belittling father who always demands more of us. The King of Wands appeared this way in my own readings after the loss of a family member. Suffering much grief and anxiety, I was glad to have the King of Wands as a companion as I led my family through the painful adjustments to our new ways of life. However, when life began to settle, his hypercompetency was not released but redirected internally. This King of Wands complex still needed something to "save" and control, which pushed me to exhaust myself trying to be ahead of every obstacle and solve every crisis (even those that were not my own).

PART 3

THE MAJOR ARCANA

CHAPTER 7

THE TRUMPS AND THE STORY OF INDIVIDUATION

*The journey of the hero is about the courage to seek the depths;
the image of creative rebirth; the eternal cycle of change
within us; the uncanny discovery that the seeker is the
mystery which the seeker seeks to know.*

—JOSEPH CAMPBELL

Throughout this book we have discussed individuation as a psychological process, but in reality we live it as a spiritual journey. Jung described this journey through the stages of alchemy; Campbell through the patterns of myth. I believe there is no better model for individuation than the procession of the Major Arcana, and if we can map out the twenty-two keys on this symbolic journey, we might truly understand this noble quest that we are all on.

The sequence of the Major Arcana has persisted as one of the tarot's greatest mysteries. This order was not universally set until the printing of the Marseille deck in the eighteenth century, and then was altered again with the Rider pack at the turn of the twentieth.* Whether ordered this way intentionally or through the wisdom of the collective unconscious, the

---

* The singular sequential difference between the Marseille deck and the Rider-Waite-Smith is the swapping of Strength and Justice, numbers 8 and 11. Waite moved Strength to the eighth place and Justice to the eleventh mostly to suit his astrological correspondences, but I believe this shift makes thematic sense as well, as we will see later.

Major Arcana plots out the story of individuation—the journey to wholeness. When we pull a trump card, it focuses our place in this journey, signaling what we've moved through and what we are approaching. In spiraling repetition, we come to these points again and again, moving always closer to the center of Self.

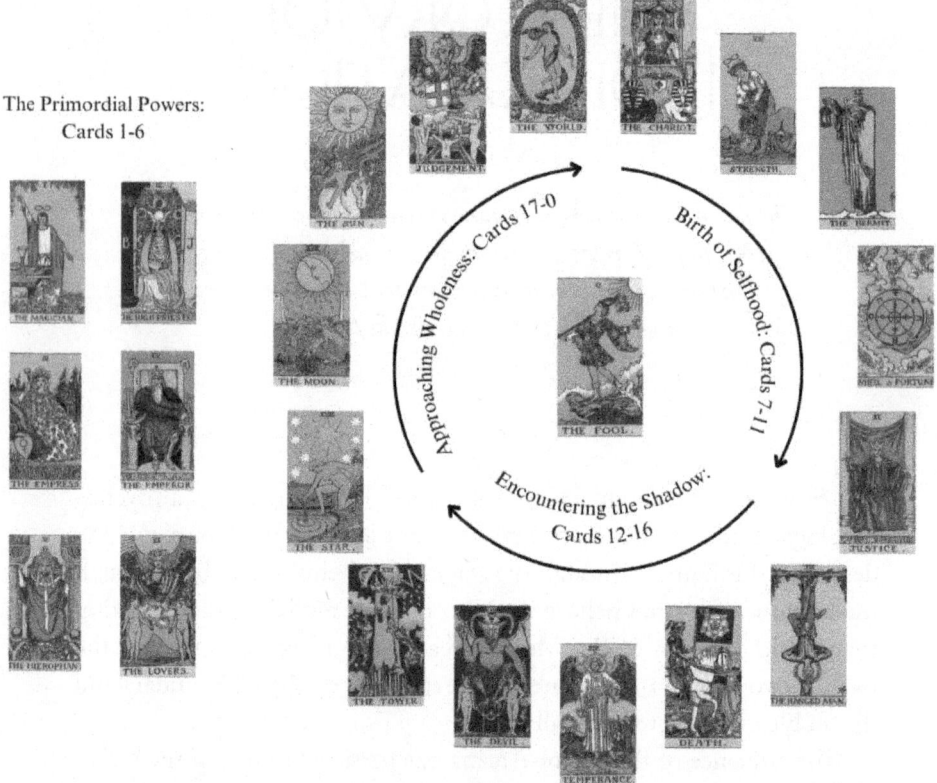

Figure 7. *Stages of Individuation in the Major Arcana*

In the archetypal tarot framework, the cards are divided into four groups that mirror the stages of the individuation journey: first the navigation of the primordial opposites, then the development of the ego, next the confrontation with the shadow, and finally the achievement of transcendence and wholeness. Each card presents an archetypal figure or experience we must meet, build relationship with, or integrate before we can continue on to the next stage. In the following chapters we will walk through these cards individually, but let us first survey what we will encounter on this glorious journey and experience the story the trumps tell of our becoming.

The first six cards of the Major Arcana present us with the primordial powers, or the archetypal Masculine and Feminine principles. With these cards we are navigating the central dualities of our existence: consciousness versus unconsciousness, nature versus society, philosophical knowledge versus lived experience. They present the primordial opposites as coupled powers, coming together as if through *hieros gamos*, the sacred marriage of goddess and god in the ancient world. When they are wed and woven into unity, the result is psychological synthesis: the birth of a new way of being and psychological growth.

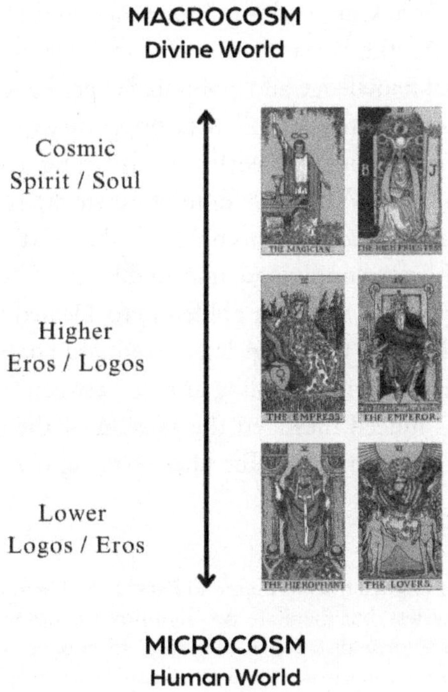
MACROCOSM
Divine World
Cosmic
Spirit / Soul
Higher
Eros / Logos
Lower
Logos / Eros
THE MAGICIAN
THE EMPRESS
THE EMPEROR
THE HIEROPHANT
THE LOVERS
MICROCOSM
Human World

Figure 8. Diagram of the Primordial Powers

In the tarot we meet these coupled powers side by side in their individual mystery. We begin in the macrocosm with the Magician and the High Priestess, who represent the most divine expression of these powers. They are the dichotomy of archetypal spirit and soul—vigorous manifestation and serene receptivity, conscious illumination and unconscious wisdom. Next, we move a little nearer to our humanity, meeting the worldly rulers as Empress and Emperor, the cosmic Mother and Father. As the forces of creation and order, they reign over nature and society, eternal life and law.

Lastly, these powers incarnate into the realm of the microcosm, and we meet them as the Hierophant and the Lovers.* Though these cards may not traditionally be understood as natural opposites, they are clearly paired by their imagery. In both we find a central figure with a hand of benediction raised over two supplicants. In the Hierophant card, this figure is the papal lord passing his knowledge on to his pupils, while in the Lovers card it is Cupid who guides Adam and Eve to love. What these cards depict is the dissemination of the vital principles of life: logos and eros, spiritual knowledge and embodied experience, reason and love.

In our holding the tension of these opposite experiences of being, they gradually come together within us, birthing a singular identity poised between them. With this foundation we are ready to begin our individuation in earnest, which comes in the next five cards as the archetypes of the developing ego, initiated by the Chariot.

In the Chariot card we see a golden hero, blessed by the canopy of stars overhead, holding the Magician's wand and adorned by the High Priestess's crescent moons. Standing at ease between the light and dark sphinxes, he has indeed mastered the tension of the opposites, and is therefore ready to begin living. The charioteer represents the emerging

---

* Because of their original titles as Pope and Popess, the Hierophant is often paired with the High Priestess, but there are two significant issues with their archetypal marriage. The first is their distance in the tarot arc, coming not side by side but two cards apart. The second issue lies in their actual meaning. The High Priestess is depicted as a goddess, enthroned in the subterranean realm of primordial unconsciousness and mystery, while the Hierophant sits firmly on a dais, poised between the earthly and the divine but clearly mortal.

ego-self who, after negotiating his inner duality, growing through both knowledge and experience, can claim that he really is someone.

But just as soon as he makes this claim, it must be tested. Strength follows, challenging us to meet the beast, to face the trials and tribulations both without and within. We must learn to do so not with resistance and aggression, but with grace and compassion. The ego must have faith in itself, developing the fortitude required to resist being torn to pieces by both its own inner impulses and the savagery of life.

If we succeed in this challenge and find the ego's resilience, we may indeed be ready to take the road of isolation inward. Now we follow the inner mentor of the Hermit, who guides us—as the Dalai Lama so wondrously describes it—to the "solitary journey toward the peaks, there to mate with the cosmos."[1] The stars of the Chariot's canopy now shine through the Hermit's lantern, lighting the way through the soulful night not as an emblem of egoic destiny but as the numinosity of the promised Self. Here we turn away from who we are trying to become in order to more deeply learn the specialness of who we innately are.

With clarity of outer self and inner, the next trial the ego must face is the spinning of fate. We have learned and mastered much within ourselves, but still, life cannot be controlled. While on the Wheel of Fortune, can we remember that life is not guaranteed to be good nor cursed to be bad? Can we resist being dizzied or trampled? Can we hold to the faith that hope will rise again? The only promise of life is that it will change. We must make peace with this fact, accepting the impermanence of all things.

Having survived the Wheel's capricious turning, Justice now welcomes us into her temple to offer us her sword of differentiation and her scales of fairness. With the wisdom we have won and the tools we've been gifted, we can successfully distinguish truth from falsehood. We can discern what is in greatest service to our growth, thus bringing us the powers of clarity and choice. At this stage—steady, strong, and sure as we are—sovereignty is ours.

Suddenly gray skies appear. Doom lurks in darkened corners. The charioteer who had been making great strides toward his destiny has been strung up to become the Hanged Man. We have entered the next phase of the journey in which we must confront the shadow—all that the ego-hero has unwittingly repressed and pushed away—and are rendered powerless. The ego despairs in this inversion, but a corona of light crowns him. This is a time of purification, when the ego learns to suspend its control. If we allow the hanging, we may indeed be blessed in the journey to come.

Still, Death is inevitable. When we surrender who we thought we were and face all that we have ignored or hidden away (our shadow), we will experience psychic dissolution. Parts of ourselves that were once strong and sure feel brittle and empty. Old loves, dreams, gifts, and strengths are all cut down by Death's scythe. We are haunted by the phrase, "I don't know who I am anymore." Yet we must not ignore what we see in the distance: the brilliant sun rising between a great stone gate and a road leading into the dawn.

As we tumble into Death's realm, Temperance comes to console us, promising that we are not abandoned there. As we see so often in myth, the psychopomp—the soul-guide—arrives to ferry the hero forth from despair. The angel of the middle way offers us a blessing, allowing us a chance to glimpse the glory we'll meet on the other side. Though everything we're experiencing now is filled with pain and fear, we must remain tempered, flexible, and receptive to unconscious energy. We must trust her soothing promise that the soul continues to move toward its goal of unity.

At last, we find ourselves at the Devil's door. The Devil is the shadow personified. He contains the darkest and most terrifying parts of who we are, the parts that the charioteer rejected to protect his place as the worthy hero. With his hand raised in mockery of the Hierophant and the Lovers enslaved to his will, the Devil now takes vengeance for our foolish attempts to deny him or exorcise his influence. We now must look at the villain hidden away in the dark recesses of our psyche and, without refusing him or being corrupted to his will, recognize him, also, as a part of ourselves.

The Tower naturally follows to break down all that has been built above the Devil's dungeon. This is the most frightening stage of the journey, but also the most liberating. Here is the moment when the life we thought we were after is ruined. For those who continue to wave off the Devil's whispered truths, the lightning bolt shatters our lives from the outside in order to make way for the revelation that must come. For those who are truly heroic and can accept what the Devil has revealed, they see that their Tower can no longer stand. Honest at last, we know that we must change, and we tear it all down.

Then, a miraculous thing: a Star—pristine, luminescent, and true—is made visible. In our final five cards of the sequence, we meet the archetypes of transcendence, and the Star rises first to remind us of what we have forgotten, what had been blocked out by that impenetrable Tower. What we glimpse here is not simply the destiny that the charioteer believed was promised, nor the caged flame the Hermit used to warm the inner dark. We are now in the cosmic realm, and the archetype we meet here is the beacon of our own sacred light, the naked, unnameable essence of who we are.

Next the primordial powers return in this celestial landscape as the Moon and the Sun: lunar and solar consciousness, the mystical realms of night and day. In the Moon card, that distant gate we first spotted across Death's valley is now only steps away, though the path is shrouded in darkness. Here we must learn to trust the unconscious intuition of the Moon, allowing ourselves to wander in the terrain of dream, fantasy, and symbol. Though disorienting, there is much to be learned here, and when the Sun eventually rises and pours out its light, we will prosper in the sudden illumination of conscious understanding. With this profound sense of consciousness, it will be as if we are reborn, and joy will break over us like a new dawn.

In these final moments of the journey, one last test is presented to us: As the angel blows its horn and awakens us back to life, can we account for all our proverbial "sins"? Can we acknowledge how we've failed, whom we've hurt, where we've turned from our right path? Do we at last have enough strength of character and fidelity to truth to pass inner judgment, without cowering or casting ourselves into hell? If we can indeed see it all, accept it all, love it all, then we can *integrate* it all. We can bring every last part of ourselves into wholeness, and we can be at peace with the entirety of our being. Then, we have embraced the Self and achieved the World. This is *at-one-ment*. This is the realization of our individuation.

Of course, the tarot does not leave us there. We have yet to encounter the Fool, the card without number. I place the Fool at the end of this sequence because it is only after we've gone through this impossible, incredible journey that we are ready to understand what the Fool is all about. The Fool is foolish because he is individuated. Remember that individuation has both a spiritual and practical definition. Spiritual individuation aims toward reconciliation with Self and the fullest expression of our being; practical individuation focuses on rejecting our inherited rules of living (given by our parents, our communities, our own internalized expectations, or society at large) so that we might find our own unique way to live. With the achievement of spiritual individuation represented in the World, practical individuation is made possible in the Fool. The Fool is fully harmonized with his authentic self and unafraid to cast the world's expectations aside. This last step of our individuation is to choose to live life utterly on our own terms. To everyone else it looks like we're walking right off a cliff, but we alone know and trust the path.

As we move through the cards themselves now, keep in mind that there are, as always, innumerable possibilities for interpretation, but we cannot (and should not) try to follow all of them. Our goal is not intellectual apprehension but psycho-spiritual comprehension, and so we must narrow our scope and spend time in contemplation. As with the Minor Arcana, allow these explorations to inspire and guide your own unique relationship with the tarot archetypes.

— CHAPTER 8 —

THE PRIMORDIAL POWERS—ARCHETYPES OF THE MASCULINE AND FEMININE

When you make the two into one, and when you make the inner like the outer and the outer like the inner, and the upper like the lower, and when you make male and female into a single one, so that the male will not be male nor the female be female . . . then you will enter the kingdom.

—GOSPEL OF THOMAS

There is a debate in the world of archetypal theory—and in the contemporary world at large—around the concept of gender bipolarity. As people liberate themselves from identities and presentations that feel constrictive or false, adopting more authentic expressions of self that challenge or surpass our inherited ideas of gender, we cannot avoid the question of what masculinity and femininity truly mean, and if they still hold any value for us.* However, as we transcend these dogmatic binaries, we must be careful not to confuse gender constructs for archetypal principles.

---

* Personally, I see this revolution in our understanding and experience of gender as proof that we are living through a paradigmatic shift away from the rigidity of patriarchy, which needs to categorize and hierarchize. The old stratifications of value no longer function when people reject those stratifications, transform, and declare their worth through their own sovereignty.

The Masculine principle is not synonymous with social masculinity, nor is the Feminine principle defined by what we think of as femininity. The Masculine and Feminine are primordial archetypes. Their meaning is universal and independent of our notions of what it means to be a man or a woman. Regardless of our gender or biology, *both* these principles exist within us in a constant state of flux and flow, and we must be wary of grasping one and rejecting the other or reducing ourselves into what we imagine to be their categorical repertoire of experience. Put simply, the Masculine and Feminine principles live in all of us all of the time as archetypes.

In Plato's *Symposium*, the philosopher Aristophanes relates a myth of humanity's origins, explaining that there were not two but three forms of human beings—male, female, and an androgynous combination of the two. The male half of this androgynous third was composed of the sun and the female half the earth. Aristophanes describes it as round as the moon with four arms and legs, four eyes, two sets of reproductive organs, and two faces. The strength of these beings threatened Zeus, and so he devised a way to weaken them by dividing them into the halves of men and women. Thus, as Aristophanes continues, "each one longed for its own other half, and so they would throw their arms about each other, weaving themselves together, wanting to grow together."[1]

This passage is often used to defend the idea of soulmates, but these two halves do not want to return to a state of togetherness, but instead want to reconcile into wholeness. This is a myth of what Jung would call the *mysterium coniunctionis*, the alchemical idea of the mysterious conjoining of opposites. The ultimate goal is to reunite the Masculine and Feminine principles within, to marry them back into the singularity of Self. This, I believe, is an essential part of the individuation journey not only for each individual, but for the collective as a whole.

Of course, without using gender constructs to define these principles, we struggle to understand their innate qualities. In Jungian studies, these archetypal energies are explored using the Greek concepts of eros and logos, which Jung identifies as "psychic relatedness" and "objective interest." In Greek mythology, Eros (whose Roman counterpart is Cupid) is the god of love and pleasure, and as a philosophical term it denotes passion and desire. In Jungian depth psychology, eros is the principle of loving relatedness invested in its ability to connect, feel, and attune to nature. Logos, on the other hand, is the Greek for "word" or "reason." Its archetypal qualities root it in the faculties of judgment, rationality, and the ability to make meaning.

There is yet another layer of we can add to the concepts of eros and logos. Although we use them interchangeably today, for most of history the concepts of spirit and soul have been distinct. In ancient and medieval alchemy, it was believed humans are tripartite beings composed of *pneuma*, *psyche*, and *soma*—Greek for spirit, soul, and body. The body is the corporeal meeting place between pneuma and psyche, holding the tension as the spirit pulls us toward the heavens and the soul draws us down into earth. Essentially, spirit is the ephemeral essence by which we approached God through the heights of knowledge, reason, and inspiration, whereas the soul is the sacred animating force that keeps us bound to living, embodied wisdom, and individual truth.

In Latin, these concepts of spirit and soul would be called *animus* and *anima*, which, as we discussed in chapter 1, were the terms Jung used for the archetypes of the inner Masculine and Feminine. Although early Jungian thought used the concepts of anima and animus to differentiate between male and female psychology, revisionist scholarship suggests that these archetypes are active to various degrees in us all. To be moved by the spirit is to be "inspired"—*in-spiritus*—seeking, as James Hillman puts it, the "God-nearness" of the peak. It is activating, invigorating, hungry for knowledge, driven to seek consciousness of itself and that which lies beyond itself. To be one with the soul, however, is to embrace the container of creation, wonder, and mystery. The soul is the vale of earthfulness, the dense landscape of feeling and longing, flowing with the lifeblood of the unconscious. Returning to the stunning words of the Dalai Lama:

> I call the high and light aspects of my being *spirit* and the dark and heavy aspect *soul*.
>
> Soul is at home in the deep, shaded valleys. Heavy torpid flowers saturated with black grow there. The rivers flow like warm syrup. They empty into huge oceans of soul.
>
> Spirit is a land of high, white peaks and glittering jewel-like lakes and flowers. Life is sparse and sounds travel great distances.[2]

The relationship of spirit and soul, logos and eros, Masculine and Feminine, is integral to the tarot. We can connect spirit to the spark of flame and logos to the clarity of air—the Masculine suits of Wands and Swords. Soul connects to the depths of water and eros to the fertility of earth—the Feminine suits of Cups and Pentacles. And in the Major Arcana, we see these principles come to life in the primordial powers: spirit flashes into being with the Magician, while logos fortifies the work of the Emperor and guides the doctrine of the Hierophant; soul blooms into being with the High Priestess, while eros awakens the creativity of the Empress and blesses the bond of the Lovers. As we move through these first six cards, we will see how the Feminine archetypes rise up from the underworld to land in the heart, while the Masculine archetypes descend from the heavens and settle in the mind.

The Magician:
The Archetype of the World-Creating Spirit

You are the laboratory and every day is an experiment.
Go and find what is new and unexpected.
—JOEL ELKES

We initiate our individuation journey with the Magician, who, as number 1 in the Major Arcana sequence, represents singularity, oneness, and pure consciousness. The Magician is perhaps the most vitalizing and mercurial card of the deck. He has appeared in many forms throughout the tarot's history: in the Marseille deck he is the wily Bateleur tricking you with his sleight of hand; in the Thoth Tarot he is the ephemeral Magus communicating with the gods; and in the Rider-Waite-Smith he is the alchemical master concentrated in his great work.

In this final form, he stands in his *laboratorium*, the lemniscate over his head signaling the transcendent insight of the Holy Spirit, and the ouroboros around his waist symbolizing eternity. On his table lies the prima materia—the primordial materials of existence at his disposal, represented as the four Aces. With one hand raised toward the heavens and the other pointed toward the earth, his stance is the physicalization of the famous hermetic maxim "As above, so below": he is ready to catch that divine breath and conduct it into being, to act as the channel between the macrocosm (the above, the without, the universe) and the microcosm (the below, the within, the psyche). What the Magician conducts is pure potentiality. His magic is manifestation, directing energy from the above to the below through the invisible wires of the unus mundus—the tapestry of interconnection woven through all things.

The core of the Magician is his inspiring quality—and we don't mean this in the sentimental sense of encouragement or motivation. Rather, this *inspiration* is defined by its etymological meaning: from the Latin root *spirare*, "to breathe," which is the same root for *spiritus*, "breath of God." As the representation of spirit, the Magician fills us with the breath of life that sparks us to seek the heavens. We kneel at his table when the world is fragrant and sparkling with possibility, when we are vibrant with creativity, when we long to be ignited.

The most direct way we experience the Magician is as a state of primed spiritual receptivity, when the spontaneous divine spark meets our concentrated focus and they alchemize into conscious action. This quality of the Magician epitomizes the energizing archetypal animus, which von Franz describes as "an enterprising spirit, courage, truthfulness, and in the highest form, spiritual profundity."[3] Within the psyche, the Magician as animus takes on the role of inspirer and strengthener, opening us to our great potential. He is, as von Franz puts it, the "incarnation of *meaning*," the inner Masculine archetype urging us to make life innovative, vital, and meaningful.

On the shadowier side of the archetype, Jungians correlate this figuration of the animus with Mercurius, the patron of the medieval alchemists (who may have directly inspired the Rider-Waite-Smith version of the card). To the alchemists, Mercurius was both "the world-creating spirit" and the spirit trapped in matter; he represented both the light of divinity and the baseness of mortality. Indeed, he was a true archetypal

Figure 9. Mercurius, "Clavis": the second key from the Twelve Keys of Basil Valentine, *engraved by Matthaeus Merian, 1618*

trickster (harkening to the Magician's earliest incarnations) suffuse with paradox, as Jung explains:

> A curious combination of typical trickster motifs can be found in the alchemical figure of Mercurius; for instance, his fondness for sly jokes and malicious pranks, his powers as a shape-shifter, his dual nature, half animal, half divine, his exposure to all kinds of tortures, and—last but not least—his approximation to the figure of a saviour.[4]

Despite these contradictions, Mercurius is the true shepherd of the magnum opus, acting as the spirit guiding the alchemists' efforts. In this way, the Magician represents how we might similarly find the center point between our inherent contradictions, so that we may successfully accomplish our own magical manifestations. To attain the Magician's powers as the channel, we must be attuned to both the higher and the lower within ourselves, receptive to inspiration and ready to act. Rather than being trapped in the stuff of this world (as the alchemists described), the Magician is *infused* within it. He is the divine creative spirit, *and* he is bound to the material world. He is both unified consciousness and paradox. He is inspirer and trickster.

In a Reading . . .

When the Magician appears with his electrified baton, we can sense that we are facing a time of inspiration, creativity, and the power of concentration without effort. He tells us to make the start and become the alchemist. However, the Magician does not come without responsibility. As Nichols writes, "The Magician's wand, like an orchestra conductor's, is an instrument for concentrating and directing energy. Energy needs direction. Only with man's conscious cooperation can it be shaped to human use."[5] When we pull the Magician, we must examine the prima materia on our tables and decide what we mean to make of it.

As the channel between the macrocosm and the microcosm, the Magician may ferry us to this connection point via synchronicity. Unconscious wisdom may appear as "messages," carried on the wings of birds or in the words of TV characters, directing us to an archetypal power trying to contact us. Now is the time to pay greater attention to these meaningful coincidences. The Magician has been known to orchestrate striking ways of getting our attention to facilitate change.

Now more than ever notice the energy within you and what meaningful action you feel drawn to take. Have you recently been flooded with a new vision? Do you feel excited by sudden ideas? Has a magical person entered your life or your dreams? All of these are signs that the archetypal Magician, that spiritual animus, has constellated in your life at this moment and draws you toward a path of revitalizing the psyche. Like the Magician, we should stand at the ready, our arms poised to catch the shocking, awe-inspiring flash of the divine spark, anticipating what we might do next.

When Reversed...

With the reversed Magician we must temper his trickster side. In this form the Magician is a rogue and a deceiver. We may feel on the edge of a breakthrough only to get distracted by a random pain, or we feel the swell of a new idea and quickly find ourselves lost in technological weeds. The Magician tricks us into thinking we've seen flashes of the divine and then pulls the energetic carpet out from under us. Answers here are unreliable, but perhaps a time of pause and gentle contemplation of what internal trickster means to thwart us is at hand.

If we overidentify with the Magician, we are also in a trap. We must be wary not to fall into visions of grandiosity or expect the burst of energy to be infinite. We might even consider if we have convinced ourselves we really are the great alchemist, envisioning ourselves as the divine channel itself rather than the mortal who is receptive to it.

Finally, the Magician reversed can suggest a lack of motivation or a disconnection from that vital spirit, which in turn results in frustration and a sense of futility. Often we try to compensate for this lack by pushing ahead mindlessly, even numbly. Then our words feel dead on the page, our efforts merely filling a quota, our studies just rote memorization. Without that spark, we channel our lives toward the mundane rather than the magical.

The answer is not to keep pushing, but to go out and find the upright Magician and reignite his spark. Read something that lights you up. Watch a movie that inspires you. Draw an image from your imagination. This is an opportunity to consciously reinitiate yourself into the highest expression of *spiritus*, the great breath of life itself.

The High Priestess
The Archetype of the Soul's Wisdom

> *Wisdom, with its deeper understanding, loves all things;*
> *for it has seen the beauty, the tenderness, and the sweetness*
> *which underlie Life's mystery.*
>
> —MANLY P. HALL

THE HIGH PRIESTESS

Out of the Magician's singularity of 1 we arrive at the High Priestess's duality of 2. Her number does not indicate a secondary authority, but her particular power. Where the Magician transmits inspired, unified consciousness, the High Priestess exposes the power in our duality and the great wisdom in the space between the light and the dark.

We do not find the High Priestess in some luminescent laboratory, but in an underworld temple of the great mysteries. Behind her a curtain hides the endless churning ocean of the deep unconscious, that psychoid space where "absolute knowledge" exists. She holds this knowledge in her scroll, and if she deems us worthy, we may indeed learn it via premonitions, intuitions, and archetypal wonder. As the governess of these unconscious depths, the High Priestess acts as the keeper of the archetypal realm, possibly making her, as Waite suggested, "the highest and holiest" card in the deck.

Just as the Magician represents the animus, the essence of spirit, the High Priestess embodies the anima, the depth of soul. As this governess of soul, the High Priestess is not the motherly anima invested in relationship (that role belongs to her sister, the Empress); rather she is the virginal anima complete in her sovereignty.* Her particular love comes not through care and nourishment but through intimacy with the

---

* Virginal here does not refer to sexual activity, but archetypal relationship. Virginity is an archetypal concept that emphasizes independence rather than partnership.

Figure 10. Sophia or Sapientia from Emblem 26 of Atalanta fugiens *by Michael Maier, 1617*

unconscious, which speaks tenderly via our subtle intuition. She acts as what James Hillman calls the "soul-spark," the swell of depth that lives equally in us as in all things.

Jung identifies this highest expression of the anima as Sophia—the goddess-like figure who beckoned the alchemists to embark upon their sacred work. While Mercurius channeled the paradoxes of divine energy to fuel the alchemical journey, Sophia (whose name is itself the Greek word for wisdom) held the secret knowledge needed to realize it. The alchemists welcomed her through the writings of the early Christian gnostics, who described Sophia as an angelic "aeon" with God at the creation of the world. In their mythology, Sophia did not act as God's servant or subordinate but stood with him, binding it all together. She is the archetypal sister to the Kabbalistic Shekinah, the emanation of the Feminine side of God guiding all things through her love and hallowed wisdom.

Perhaps the best explanation of the High Priestess's remarkable power of cosmic wisdom comes from a sixteenth-century German shoemaker and mystic, Jakob Böhme. Böhme's visions of Sophia depicted her as the reflective matrix through which God witnessed his own potentiality, thus enabling him to create the universe. Because of her unique gift to refract God's mysteries, the universe was spared from one-dimensionality and thrived with wondrous richness of multiplicity. We might think of it this way: just as the moon makes it possible to see the full radiance of the sun, Sophia (and the High Priestess) reflects back the ultimate unknowable mysteries of being in a vivid multicolor display, presenting divine wisdom not as something distant and enigmatic but suffuse in everything.

For us, the High Priestess is the prism of the in-between, mediating transcendence and immanence—higher understanding and deeper knowing. We enter her subterranean domain to beg her to reveal what she knows about our souls and then hope to draw it back up to the surface. The High Priestess does not reveal her secrets lightly, and so when she calls upon us to offer her holy wisdom or whisper secrets of our soul's true power, we must listen.

Of course, when she deigns to speak to us, we can, like the thirsting alchemists, become addicted to her milk of knowledge. To try to enter her temple without invitation is to profane her holiness. We cannot absorb her wisdom without her gifting it to us. As sixteenth-century alchemist Michael Maier puts it: "He that without a key enters into the Garden which is every way enclosed is like a Thief who coming in the dark night can discern nothing that grows in the Garden, nor enjoy what he steals thence."[6] We might try to grab for her secrets, but if she does not offer them willingly, we will not be able to make sense of them. We must remember that we are only devotees to her wisdom, eager to seek, learn, and do her reverence.

In a Reading . . .

When we pull the High Priestess, there is a direct invitation to consider the intuitive wisdom we hold in our centers. In contrast to the Magician's activity, the High Priestess invites us into a state of necessary passivity, silently reading from our inner scrolls. We have been beckoned into her temple to listen to what she says through the voice of our own deeper knowing.

Often this card arrives when we are poised between opposites and our faculty of differentiation is either inactive or out of its depth. Our first impulse is to struggle to move forward, but here is the opportunity to sink inward. In these cases she asks us to submerge into the non-thinking space, to be in touch only with intuition, to learn something previously unconsidered, achieved not by conscious analysis but by quiet knowing.

As the representative of the soul, the High Priestess illuminates our innate destiny. She points us toward our unique talents and our particular longings, reminding us of what is meant for us. Like the Magician, she may appear as the anima in dreams and fantasies, taking shape as a goddess, angel, or sorceress. This is a time of meditation and contemplative exploration of the unconscious. It is an opportunity to cultivate trust in the intuitive visions and clairvoyant flashes that arrive from the depths.

Very simply, you may want to ask the High Priestess what she has come to tell you and silently await the answer.

When Reversed . . .

Reversed, the High Priestess can sometimes come with a scolding demeanor, rebuking us for willfully tuning out the intuitive wisdom she's been whispering to us. We have received her summons, but declined to answer. I have found that in these cases the High Priestess's appearance is in no way casual, as she only deigns to emerge from her temple on matters of utmost importance. When inverted, she demands that we acknowledge the wisdom that has been telling us exactly who we are. Perhaps you've been afraid to accept it, but now you must. Go quiet and enter the intuitive place and you'll likely find the direction is already awaiting you.

Another possibility for the inverted High Priestess is the experience of disconnection from soul. Alienated from her damp, fecund temple and the cool mist of her flowing waters, life feels arid, dry, and empty. Jung noted that when we lose the intimacy with soul, our spirituality may become preoccupied with procedure or doctrine over intuition. We may be fixated on the right performance of our practices because we can no longer feel their depth.

We can also fall into the trap of being overly identified with the High Priestess. Her allure is undeniable for the mystic, the seeker, the diviner, but just as we cannot be the Magician reaching up into the heavens, we are not the High Priestess holding the scrolls of knowledge. To become her apprentice, we must go into the dark where worldly knowledge is rendered meaningless; we must first not know before we can learn. To mistake our love of holiness and mystery as proof of our participation in her divine power is to fall prey to a messy inflation, one that she will force us to contend with.

The Empress:
The Archetype of the Great Mother

> *Earth laughs in flowers, and the Mother laughs within every seed that grows, in every pulse of life.*
> —RALPH WALDO EMERSON

Just as the Magician and the High Priestess reflect the divine pairing of Masculine and Feminine as spirit and soul, the Empress and the Emperor open us to another variation of this cosmic marriage. Together they are the archetypal Mother and Father and the primordial dichotomy of Nature and Order. The Empress generates the endless dynamic universe, while the Emperor contains it with structures, law, and reason.

As the archetypal Mother, the Empress nourishes and nurtures us, but her significance extends beyond the personal maternal relationship. She is the Great Mother, the creatrix of life in all its forms, substances, and abundances. Her diadem of twelve stars (like the twelve zodiacal signs) suggests her cosmic rulership over nature, while the wild garden around her shows her submersion in it. She does not sit in austerity as her sister the High Priestess and her husband the Emperor, but lazes on a cushion in a flowing gown, showing her embrace of the erotic through relationship, sensuality, beauty, and care. The Empress rules over the world of matter, and all she touches is made fertile. Her blood flowing with the prima materia, she is in ecstatic love with all she births into the world.

Many tarot scholars have wondered at the placement of the Empress before the Emperor, but again, this does not intimate rank. Rather the Empress is the third in the Major Arcana sequence because the 3 is dynamic and oriented toward growth. After the initial thesis of the Magician's purity of consciousness and the antithesis of the High Priestess's depth of unconsciousness, we have arrived at a synthesis. A dynamic third way comes through that allows us to gestate our own psychological development.* She offers us spaces to grow, adapt, play, try. She concretizes our abstract revelations into lived experience, lending us her remarkable powers of creation. The Empress cocoons us in love and safety and nurtures whatever must come forth.

The Empress is the matrix of life pregnant with herself. As personified Nature, she is earth and root and river, but she is also the divine Eve, the first flesh and bone mother whom the world has been taught to denigrate. She possesses the womb of creative potential, the container where true psycho-spiritual birth takes place. As depth psychologist Marion Woodman writes, "When the conscious ego is able to release repressed psychic energy, or reconnects with unconscious body energy, or makes a decision on its own behalf, that new energy is symbolized as new life."[7] We embody the Empress as we deliver ourselves—revivified, transfigured, *new*.

Archetypally, the Empress as the Great Mother displays the power to both create life and devour it, as she has throughout history. However, since the establishment of patriarchy, the world has turned against this natural expression of her archetypal power and depicted her as a monster, demon, or dragon that the bootstrapping young hero must dominate and defeat. In the legend of the mother goddess–turned-demoness

Figure 11. Battle between Marduk and Tiamat, from the Temple of Ninurta, c. 865 BC

---

* There is a common misconception that the true nature of the Feminine principle is passive, but the dynamic power of the Empress demonstrates that the Feminine principle can be equally active, just as the Masculine principle can, at times, be passive.

Tiamat, the demigod Marduk faces in her battle, trapping her, murdering her, and cutting her in two. From her severed carcass he creates heaven and earth, and thus it is the patriarchal hero who becomes lifegiver. The Great Mother is diabolized into a purely monstrous entity, utterly devoid of love.

This denigration of the Mother is a great darkness in our contemporary collective shadow. As we distance ourselves from our planet and its rhythms, we lose connection to the source of our being. As Jungian Erich Neumann writes:

> Devaluation of the Earth, hostility towards the Earth, fear of the Earth: these are all from the psychological point of view the expression of a weak patriarchal consciousness that knows no other way to help itself than to withdraw violently from the fascinating and overwhelming domain of the Earthly ... [which] is fused together with the archaic image of the Mother Goddess.[8]

To embrace the Empress, we embrace the earth. We embrace not only what is beautiful and bountiful in nature, but what is also "fascinating and overwhelming." Then we might indeed be bound to the matrix of being. We might experience the true creative wonder in life and its most vital, hard-won, and transformative lessons.

In a Reading . . .

The Empress indicates an opportunity for new life to be born. This might come in a more literal sense as a new role or life change, but it might equally be a new orientation, attitude, or sense of purpose. When we draw her, we know we are in the chrysalis of psychological metamorphosis, or an experience of inner gestation. This is an important time to notice dreams of pregnancy, gardening, squeezing through tunnels, or any other birth-related symbols.

Another possibility is that we've adopted her power as the matrix of life and are entering a period of vibrant creativity. Unlike the Magician, her creativity is not about inspiration but conception. Her power appears in our cells, our hands, and through it we love our work into being. She comes to tell us it's time to embrace our longings—whether those be sensual, artistic, or spiritual. She encourages us to experience ourselves as the Maker and also gives us permission to enjoy our state of fullness, taking pleasure in our abundance, our bodies, or our creative flow.

Finally, returning to the archetype of the Mother, we can meet the Empress as the anima or inner Feminine in her maternal role. She brings our attention to our personal relationship with our mothers and maternal figures, inviting us to reconsider past or current relationships and needed reconciliations. She may also appear as a patroness of our own journeys through motherhood. When encountering her this way, we must remember that the Empress is not a prototype, but an archetype. It is through our innate relationship with her that we know what a mother can be, but we must not forget our humanness.

When Reversed . . .

Reversed, the Empress may appear in us as that Terrible Mother. This might be a simple call to reconnect to the primal maternal love, or it may indicate a more rooted complex around the Mother archetype. Whether instigated by our personal relationship to our own mothers or from the archetype itself, symptoms of a negative mother complex may include constant self-criticism, anxious attachment, rejection of the maternal, or an inability to nurture. If we experience these and pull the Empress inverted, it may be a serious call to face this complex.

Often with such powerful archetypes, we experience them as projections, either casting them onto others or having them forced upon us. In these cases she might appear as the shrew, the punishing mother, or the monstress. A friend of mine suffered months of mistreatment by his boss, leading him and his coworkers to project this Terrible Mother onto her. They would complain about her throughout their lunch hour and obstinately rebel against her many castigations and trivial rules. It became clear that, unconsciously, their relationship had warped from employer-employees to mother-children. Sure enough, when one coworker finally "talked back," my friend and the rest were terminated. When working with projections of this nature, our goal is to recall it back into our own psyches, inquiring what about the Empress we find in this person or what they seem to find in us. With this sort of conscientious inner work, we might eventually restore the archetype to its rightful place and cleanse our relationships.

A final possibility for the reversed Empress is that we have been gestating too long. The Empress can turn indulgent, relaxing into the stagnancy of convalescence before delivery. It can be a period of rosy excitement, but at some point we must give birth: we must harness the dynamism of the Empress and find the courage to bring the new thing into reality. Now is the time to induce labor and create. As Woodman reminds, if you wait too long, the process may be aborted, and you may lose the sacred opportunity for growth.

The Emperor:
The Archetype of the Father-Patriarch

>*The father's love gives strength to the heart,
>a force that cannot be seen,
>yet is present in all things.*
>—RUMI

For many, drawing the Emperor only disappoints. He may make us feel hostile to the hierarchical systems in our world or rebellious against the authorities we have projected him onto. But we must remember that all archetypes have both a negative and positive pole, and though for many of us the Emperor bears the lance of patriarchal wounding, he is not the patriarchy itself. In his positive aspect, the Emperor rules without betraying his balanced marriage to the Empress and the Feminine principle.

This sacred partnership was well-established in the ancient world. Civilizations of the Near East annually celebrated the death and subsequent rebirth of their father god Tammuz, both of which happened through the mother goddess Inanna. To them, this was not brutality but the primacy of nature. Their cosmology accepted that the Masculine father was destined to inseminate, support, and ultimately sacrifice itself to the Feminine life-bearer. Of course, as we know from the story of Tiamat and Marduk, this worldview would eventually be supplanted by one of patriarchal dominance, eclipsing the reverential potency of nature with force of social rule.

The point here is not to suggest that the Masculine principle is subordinate to the Feminine, but rather that the progression from the Mother to the Father holds archetypal significance. The Empress is the matrix of life, the raw creative potency that must first exist in order for the Emperor to have purpose. The Masculine needs the primordial chaos of the Feminine to make a structured world, just as Marduk needs the body of the great goddess to form the heavens and the earth. As Nichols puts it, the Emperor's role is to "bring order to the Empress's garden which, if left to grow by itself, can become a jungle."[9] The Empress and Emperor are a wedded pair that work in cooperation. The Empress creates life, but the Emperor gives it order and direction.

To truly understand the Emperor, we must rescue his benevolence. At his core, the Emperor is the archetypal Father, the one who gives us the rules we need to develop and function in the world. While Mother launches us into the primitive experience of living, Father gives us the tools to organize it into something, to establish its parameters and meanings. With his grasp over logos, he guides us to our most fortified experiences of reason, strength, and clarity of will. The Emperor caps and contains the open-ended universe, protecting our individuation by creating the walls and laws we need to safely explore, grow, and change.

As number 4 in the tarot sequence, the Emperor represents the first stage of stasis and completion. The Magician inspired our conscious direction; the High Priestess revealed our unconscious wisdom; and from that came the dynamic third in the Empress that births a new way of life. Like Tammuz born from Inanna, the Emperor emerges from her as the fourth: the force of will that brings a sense of stability and sovereignty to the psyche. Now we have navigated our primordial binaries and at last ceased our oscillation to find a persevering solidity and cohesion.

Of course, as the Emperor-patriarch, we must not forget his impulse for rigidity that prevents rather than encourages change, newness, and adaptation. When this happens, the Emperor defends not the wondrous creativity of the universe, but his own imposed order. The Empress's dynamic cycles of destruction and rebirth become the greatest threat to his control, and so rather than contain this chaos, he dominates it, imposing his hierarchies and paralyzing the dynamism of the psyche. Nature itself becomes the evil that must be defeated; social law becomes the supreme doctrine; and we are bound to the Emperor's will alone.

Returning to the medieval legend of Perceval and the Holy Grail, we find the Emperor as the Fisher King, alone and maimed in his barren wasteland stripped of its fertility. The hero Perceval (a stand-in for ourselves) has the opportunity to heal the king and restore the proper order of things if he asks the right question: *whom does the grail serve?* The grail, the cup of reciprocity and love, belongs also to the Emperor. It serves not one, but all the world, and this is also the belief of the positive Emperor, who wants only to protect, support, and restore the bounty of the land he loves.

In a Reading . . .

The Emperor teaches us how to create stability and order within ourselves. As the archetype of the inner Father, he helps us establish the rules by which we can safely explore and expand. When we draw him, we may need to create a more structured reality to focus our development or prevent ourselves from being swept away by the dynamic yet chaotic impulse to perpetually create and grow. When we can welcome both the Empress and Emperor onto our intrapsychic team, we can accomplish so much—fruitful organization, contained abundance, autonomous creative living.

The Emperor also calls us to cultivate a sense of personal authority. He encourages us to hold to our resolve and defend ourselves against submission to others' wills. Now is the time to approach our problems with a defined rational process and resolutely uphold our boundaries. As Emperor and Father, his law is final, and that is sometimes a necessary attitude when we wish to enforce our sole sovereignty over how to live.

Like the Empress, the Emperor can also point to the animus in his paternal role. In this way we may be called to contemplate our relationships with our fathers or father figures or how we embrace fatherhood ourselves. Commonly we may seek this benevolent father archetype outside of ourselves, projecting him onto another, which can indeed help adapt him more solidly into our psyches.

When Reversed . . .

Frustrated in his neglected position, the inverted Emperor tries to dominate rather than relate. When we do not listen to the negative father-animus's directives and demands, he can turn critical and belligerent, wreaking havoc on our relationships with ourselves and others. In these cases the inner critic is more than just an internal heckling; it is an imposing, tyrannical force in the psyche. It expands to archetypal proportions and must be approached with severity and care.

Upon pulling the inverted Emperor for a client who was excited about starting her own business, she identified him as her strong, uncompromising inner critic. Though most of the other cards were positive and supportive, I noticed a growing discomfort in her. When I questioned this, she confessed that all these encouragements were being swatted away by that inner critic, who demoralized her and sneered that she'd never have what it takes. It was clear that she would have to develop the courage to confront this negative animus complex, or else fail to live her life. In such instances the Emperor has betrayed his vow to protect the generative and vulnerable growth of the Empress and has indeed become a negative patriarch dominating and tearing us down.

Again, as with the Empress, we may also encounter the inverted Emperor as a Father complex. In this way he may appear to us as the internalized voice of our real fathers, whom we are either rebelling against or trying to please. Or we may project the archetypal Father onto someone in our lives, adopting behaviors that unconsciously call out for their paternal attention, be it punishment or praise.

The Hierophant:
Logos and the Archetype of the Spiritual Teacher

> *The possession of knowledge does not
> kill the sense of wonder and mystery.
> There is always more mystery.*
>
> —ANAÏS NIN

We've oscillated between the primordial dichotomies of divine spirit and soul and the archetypal Mother and Father, and now we come to the last pairing of wedded opposites as the *lived* principles of logos and eros exemplified by the Hierophant and the Lovers.

The Hierophant is one of the most controversial and confusing cards in the deck, being viewed as a symbol of hierarchy and control. To understand the true nature of the Hierophant, we must drop into the mindset of the tarot's fifteenth-century creators. The Pope (the original name for the Hierophant) held supreme rulership not by social law but holy law. He was called the pontiff, a title that originated from the Latin word for "bridge," because he was the living passage between God's divine mind and the Church's teaching.

Today, we are less likely to turn toward popes and organized religion for our spiritual direction, and so it may seem as if this card has lost some of its archetypal resonance. However, his more ancient origins better encapsulate his archetypal role for us. In ancient Greece, the hierophant—drawn from the words *hieros* meaning "sacred," and *phainein*, "to reveal, bring to light"—was the priest who brought worshippers into the holy rites. His task was to act not as lord but as intermediary facilitating the people's understanding of the divine mysteries.

Philosopher Mircea Eliade explains the importance of this intermediary role, and how we might also experience it as a spontaneous, internal process he calls *hierophany*:

> [*Hierophany*] expresses no more than is implicit in its etymological content, *i.e.*, that *something sacred shows itself to us.* . . . The sacred tree, the sacred stone are not adored as stone or tree; they are worshipped precisely because they are *hierophanies*, because they show something that is no longer stone or tree but the *sacred*.[10]

This is a striking summation of the Hierophant's purpose. He guides us into the temple and shows us the words in the book, the colors on the canvas, the stars in the night sky, and communicates what is wholly *sacred* within them. It is by his teaching that we examine tangible reality and suddenly discern the greater mystery within it.

As with each of these first six cards of the Major Arcana sequence, the work of the Hierophant is to unite the opposites—not through *coniunctio* of partnership (that's the task of the Lovers), but through philosophy. This is the principle of logos in action. He sits austerely, hand raised in benediction, two priests at his feet eagerly awaiting his lessons. This threefold element is emphasized by his three-tiered headdress and the triple cross he holds. These symbolize the divine, intellectual, and physical worlds—the descending dissemination of the word, logos, spiritual knowledge. He will speak this doctrine and facilitate the hierophany: his teaching will act as the bridge by which higher knowledge crosses to become a lived mystery.

The Hierophant, therefore, appears to us as the archetypal spiritual guide, whether he be guru or priest. He is the mortal authority over God's mystery—the scribe and steward of hermetic knowledge. The keys at his feet are not merely symbolic of his unique power to peek into the beyond, but suggest his ability to access and dispense its wisdom at his own discretion. His purpose, ultimately, is to guide us to our own seat of inner authority where we offer the benediction to ourselves. Just as the ancient hierophant revealed the mysteries so that initiates might encounter them within their own depths, so too, do we absorb the lessons from our teachers to awaken our own inner source of knowledge. Only then will we discover our spiritual authority, truly see the sacred, and learn to live the teachings themselves.

However, we must remember that though he has the special privilege of *revealing* the sacred, unlike the High Priestess he does not *possess* it.

His power is to disseminate the knowledge he accesses, which when abused, produces hierarchical ladders, dogma, and orthodoxy. Then the Hierophant becomes a version of the Devil, who sits in his mocking pose, inverting the sacred back into the profane and inflating the profane to eclipse the sacred.*

As Jung warned, one of the greatest crises of humankind in the twentieth century is the loss of religion, not because we need a God to follow, but because with no designated pathways to the divine we do not know how to find it within ourselves. This is not a call to reclaim the defunct religious practices of the past, but to center the religious function. This function or natural propensity toward religious experience opens us back to Eliade's idea of the sacred, learning how it can coexist with and reenchant the temporal monotony of daily life.

In a Reading . . .

As the lived experience of logos, the Hierophant calls us to the spiritual path through learning and intellectual discovery. It is time to accept the pull of the religious function and illuminate our understanding of the divine. This may require that we first find a true Hierophant mentor to guide our journey—be they online educators, family members, or spiritual leaders. However, we must remember that though we learn from our teachers, we ultimately find the spiritual truth within ourselves. We already hold all the wisdom; our task is to locate it within, listen, and abide by its teaching.

The Hierophant may also be encouraging us to tap into our sense of spiritual authority and leadership. We are called to take ownership of the knowledge we have learned and cultivated throughout our (usually long and effortful) study. Perhaps that means literally accepting positions of guiding others or simply initiating the spiritual paths we feel called to follow. As I mentioned in an earlier chapter, for years I projected the Hierophant archetype onto many personal teachers and was hungry for the knowledge I knew they possessed. I listened carefully and read constantly, and still I always felt that *they* held the truths I was merely circling

---

* Referencing the title of Eliade's book, we do not mean *profane* as irreverent or disrespectful, but in its older context as simply mundane, secular or "not consecrated."

around. When I at last began my own career teaching and writing about the tarot, I finally embraced the Hierophant within me, who helped me alchemize all that I had learned into my own personal wisdom and expertise. This can be the purpose he serves for us, if we allow ourselves to embrace our intuitive authority.

When Reversed . . .

When the Hierophant comes reversed, it may be time to challenge the pontiff. For anyone in a hierarchical setting, be it academia, the corporate world, or strict social groups, we must discern when doctrine becomes dogma. When those above us become our masters rather than our guides, it may be time to rebel and forge our own path.

Another possibility with the inverted Hierophant is that we have projected him onto our mentors and teachers so vigorously that we have mistaken them for prophets. This is the archetypal projection at the heart of many cults and university classrooms. Any teacher or mentor who claims to own a piece of higher knowledge (legitimately or not) can captivate us with their charisma and wisdom.

Lastly, and especially for those engaging in spiritual work, the Hierophant inverted can signify that we've become intoxicated and inflated by the spiritual pilgrimage. When we have been labeled the gurus ourselves, we can fall victim to this potent archetypal possession.* As Jung warns, when we don't have the proper humility in our work with the sacred, "the greater the danger of our putting the divine germ within us to some ridiculous or demoniacal use, puffing ourselves up with it instead of remaining conscious that we are no more than the Stable in which the Lord is born." We forget that we are only the translators of the knowledge, and use our keys to gatekeep and lock it within our control alone.

---

* Jung used the term *archetypal possession* to describe the cases when we lose our identity to the archetype rather than form relationship with it.

The Lovers:
Eros and the Archetype of the Sacred Marriage

> *Love is born into every human being; it calls back the halves*
> *of our original nature together; it tries to make one out of two*
> *and heal the wound of human nature.*
>
> —PLATO

We come now to the last stage of our negotiation of the primordial dichotomies with the embrace of eros, bringing together Masculine and Feminine in the *mysterium coniunctionis*, the sacred marriage.

We know this card is about love, but to understand its archetypal depth, we must examine it in juxtaposition to its opposite, the Hierophant. Just as he sat atop his dais as the keeper of the holy word of logos, two supplicants receiving his lessons at his feet, the Lovers are posed below the god Eros himself, enthralled by his magic of love.*

Here the sacred transformative agent is not the preached doctrine but the personal experience of relationship. Both contain lessons of supreme mystery and spiritual revelation: the first is taught through the portal of the mind and spirit, the second is experienced through the heart and the soul. The supplicants bow their heads and *learn*; the man and woman stand naked and *feel*.

As Jung often reminded, intellectual understanding is essential to consciously directing our individuation, but relationship and experience are how we live it. The erotic experience (as in being of eros, not sex),

---

* While this angelic figure is commonly identified as the archangel Raphael as first suggested by tarot scholar Paul Foster Case, I think is more appropriately the god Eros/Cupid. Looking throughout the history of the tarot, it is always Cupid pictured above the Lovers, sometimes watching, sometimes shooting his arrow of *amour*. Here we see the same figure, only in his Greek depiction as a winged youth rather than the Roman cherub.

whether it comes through physical, romantic, familial, or platonic relationship, is the embrace of the *Other*. Through this embrace we enter an alchemical exchange. As Jung puts it, "The meeting of two personalities is like the contact of two chemical substances: if there is any reaction, both are transformed."[11]

Figure 12. *Chemical Marriage of Sun and Moon from* Rosarium Philosophorum *by Jaroš Griemiller, 1578*

When the Lovers step together into the alembic, their goal is to fully witness and experience the soul of the Other. The alchemists depicted this great mystery in their concept of the mysterium coniunctionis, the "chymical wedding" of Masculine and Feminine into a single being. For us, this Other we are seeking is not external but internal: our anima or animus, our inner beloved, who, when embraced, might indeed make us feel whole.

Of course, much of this inward searching is reflected in our outer life, and we meet the Other in relationships with real people. In this way, the great struggle of love is to experience our real-world others as *they* are and not as *we* are. This is the trap of either projection, in which we cast the reflection of our own unconscious visions onto the other, or what depth psychologists call the *participation mystique*, in which the lines between self and other blur and the two become indistinguishable.

In the Greek myth of Psyche and Eros, the supreme beauty of the mortal princess Psyche draws the envy of the goddess of beauty herself, Aphrodite. As punishment, Aphrodite sends her son Eros to pierce her with one of his arrows and make her fall in love with someone hideous and vile, but instead she is brought to Eros's palace in the forest. Her husband comes to her at night, entirely hidden by the dark. When Psyche's sisters visit they convince her to light a lamp over his face and see what sort of beast she has married. That night, as Psyche suspends her lamp over her husband's sleeping face, she discovers he is no beast at all but the resplendent god Eros. In the same moment, his arrow scrapes her thigh as her lamp's oil drips onto his skin. Psyche is engulfed by love just as Eros wakes and furiously flees.

A profound heroine's journey is initiated for Psyche, but something essential has already been alchemized, as Neumann writes:

> Psyche dissolves her *participation mystique* with her partner and flings herself and him into the destiny of separation that is consciousness. Love as an expression of feminine wholeness is not possible in the dark, as a merely unconscious process; an authentic encounter with another involves consciousness, hence also the aspect of suffering and separation.[12]

Psyche betrays Eros's demand to remain in the participation mystique, symbolized by their nighttime unions in the darkness of unconsciousness, when they cannot distinguish the other's individuality. Now she must quest for the true identity of both herself and her beloved. This is the same quest we embark on with our lovers. Psyche's tasks demonstrate how we might also transform: she must sort the grain and learn discernment; face the rams and learn temperament; collect the vile water and distill resentments; descend into the unconscious and find her own heroic will. And then, when all else is accomplished, she must return to seek forgiveness and learn, in turn, to forgive. The Lovers shows us the necessity and power of love, relationship, and the bliss of the embrace of the Other, if we can withstand the tests it presents.

In a Reading . . .

Traditionally, we read the Lovers as finding "the one" or being in love. While it can come up this way, we also may be called to investigate our personal experience of eros and its desire, connection, and relatedness. Whether with a romantic partner, friend, or parent, we may need to examine how well we love them and what motivates that love. Can we in some way see them more truly, without projections and entanglements? Can we discover a more honest connection to their authentic self rather than our ideas of it? Can we love without bonds, letting it be, as poet Khalil Gibran puts it, "a moving sea between the shores of your souls"?[13]

The Lovers may also come as an invitation to consider our relationship to the inner Other. We may dream of the anima/animus or project them onto real people through infatuations and fantasies. The task here is to bring this inner Other into the alembic with us. We may need the spirited essence of the Magician-animus to inseminate us with inspired consciousness, or we may need the soulful anima in the High Priestess to draw us into our more tender, intuitive depths. I often encounter the card appearing this way with querents who feel stuck, unmotivated, or having lost their sense of meaning. Just as meeting someone new and falling in love can reawaken us to life's wonder, seeking the inner image of the beloved as animus or anima can reforge our relationship to spirit or soul. We must seek that holy experience of coniunctio within ourselves.

When Reversed . . .

The Lovers inverted commonly points to problematic projections that are inhibiting our personal development or the potential of our relationship. We may see this person, like Psyche, as either god or monster, blinded by their perfection or their awfulness. It's true that such projections often branch out of a genuine sentiment, such as being captivated by another's charm or infuriated by their laziness. But when we fail to see a real, human person suffused with both gifts and flaws, it's not only them we're looking at but a rejected part of ourselves. The task is to go seeking the lost beloved as they really are in order to determine the strength and truth of our love.

Finally, just as we saw the Devil's mockery of the Hierophant, we also see his bondage of the Lovers. Symbolically, this shows the prison that love or relationship can become. When the Lovers comes up reversed, we should consider how the erotic has entrapped us. Perhaps we are indeed lost in a state of participation mystique and have abandoned our selfhood to codependency. Or perhaps we have developed an unhealthy relationship to sex or a toxicity in our partnerships. When we become chained to our desperation to be loved or submit to relationships that harm us or enmesh ourselves in one-sided projections, we are trapped. The love of the Other should be free, generous, and honest; otherwise it has been corrupted.

CHAPTER 9

BIRTH OF SELFHOOD—ARCHETYPES OF THE DEVELOPING EGO

*Man's main task in life is to give birth to himself,
to become what he potentially is.*
—ERICH FROMM

Having negotiated our inner dichotomies, we are now ready to fully birth ourselves by following the archetypes of the developing ego. The Chariot appears first as the heroic seat of the ego, pursuing our emerging identity; next we pass through inner and outer trials, cultivating faith and fortitude with Strength; then we turn away from the extraverted journey and toward the introverted one, following the Hermit into self-intimate solitude; next the Wheel of Fortune teaches us how to make necessary peace with fate; and finally we cultivate discernment, certainty, and loyalty to truth beside Justice.

In order to fully understand the importance of this stage, we must understand the importance of the ego. As we mentioned in chapter 1, in Eastern spiritualities the ego is seen as the entrenchment to our limited ideas of selfhood that must be transcended for enlightenment; in Western thought, however, the ego is the part of us that consciously steers the psyche toward its revelation. It is necessary in our pursuit of individuated selfhood, for, as Jung once put it, the ego functions like a workshop where we build the self.

With the following five cards, the self we speak of is in lowercase. The uppercase Self—the Self transcending ego—is not something we will encounter directly until we are tied up with the Hanged Man. The differentiation between the ego-self and the capital-*S* Self can be difficult to grasp. Without realizing it, we tend to experience ourselves in duality, as both the one who wonders and the one who knows, the one embroiled in the struggle and the one who watches from a distance. In his memoir, Jung himself describes these unique viewpoints appearing early in life and calls them personalities No. 1 and No. 2, the first being a nineteenth-century schoolboy and the second a timeless sage. That No. 1 personality is the ego, the immediate I, while the No. 2 is the voice of the Self, the remote I. Though it is the immediate I that feels present in life and propels it forward, it is the remote I that observes and urges us toward the right path. As the ninth-century Chinese monk Tung-Shan describes it:

> If you look for the truth outside yourself,
> it gets farther and farther away.
> Today, I walk alone,
> I meet him everywhere I step.
> He is the same as me,
> yet I am not him.
> Only if you understand it in this way
> will you merge with the way things are.[1]

At this stage of the journey, our egos expand and stir with desire, seeking victory rather than unity. This is natural and right, as we quest toward becoming. In order to successfully endure the efforts of our individuation, our egos must be sure and strong. Ego-strength is not about dominance or rooting out vulnerability, but about psychological resilience and flexibility. When our objective is living authentically, it is the fortified ego's willpower that drives us ever nearer to the center point of the Self.

The warning here is that it is easy to mistake the desires of the ego for the end goal of the journey. We all fall into the trap of believing that our great purpose is to publish that book, raise successful children, retire with wealth and respect. These are all vital motivators in our individuation, but they are not the goal. The goal is not the triumph or glorification of the ego, but reconciliation with the Self; or, as Tung-Shan puts it, to "merge with the way things are." Therefore, though this phase of the journey guides us to develop the ego—the sense of who we are and what our lives are about—we must remember that it is only a small part of the vast expanse of our identity. The ego carries our personal, conscious sense of selfhood, with its many longings, skills, and fears. The Self, however, encompasses both the conscious *and* unconscious, the seen and the unseen. The ego knows only itself. The Self knows it all.

This upward arc of the ego is only one stage of our journey. In our contemporary world centered around progress and productivity, we push ourselves to always remain in this phase, to always be growing, pursuing, becoming. But as the tarot shows us, immediately after its exhilarating development, the ego suffers crisis and disintegration. We must build ourselves up, then we must break ourselves down. Only then can we witness all of ourselves and embrace it into the whole of who we are. So though the journey will eventually have us challenge all that we now quest after, we must traverse this phase with all seriousness.

In the next five cards, we will learn how to develop the strength and flexibility of the ego. We will embrace our passions, adapt to our skills, glimpse our weaknesses. We will follow both the extraverted and introverted paths of self-discovery, surviving and thriving through many trials, embracing the call to be the hero. We will know ourselves and become ourselves, preparing for the further journey of reunion with Self and wholeness.

The Chariot:
The Archetype of Ego in Motion

> *How can you follow the course of your life
> if you do not let it flow?*
>
> —LAO TZU

While we tend to focus on the golden-haired hero, the card's title directs our attention not to the charioteer but his vehicle. Vehicles are symbols for the psyche in motion steered by our ego, showing how we move through our lives. It represents the drive of the libido, that life force energy carrying our appetite for growth, progress, and development.

In the tarot, the Chariot is this symbolic vehicle of the libido, transporting us from one pursuit to the next to the next. We often associate this card with willpower, or forceful control of our psychic energy, reading it as a directive to determinedly go after our plans. But libidinal energy is not truly ours to control, as Jung explains: "It does not lie in our power to transfer 'disposable' energy at will to a rationally chosen object.... However much energy may be present, we cannot make it serviceable until we have succeeded in finding the right gradient."[2] While the ego can focus our attention and energy on a certain goal, if there is no gradient—or natural unconscious inclination toward it—we cannot bend our energy its way by will alone. It is when the ego and the unconscious are in agreement that the libido spins like wheels down a slope. This is when we successfully propel ourselves toward our aims, feeling very much the triumphant hero barreling toward his destiny.

The Chariot card directly depicts this paradox of ego development without willful control. A phrase we often hear with this card is to "take the reins," and it comes as a shock when we look more closely and see that there aren't any reins at all, though the charioteer's calm and certain demeanor tricks us into believing they're there. What this symbolizes is that the charioteer does not need to push and pull to move forward. The ego in alignment with the unconscious produces a natural gradient for that libidinal energy to move us through life with vigor and grace.

Returning to the charioteer himself, we find him standing, solid and engaged, between unconscious motive and conscious direction. Guided by the canopy of stars above and loyal to the unfolding path ahead, he is ready to claim his unique selfhood and begin the great task of becoming someone. The Chariot-hero is not a conqueror but an integrator. Like the High Priestess between her pillars, he rests unthreatened by the tension of his white and black sphinxes, representing both the primordial dichotomies of the previous six cards as well as the ego poised between persona and shadow. He is swayed neither by false ideals nor hidden fears, and is secure in his answer to the quintessential question: *who am I?*

Of course, this quest of selfhood does not come without risk. In the Greek myth of Phaethon, the young hero enters the grand hall of his father, the sun god Helios, desperate to be recognized and accepted as his son. Helios swears to grant him any request, but when Phaethon demands to drive the great sun chariot across the sky—a task he knows is far beyond the boy's abilities—he pleads with his son to reconsider. Phaethon resolutely takes the reins, but despite his determination to prove himself, he is unable to wrangle the fiery horses. The chariot veers wildly, unleashing catastrophe upon the earth. To prevent further destruction, Zeus strikes him down with a thunderbolt, and Phaethon plummets into the sea.

This is a classic myth of hubris, or what depth psychologists call inflation. Inflation, as we briefly noted, occurs in the psyche when the ego expands beyond its proper limits, overestimating its powers and centering its ambitions above more judicious wisdom. The ego becomes immune to greater understanding and too inflexible to follow the libido's shifting flow. As Jung puts it, the inflated ego is "incapable of learning from the past . . . and incapable of drawing right conclusions about the future. . . . [It] is hypnotized by itself and therefore cannot be argued with."[3]

This is not to say inflation is altogether a bad thing. In fact, we could even argue it is an inevitable and necessary part of psychic development. While the goal of individuation is to arrive at a state of wholeness, the process requires us to assert our conscious autonomy against the subsuming nature of unconsciousness. This means that we must, like Phaethon, heroically walk up to the gates of the gods and present ourselves, reaching far beyond our past hesitations and limitations so that we may grab for our highest potential.

The Chariot encourages us to claim our inner power while moving with the natural flow of the libido, and never against it. It shows that when we steer our life-chariots by the wisdom of unconscious motivation, rather than willful force or hubristic desire, we cover much ground and win much success. The Chariot is the first initiation of the ego into its identity and must be driven humbly.

In a Reading . . .

Pulling the Chariot tells you to pursue the sincere and solidifying knowledge of who you are. Traditionally we associate the Chariot with the classic mythic hero, but the Chariot is not only about heroism, nor is it solely about achievement or championship. With the Chariot we are meant to question how we are directing ourselves on this journey and who we know ourselves to be. We are asked to cultivate a sense of confidence in our actions, follow the draw of our libidinal energy, and resist the urge to surrender in the face of defeat. Of all the cards of the tarot, this one most encourages us to pursue what we want, building momentum as we become the active center of our lives.

This card can be a powerful confirmation when we are considering initiating a new path or when we feel that we are gaining a new clarity about who we really are. If you have been questioning whether you are ready and able, the Chariot generally confirms that you are. It points to activity and achievement, encouraging us to go after our dreams and passions and make something of ourselves. But, at the same time, it also reminds us that we must be harmonized with the pull of our libido, always remaining faithful to that essential life force. The Chariot signifies your life—the vehicle of your psyche, your soul—is ready to be lived.

When Reversed . . .

Reversed, the Chariot indicates that we, like Phaethon, may be overestimating our powers and dooming ourselves to plummet back to earth. It points to an inflation in which we become obsessed with grandeur or cocooned in arrogance. The inflated alchemist believed it was his knowledge rather than the process that turned lead into gold, just as the inflated tarot reader believes it is her wisdom rather than the cards' that holds the answers her querent seeks. When we believe our power or will is the supreme force in our psyches, the only solution is a tragic reconciliation with our limits. Then we enter a deflation, the state of alienation from the greater Self, and we believe ourselves to be nothing and no one.

Alternatively, the Chariot reversed points to stagnancy or loss of control to unconscious impulses. When we find ourselves in broken-down cars in the dreamworld, or when we're holding the wheel straight but still spinning in loops, it is a sign that the libido has turned off or deviated from its course. This is the time to take a step backward in the journey. You aren't yet ready for the coming phases until the Chariot is righted. Pay closer attention to where the energy naturally moves, rather than where you want it to move. Practice asking the question *who am I?* Be unsure but curious about the answer.

Strength:
The Archetype of Ego-Resilience

It is not the mountain we conquer, but ourselves.
—EDMUND HILLARY

An obscure apocryphal text titled the Acts of Paul and Thecla tells us the story of a first-century woman, who, by her own unfailing determination, willed herself to sainthood. Days before her wedding, St. Paul arrives in her hometown and preaches outside her window, proclaiming the good news. Thecla knows instantly that she is meant to abandon her destined life as a wife and mother and become a servant of Christ, but Paul refuses to baptize her. Undeterred, Thecla follows Paul hundreds of miles to Antioch, all the while begging him for baptism. In Antioch, a prominent nobleman forces himself on her, and when she fights back, she is ordered by the governor to be put to death by mauling.

Though the women of the city shout their protests, Thecla is brought to the arena, stripped, and bound to a lioness. The lioness does not attack, however, and instead licks Thecla's feet. She faces lions, bears, and bulls, and the lioness sacrifices herself defending her. As yet more wild beasts charge her, Thecla flees to a pool at the center of the arena, and in the moment before her death, brings the water to her head and baptizes herself. Moved, the women cast down flowers and sweet-smelling herbs, lulling the beasts to sleep. The governor asks, aghast, "Who art thou?" to which Thecla declares, at last, "I, indeed, am a servant of the living God."

Thecla is a paragon of Strength. She exemplifies the duality of this archetype, which counsels us on the commitment to our selfhood and the relationship with our instinctual nature. Traditional keywords we associate with the Strength card are courage, confidence, and self-control, but as Thecla demonstrates, it is also about faith, fortitude, and an unfailing dedication to the true self. It is about knowing and holding the identity of the ego—protecting who we are, who we've always been, and who we know we're meant to become with unfaltering care.

We might think of Strength as the brute force it takes to dominate and triumph, but the imagery of the card reveals an entirely different secret. Rather than an aggressive warrior, we find a maiden dappled in floral garlands as she parts a lion's mouth.* The paradox emphasized is that rather than force being the necessary drive to tame the beast, it's gentility, purity, and love.

The beast itself is a symbol of the instinctual side of the psyche, the part that is motivated by our primal unconscious. The instincts that were natural and necessary for the primitive world have, in contemporary society, largely been suppressed into collective shadow and acted out unconsciously. The instinct for nourishment becomes the entrepreneur's greed; the instinct for self-defense becomes the competitor's urge to sabotage; the instinct to form community becomes the adolescent's desperation to belong. Jung argues that our instincts also include more complex needs, such as creativity, self-reflection, and spirituality (as Thecla demonstrates). When repressed, any of these instincts can breed an inner voraciousness that devours the ego's conscious ability to analyze and mediate our actions. We become swamped by unconscious energy that can quickly overwhelm us if not consciously understood and thoughtfully directed.

Thus, we need an inner lion-tamer, a figure to hold our fearful, intense, needy impulses close, to meet them not with harsh criticisms and a club, but with appreciation, softness, and sweet-smelling herbs. To combat or flee the inner beast is to remain separated from it, to remain as prey to our instincts rather than companion to them. As Jung suggests, when we encounter the inner lion, our best stance is to say: "Please, come and devour me." The work here is to embrace the unconscious contents, befriending

---

* In the earliest decks, as in the Visconti-Sforza, Strength was commonly portrayed as an aggressive Herculean figure wrestling a beast, his club poised ready to strike. However, in an even earlier 15th-century deck, the Visconti di Modrone, Strength is depicted as the woman astride the lion, her hands easily parting its razor-sharp jaws as if opening a book. Five hundred years later, this is the image that prevails—clearly capturing something more interesting or nuanced to the archetypal imagination.

and consoling them, so that we may consciously integrate them as expressions of the essential vigor of life.

Strength is the natural follow-up to the initiation of the Chariot's crusade, because once we begin the quest of finding out who we are, we will inevitably be met by both these overwhelming unconscious forces and the external trials of our ego-development. Thus we are faced with the problem of "tribulation calling out for transcendence," as Jungian analyst Edward Edinger so aptly describes it. We are pressured on two fronts—internally and externally—and must cultivate the resilience to hold fiercely to our ego center despite the many threats and challenges that impede us.

Like Thecla, when we know who we are, we can walk into the arena and befriend the beast, letting it inspire our courage and protect us from psychological harm. It is neither by force nor fleeing that we will be saved from the intensity of our depths or the threats of the world, but compassion (from the Latin *com*, "together," and *passio*, "to suffer, endure"). We must have faith in the calling and not try to evade the dangers that will inevitably come. We must rise with them.

In a Reading . . .

Strength tends to be one of those cards we gloss over, mutely accepting that we should be firmer or braver, but Strength is a card of true empowerment. It both encourages us to recognize the force within us and challenges us to become receptive to it. Perhaps those powerful instinctual aspects of self we've repressed since childhood—be they intense emotions, sexual desires, discouraged talents, or any other rejected parts—are calling to be expressed. Perhaps those vital, human flares of fury, love, determination, despair are raging beneath our fronts of control and need to be tamed or embraced as parts of our nature. And perhaps, if we can bond with these instincts and form relationship with them—like Thecla—we might even learn to draw from their ferocity for both defense and encouragement.

We must learn how to open and close the lion's mouth at will. When Strength arrives before us, now is the time to consider what parts of ourselves we have tried to cage, what parts we have allowed to rampage, and how we can more consciously form an intimacy with this raw potency within us.

Finally, Strength reminds us that we are never too weak to meet those savage moments of life and claim who we are. The mantra I like to conjure with Strength is *faith and fortitude, fortitude and faith*. When we truly know who we are, when our instincts rise and meaningfully guide our will, then we can embrace our wild souls living in balance with our conscious quest of individuation.

When Reversed . . .

We may feel that Strength inverted scolds us for being weak, but more often it points to a loss of faith in our resilience. We may be plagued with doubt that we are who we believe ourselves to be or worry that we've pushed ourselves into territory we don't have the tenacity to traverse. Of course, the medicine here is to reconnect to the vitality of Strength, as well as our faith that there is still power within us. There is no gauge of how much strength we might possess. The muscle of inner fortitude cannot atrophy.

Another possibility is that we are letting our instincts eat us up. We may become indulgent with our emotions and our passions, which may be manifesting as uncontrolled indulgence, tantrums, or panic. Despite our progress, we might regress to a semi-juvenile state and sabotage our development. Maybe you awaken your creativity, but explode with rage when offered a critique; or perhaps you begin to explore your suppressed sexuality and thoughtlessly betray your partner in the process. Releasing our wild, instinctual side is freeing but cannot be done without the help of the lion-tamer, meeting that inner beast always with grace, tenderness, and compassion.

The Hermit:
The Archetype of the Mystic Mentor

> *I have been and still am a seeker, but I have ceased to question stars and books; I have begun to listen to the teaching my blood whispers to me.*
>
> —HERMANN HESSE

After discovering the ego-center, then developing its resilience, we are now ready to follow the Hermit's lantern into the cave—the portal of inner truth.

The Hermit is a very familiar archetype to us, appearing again and again in both our ancient and contemporary stories. He is the Wise Old Man, the sage-like mentor who guides our right path, manifesting in characters like Gandalf, Yoda, Dumbledore, and Merlin.

As Jung illuminates, the Wise Old Man acts as a symbolic prefiguration of the enlightened hero. His age and wisdom tell us that he long ago successfully passed through his own egoic journey and is now attuned to his higher nature—to the Self. While he generally appears white-bearded and cloaked, he might also show up as the benevolent old crone or the faceless guardian of the wood. The Hermit can shift in dress, power, gender, or status, but his essence remains consistent: he is the old sage who has abandoned the chains of society and instead bound himself to spirit, nature, and wisdom. What he teaches us is, as Jung puts it, "the actuality of the soul." He is the mirror of our coming awakening and reconciliation with our calling, guiding us toward the path he has already walked, the path into the inner world where we discover our most unique and powerful gifts.

With Strength's lessons of faith, fortitude, and how to survive the inner wilderness, we are ready to follow the Hermit deep into the forest or high up the peak. Though he himself seems enlightened, the Hermit is not about the great revelation of spiritual knowledge. He is, like the

Chariot, a card of motion. We do not crouch beside him in the cave, but trail behind him on the snowy path, his lantern raised to light our forward steps. As the author of *Meditations on the Tarot: A Journey into Christian Hermeticism* writes:

> The Hermit is neither deep in meditation or study nor is he engaged in work or action. He is walking. This means to say that he manifests a third state beyond that of contemplation and action ... the term of synthesis, namely that of the heart. For it is the heart where contemplation and action are united, where knowledge becomes will and where will becomes knowledge.[4]

The Hermit is walking, always walking, following the Star held at the level of the heart. The Hermit's movement is symbolic of his active contemplation. He is in pursuit of his own inner light, the numinous essence of his selfhood, which is brightest when we find ourselves quiet and alone.

In contemplation of our selfhood, the Hermit opens us to mysticism, which can only be experienced through the solitary heart, not the searching mind. This is the key difference between the Hermit and the Hierophant, whom many beginner readers struggle to differentiate. The Hermit's mysticism stands in stark contrast to the Hierophant's orthodoxy. While the latter gives us a dependable dogma to structure our spiritual learning, the former invites us into the ecstatic wonder of feeling the mystery itself. It really can't be said any better than in the words of the great Sufi mystic Rumi, "This Love is beyond the study of theology, / that old trickery and hypocrisy."[5]

The Chariot initiated us onto the extraverted path of purpose, but if we become too focused on progress, we can easily be swept up in the outer life and the achievements of the ego or persona. In these cases we fall victim to mass-mindedness, which may offer connection and community (or the illusion of it), but ultimately costs us the opportunity to individuate and learn our own truths. The Hermit appears to prevent this, drawing us into the introverted path of soul-seeking. However, for some of us this path, too, can become an enticing detour. Sometimes the Hermit takes us too high up the mountain, captivating us with the view, and it can become increasingly difficult to find our way back. This is when the Hermit's call becomes hermitage and we reject society altogether.

To remain in indefinite isolation is to deny life and thus hide away in petrifaction. The Hermit's cell is no home. We must learn to bring forth our individual experience and wisdom, and actually *live it*.

In a Reading . . .

When we draw the Hermit, we are directly called to pull back from the extraverted life and turn our attention toward the introverted one. Often we bristle at the idea of taking time off work or doing a solo camping trip, but of course, we know that the cards' invitations are more metaphorical than literal. When we retract ourselves from the relentless drive to *do*, our libidinal energy reconcentrates on the quieter, simpler path of our truth. We connect back to the heart, to the feeling of who we are rather than the performance of it.

The Hermit can appear with a strong message to recede. Maybe you need to turn away from world events or pause your focus on the next achievement or momentarily take away the burden of caretaking. Whether speaking through the voice of an external mentor or arriving as an inner calling, the Hermit encourages us to separate from the world and enter solitude. He invites us into that inner cave where there is nothing to meet but the beating of our heart and the whispering of our soul. In this solitude we learn mindfulness, awareness, and hear the wisdom guiding us toward the forward path.

This inner cave, again, is metaphorical—interior moments carved into our busy days—but sometimes the Hermit urges us to take the path less trodden and really go out and settle on some distant hill. Jung entered this space in his own remote attic office while he recorded his inner fantasies in his *Red Book*. Joseph Campbell quit his PhD program and lived alone in the woods for five years where he did nothing but read and wonder. Sometimes we really do have to find out who we are in a space where society cannot interrupt and impose its perspectives before we truly learn who we are.

When Reversed . . .

For those committed to the inward path, we can easily become possessed by the Hermit. When inverted, rather than following the Hermit's lantern through the dark, we may believe that we have become the Wise One, the mystic, the soul-guide. This is common with the Hermit because, from our isolated view, we cannot see all those who have earned the same wisdom. We fall victim to the illusion that we alone have won the truth.

Alternatively, the Hermit inverted can point to what Jung called the archetype of the Senex, a Latin term meaning old man—which exists in opposition to the archetype of the Puer—Latin for boy. Alienated from the vitality of the youthful Puer, the Senex turns rigid, aloof, and resistant to change and connection. When the Hermit languishes too long in the comfort of his isolation, he can harden into the Senex, thus losing all the spark and thrill of life. Then he is nothing but an old man hiding in a cave with no real life to be lived.

When the Hermit shows up reversed, it's time to emerge from isolation. If we linger too long, our solitude will sour into loneliness. We must continue the journey initiated by the charioteer and regain some motion in the psyche, restarting the motor of our individuation.

The Wheel of Fortune:
The Archetypal Negotiation of Circumference and Center

> "Inconstancy is my very essence," says the wheel. Rise up on my spokes if you like but don't complain when you're cast back down into the depths. . . . Mutability is our tragedy, but it's also our hope. The worst of times, like the best, are always passing away.
>
> —BOETHIUS

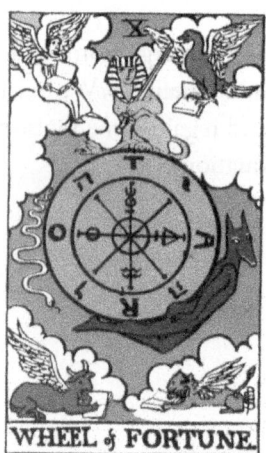

In AD 523, a Roman senator awaiting his execution wrote a profound philosophical treatise on the acceptance of fate. Boethius had lived a successful life as a scholar and politician, enjoying great wealth and prestige until his enemies accused him of treason. In the months of his imprisonment, he devoted himself to understanding the greater meaning of his sudden reversal of fortune. The work that came from this effort is *The Consolation of Philosophy*—a dialectic between himself, the goddess figure Lady Fortuna (Fate), and the personified Philosophy. Philosophy consoles Boethius by convincing him that true happiness does not come from the fleeting pleasures of material wealth, but from the rewards of spiritual wealth. This, Philosophy argues, is the pursuit of wisdom and what all true seekers of fortune are after.

The Wheel of Fortune is one of the cards that is often interpreted too literally, being read mostly as good or bad fate. However, the card opens us up to the deeper mystery that Boethius himself proposed fifteen hundred years ago: happiness comes when we can thank Fortune for the favors she has given us, rather than "complain as if what you have lost was fully your own."[6] If we can release our sense of entitlement to good fortune, then we are available to gratitude and immune to despair. Then we can accept the impermanence of life, trusting that the Wheel will continue to spin, knowing that we are bound to perpetually cycle through abundance and lack, love and loss, joy and fear.

As a Christian, Boethius believed that all things worked toward the highest "Good" and that without God's all-knowing vision we can't see that everything we encounter on the long, winding path of suffering and celebration has purpose. But there is yet a deeper, more mystical point of interpretation in the Wheel of Fortune. As Boethius himself says: "everything is the freer from Fate the closer it seeks the centre of things."[7] The secret of the Wheel is that motion happens at the circumference, but the center is always still. Our daily lives are in constant rotation, managing the blessings and pains of living. However, that innermost point—the Self—is immovable. (As Friedrich Nietzsche put it, "The middle is everywhere. Crooked is the path of eternity."[8]) It is this place, not some imagined end, that we are trying to approach on the mystical path of our individuation.

The Wheel of Fortune and its many symbolic elements represent the paradoxical fluidity and fixedness of life, orienting us always to question whether we are moving with it or against it. The four creatures on the Wheel—the Lion, the Ox, the Man, and the Eagle—represent the four corners of existence via the four fixed astrological signs, while Anubis, the Egyptian god who shepherds souls to heaven, ascends, and Typhon, the monstrous Greek titan who failed to overthrow Zeus, descends. The sphinx atop the wheel reminds us of the riddling mystery that is life, while the letters within it spell out TARO, ROTA (Latin for wheel), and TORA (the sacred book held by the High Priestess), showing that the simple rearrangement of the letters (or a rearrangement of fate) opens up unexpected possibilities.

The Wheel of Fortune tells us that fate is neutral. While we must have faith that the universe conspires for our highest good, we will not be spared life's volatility, nor promised contentment. This is why, I believe, the Wheel of Fortune appears at the midpoint of the Major Arcana story, near the end of the ego's development. After the charioteer emerges, taming his own instincts with Strength, connecting to his inner truth in the Hermit's solitude, he must now learn to navigate the inherent chaos and fickleness of fate. Learning this lesson will be one of the greatest supports we have for cultivating genuine inner peace no matter what comes to threaten us. (And with the Hanged Man a few cards away, we know something is indeed on the horizon.)

When gripped to the Wheel's circumference, our contentment and peace become shackled to our position on it. As Campbell writes, when on the rim of the Wheel of Fortune, "you will be either above, going down, at the bottom, or coming up. But if you are at the hub, you're in the same place all the time."[9] The question we are posed is how might we live life with its ever-shifting conditions, challenges, and successes in the same place all the time. The task with the Wheel of Fortune is that we move from the rim to the hub, from the circumference of life to its center.

In a Reading . . .

The Wheel of Fortune often tells us that the Wheel is spinning of its own volition and our conditions are about to change. It is one of the few cards of the tarot where its interior, psycho-spiritual significance almost always goes hand in hand with a real external shift. These are not the catastrophic changes that come with the Tower, but they can be nonetheless jarring as we find ourselves in new promotions, suddenly single, or navigating other unexpected circumstances.

The Wheel of Fortune can indicate "good fortune," but it can also point to a cyclical return to a place we've already been. We all experience the return to old wounds and learned lessons, which may make us worry that we've moved backward. However, we should think of the Wheel in three-dimensional form. As Woodman often reminds in her writings, life is neither a circle nor a line but a spiral: "We continue to learn the same things again and again at each spiral in the path, each time taking the understanding deeper, each time embodying it more, each time able to recall it more quickly in demanding times."[10]

Now is the time to be open to change and receptive to new (or old) lessons. It is also an opportunity to focus on the center and a sense of presence through the tides of life. Trust that life will right itself and also that your luck will not hold forever. The point is to not resist, to accept your place on the Wheel and hold on to hope that a new turn is always on its way.

When Reversed . . .

When the Wheel is turned upside down, we often find ourselves spinning in place. Rather than seeking deeper insight, we may be stuck in patterns that we perceive as "bad fate." Perhaps this looks like encountering the same militant boss at every job or discovering the same emotional neglect in every new romantic partner or always oversleeping on days of important meetings. When we keep hitting the same obstructions in our path, we are living in a closed circuit. When we deny our accountability and blame it all on bad luck or some karmic loop, we can turn fatalistic and believe ourselves doomed to perpetual failure.

The Wheel of Fortune inverted encourages us to take up the responsibility of seeking meaningful change. Jung is often (mis)quoted as saying, "Until you make the unconscious conscious, it will direct your life and you will call it fate," which is a pithy paraphrase of what he actually said:

> The psychological rule says that when an inner situation is not made conscious it happens outside, as fate. That is to say, when the individual remains undivided and does not become conscious of his inner opposite, the world must perforce (necessarily), act out the conflict and be torn into opposing halves.[11]

Though we cannot control who our bosses are or what our partners do or whether or not our alarms will sound, we are playing some part in the pattern. When we do not examine our inner oppositions and conflicts, the outer world—the Wheel of Fortune—plays them out unconsciously and synchronistically, and, of course, we'll throw our hands up and call it fate.

Justice:
The Archetype of Balanced Truth

The content of your character is your choice. Day by day, what you choose, what you think and what you do is who you become.

—HERACLITUS

Along with Strength (aka Fortitude) and Temperance, Justice represents one of the four cardinal virtues that were so important to the medieval world in which the tarot was born. Though emphasized in Christian morality, these cardinal virtues actually originated from Hellenistic philosophy and are attributed to Plato, who wrote that good character was "wise, brave, temperate, and just."* What these virtues are ultimately about is mediation, or in depth psychology terms, the balanced path through the opposites. This is what the early Major Arcana prepare us for and what the middle Major Arcana achieve. Strength mediates instinct and control, our wildness and tenderness; Temperance mediates the mundane and the sacred, our mortal need and our spiritual longing; and Justice mediates, as Aristotle might put it, selfishness and selflessness, or to the Kabbalists, severity and mercy.

The Kabbalistic viewpoint is particularly useful in discussing the deeper meaning of Justice for our psycho-spiritual development. On the Kabbalistic Tree of Life there are two pillars—one black and one white—which also appear on either side of the High Priestess. On the left is the dark pillar Boaz, the pillar of severity; on the right is the light pillar Jachin, the pillar of mercy. In between—where the High

---

* The fourth virtue, prudence or wisdom, is notably absent from the deck. Many tarot scholars have speculated on this, and many theories have been offered. Some believe prudence was the original name for the Hermit. Some insist it must be hidden within the High Priestess/Popess via her scroll—a common symbol attached to prudence. Still others argue that the Hanged Man is a perversion of prudence. Though there is no consensus, it is one of those fantastic mysteries of the tarot.

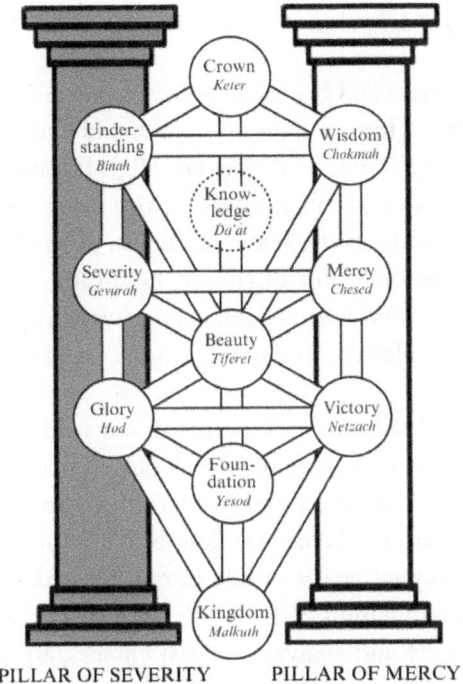

Figure 13. Simplified Kabbalistic Tree of Life

Figure 14. Justice and the High Priestess from the Rider-Waite deck

Priestess sits—is an invisible, unnamed pillar associated with mildness or balance.

The High Priestess and Justice sit between the same pillars, as Waite writes, "the pillars of Justice open into one world and the pillars of the High Priestess into another."[12] Where the High Priestess holds her balanced wisdom in unconscious mystery, Justice brings it into conscious action. Justice is firmly in the plane of choice, planted between mercy and severity, compassion and discipline, expansion and containment. She does not simply meditate on equilibrium, but actively hones her skill to sort through complexity, develop discernment, and facilitate mildness between extremes.

Justice is one of the strongest points in our individuation arc. Her purpose is to protect and serve the developing ego, using her scales to harmonize our inner tensions and her sword to cut away that which keeps us unconscious, stuck, or powerless. She is loyal only to truth and is willing to take any action (be it mild or radical) to defend it. She does not balk at self-examination. Side by side with Justice, we learn to look more critically at life and analyze our past choices, attitudes, reactions, and expectations so that we may understand ourselves more wholly and honestly. Then, with that understanding, we can intentionally serve our authenticity, autonomy, and growth.

In her mythological origins, Justice derives from the Greek titan Themis, the daughter of Uranus and Gaia, deities of heaven and earth. With Zeus she bore the three Horae, the personified seasons and the goddesses of justice, law, and peace, and the Moirai (the Fates), the three goddesses that arranged human destinies. Symbolically, we might see these two sets of divinities as representatives of the two tools at Themis's (and Justice's) disposal. Her scale of natural, lawful balance indicates her receptivity and fairness, while her sword of discernment and power protects the rightful order of life's unfolding.

Where Justice differs from Themis is that she has stripped off her blindfold: the symbol of impartiality. Justice has her eyes very much open—as she must. When we blindly abide by the laws given to us, whether from society, family, or past versions of self, we cannot judge our own emerging truth. We fail Justice when we surrender our agency to external conditions or influences, regressing back into the unconscious acceptance of what we're told is "true." In these cases, it is as if we have dropped Excalibur back into the lake and a crucial stage of the process has been lost.

We must not be impartial because our loyalty lies with our authentic selves and our own individuation. At this point in the tarot sequence, we must begin to take responsibility for our decisions and our direction in life. We can no longer blame the Wheel's capricious turning. We can no longer linger in the Hermit's cave or battle out our passions with Strength. Now we must follow the straight line of the sword as it points toward our truest self.

In a Reading . . .

Justice asks us to lean into our powers of discrimination, discerning truth from falsehood, impulse from intuition, need from fear. After the chaos of the Wheel of Fortune in which we could not tell up from down, we must ground into what is stationary and strong and from that place direct our lives.

We must critically analyze what in our lives actually serves us and what we serve in ourselves. For example, we might ask how we allow ourselves to be taken advantage of and consider how we take advantage of others; we might examine where we should moderate our manipulations or erect stronger boundaries. If we find that what we serve is anything other than authentic, uncorrupted truth, Justice can help us raise our own swords to draw new lines in the sand or cut away problematic patterns.

Though she sits passively on her throne, Justice is a card of action. With her unrelenting devotion to truth and fairness, Justice empowers us to make the choices we know are right. She demands honesty above all, which in turn fortifies us in taking responsibility for our own failures, deceptions, and excuses. Often Justice arrives when we already know what is right, but acting upon it, for whatever reason, unnerves us. We must remember that Justice sits equally between severity and mercy. Sometimes harshness is healthy, and sometimes forgiveness is necessary. This negotiation is the path to true mildness and balance. The test of learning Justice is the ability to make fair judgments because, deep down, we know they're right. If we can master her fearlessness and devotion, her willingness to serve all that is for our greater good, we will find ourselves much bolstered.

When Reversed...

With inverted Justice we double down on our biases and prejudice. Self-protection becomes self-defensiveness, and everything and everyone else are to blame. When we betray our integrity or act falsely, coming to terms with these actions can threaten our fragile sense of self. Our egos feel too weak to bear the sharp edge of that necessary judgment. Thus we project the criticism outward or ignore our blaring misjudgments or apply Justice's natural skill to ward off truth rather than serve it. We refuse honesty and accountability as we stubbornly tie the blindfold back over our eyes.

Another possibility is that we're struggling to maintain the discernment that we established while the card was right side up. It is difficult to preserve the decisions we know were right, particularly when they alienate us from those we care about or things we love. For gentler personalities, they may make us feel quite the villain. Even Themis, the goddess of justice, struggled to discern and defend the choice she knew she must make. It was she who turned the tide in the titanomachy, overthrowing her own family on behalf of the rising gods of Olympus. But she trusted her critical wisdom, knowing that their reign had ended and that she must make her terrible choice to serve the greater good. We must protect and serve what is authentic and true, whether in us or the world around us, and defend what is right with clarity and solidity.

CHAPTER 10

ENCOUNTERING THE SHADOW—ARCHETYPES OF DESCENT

A life truly lived constantly burns away veils of illusion, burns away what is no longer relevant, gradually reveals our essence, until, at last, we are strong enough to stand in our naked truth.

—MARION WOODMAN

From the Great Above she opened her ear to the Great Below.

From the Great Above the goddess opened her ear to the Great Below.

From the Great Above Inanna opened her ear to the Great Below.

These famous lines begin a four-thousand-year-old Sumerian poem in which Inanna, the Queen of Heaven, journeys out of her empyrean kingdom and into the pit of the underworld to visit her sister Ereshkigal, Queen of the Dead. Dressed in finery and beads and golden rings, the crown of heaven upon her head and her magic scepter in hand, the great goddess arrives at the gates of the underworld. Inanna knocks, demanding entrance, but Ereshkigal orders the seven gates bolted until she removes her royal garments. Gate by gate Inanna strips away the vestiges of her beauty, power, and glory, until she finally enters the inner lair, naked and humbled. There, without warning or cause, she is put on trial, found guilty, and slain.

With the Chariot through Justice we were dressing ourselves in the raiment of our selfhood, learning who we are, what we want, and what it takes to get it. Now the direction of our journey has reversed. As we meet the Hanged Man, then Death, Temperance, the Devil, and finally the Tower, we are on a quest of undressing, stripping away, breaking apart. Like Inanna, we are asked to humble ourselves, to relinquish our identity as the luminous hero and stand in our bare truth. It is only in this state that we may approach the throne of the shadow sister, our inner enemy.

Mythologically, we call this passage *katabasis*, the journey down from the land of light and the living into the realm of dark and the dead. In Jungian language, it is the confrontation with the shadow, the descent into the unconscious realm that holds all that we have cast away or lost. As we quested to strengthen the ego, gathering more and more under the umbrella of *What I Am*, we were simultaneously casting off more and more into *What I Am Not*. The more secure we feel in the ego as hero, the more we must deny the inner villain—the shadow that has been growing in parallel beneath us all along. As Robert Johnson writes, "This is one of Jung's greatest insights: that the ego and the shadow come from the same source and exactly balance each other. To make light is to make shadow; one cannot exist without the other."[1] In order for the ego to develop and move us closer to our potential, it must believe in its purity and deny its depravity. If we are to be honest, our insincerity must be driven out; if we are to pursue ambition, our idleness must be refused. Whatever we claim as our conscious power and goodness, some other side must be rejected as wicked and weak.

However, nothing is truly cast away. Poet Robert Bly calls this rejected shadow material the "long bag we drag behind us." What is rejected by the ego is discarded into the shadow, and we continue to carry it with us as it subtly haunts and disturbs us. The contents of this bag are not only the muck within us, but the gold. Jung is said to have suggested that 90 percent of the shadow is actually this "gold," or the repressed content containing our hidden skills, forgotten beauty, swallowed potentials. In order to move forward in our individuation, we must descend into shadow and sort through the muck in order to rescue this gold.

The tarot shows us the stages of this descent. The charioteer is disarmed and strung up on a tree before the ego-self he has known is annihilated in death. Next he will be prepared for passage into the underworld by the angel of purification, who, as psychopomp, will deliver him to the gate of the shadow enemy. Finally, he will watch as the life he once labored to build turns desolate and crumbles to ash. It is a horrifying journey, but a necessary one. What the tarot shows us is that the natural path of individuation is a cyclic building up and breaking down, pursuing who we are and then reconciling with all that was lost in that pursuit. This is a place where fear follows us through every turn and shame is a constant weight on our hearts, but we must not submit to despair. The story does not end here. There is one final stage of our journey—the *anabasis*, the ascent, the transcendent rise into integrated unity.

Inanna was not abandoned to the tortures of the underworld, and neither are we. She is saved and rises, even more resplendent, to take back her throne. We, too, will regain the potency of our selfhood, but through the courage and wisdom only won when we face this gauntlet of suffering. As we make our own journey of katabasis now, keep in mind that all we are asked to do is hold the tension, remain faithful to our goal of becoming, and remember the promised return. The soul waits somewhere beyond this morbid landscape, patiently anticipating our reconciliation with its light.

The Hanged Man:
The Archetype of Sacrificing Self

> *I don't know Who—or what—put the question,*
> *I don't know when it was put. I don't even remember answering.*
> *But at some moment I did answer Yes to Someone—or Something—*
> *and from that hour I was certain that existence is meaningful and*
> *that, therefore, my life, in self-surrender, had a goal.*
>
> —DAG HAMMARSKJÖLD

I first encountered the Hanged Man when I was fourteen. My friend had invited me to a makeshift carnival held in her church's parking lot, and we brazenly hopped onto the one ride that not only lifted you off the ground but made a full 360° revolution. We spun around and around, shrieking happily, until suddenly we jolted to a stop and found ourselves completely upside down. At first we giggled, watching each other turn tomato red as our heads engorged with blood. But soon the giddiness wore away as my brain buzzed and throbbed and my organs slowly sagged their enormous weight onto my lungs. Five minutes passed, ten, twenty, and the panic became the worst of the pain. It was not only death I feared, but the terrible wrongness of things: the sky, the feel of my body, my friend's face—all horrifically inverted. A metal bar was the only thing between me and my end, and with each second that passed I was sure I couldn't bear another.

When we talk about the Hanged Man, we typically use phrases like "surrender" and "letting go," but we have a tendency in tarot to bypass the archetypal truth in uncomfortable cards and replace it with innocuous aphorisms that wash away its wisdom. As I learned firsthand, to hang is to suffer. It was once the common punishment reserved for deplorables—thieves, tricksters, traitors, false prophets—because before the release of death comes ridicule, agony, and confusion; it strips them of the most basic comfort of the solid earth beneath them.

However, despite his undoubted delirium and despair, the man hangs in perfect stillness, as if in meditation. This does not signal that he lets go of his suffering, but that he gives in to it. The Hanged Man's serenity comes from his acceptance that his suffering is also sacrifice.

Sacrifice is indeed the archetypal heart of the Hanged Man. The image itself seems directly drawn from the mythology of the Norse deity Odin, who, though himself the god of wisdom, yearned for the greater wisdom within the runes. Odin gazed down at the work of the rune-casting Norns—the fate-makers who tended to the world tree Yggdrasil—and knew that to earn their secrets he would have to make himself worthy. He hung himself from Yggdrasil, refused food and water, and stabbed himself with a spear: "I know that I hung, on a wind-rocked tree, nine whole nights, with a spear wounded, and to Odin offered, myself to myself; on that tree, of which no one knows from what root it springs."[2] After nine long days and nights, Odin made his final offering by plucking out his eye, and his great sacrifice at last earned him the runes and the wisdom he sought.

Another story we connect to the Hanged Man is Jesus's crucifixion. While Jesus did not sacrifice himself to gain wisdom, he knew his suffering was the only path to embracing his full divinity. ("Father, if you are willing, take this cup from me; yet not my will, but yours be done.") We may not meet this suffering enthusiastically, but we nonetheless allow it, knowing it is the portal to the highest self. It is this knowledge that brings, as Waite describes it, the "deep entrancement" that rests on the Hanged Man's face. He knows that his hanging will draw him into the realm of Death, where the only path leads past the Devil's gate, but he also knows that it continues on, following the light of the Star which illuminates the way to glorious union with the Self, the soul.

We do not choose to be hung, but it is when we are in these paralyzed states that we have the opportunity to accept the inversion, embrace the not knowing, move our center point inward, cast our eyes downward at the roots of the tree whose origin will always be beyond our sight. This is why the man bears a golden nimbus around his head. He has sanctified this moment of suffering by surrendering his ego's need for supremacy and control. He has consented to the suspension and redirected the center of the personality from the ego-self toward the sacred Self. This is a crucial, radical shift in our tarot journey of individuation, and if this sacrifice is successful, as Jung says, it "bears blessed fruit." Peace can be won if we surrender to the hanging.

In a Reading . . .

In our lived experience, the Hanged Man rarely feels holy. We tend to pull this card when we are suffering those excruciating moments of helplessness, confusion, and disorientation. However, the opportunity the Hanged Man presents is truly a blessed one: instead of thrashing against the suffering, we can allow ourselves to hang. We can sacrifice our old strategies of survival on the cross of our transformation. We can allow ourselves to be uncomfortable, unsure, unmotivated, laying ourselves bare to the new wisdom that had been waiting to emerge from within our depths.

Gravity has been reversed, and though we might not see it now, we are being pulled equally between the earth and heaven, between the mundane and the numinous within us. The lesson in the Hanged Man may seem mysterious, but it's actually quite simple. The plain and bitter truth is that sometimes we must *be where we are.* The burden of the Hanged Man is to hang. Answers do not serve here, nor are there any to be found. This is a moment of inwardness. It is an opportunity to learn by way of allowing. Our task now is to resist the urge to struggle and unbind ourselves. Instead, we must breathe and remember that our suffering is sanctified and makes us ready for a metamorphosis we can't yet fathom.

When Reversed . . .

When the Hanged Man is reversed, we still struggle with our ropes and fight to get back upright. This desperation clings to our (diminishing) ego-control and prevents illumination. The suffering is made meaningless.

A client received a disappointing (though non-life-threatening) diagnosis and came to me seeking clarity on how to accept this news and redirect her life forward. When the Hanged Man arrived inverted, I asked if rather than pressuring herself to choose a new direction, she could first allow a moment of surrender, seeking acceptance of what is. My client irritatedly replied that she had pulled this card for herself many times and had enough of its message; she wanted to know how to push through the diagnosis, not how to make peace with it. As professional tarotists know, it is exactly this resistant attitude that makes a card repeatedly come up. The radical (and wise) choice of the Hanged Man is to be in the tension of where we are.

With the inverted Hanged Man we have unwittingly suspended our individuation. We may resist sacrificing old attachments, patterns, and ways of being. We may be holding on to our parents' projections or clinging to old identities we've outgrown or living out someone else's ideas of who we are. We become tangled in the knots of who we have been that simply no longer fit, and that stuckness becomes a source of self-pity, which prevents us from learning the humility and serenity of the Hanged Man.

When we try to stand the Hanged Man up on his feet, we are corrupting the archetype. The inversion is necessary. It's a symbol of the sudden suspension of who we are so that we might learn what deeper wisdom exists within. To eventually land upright again, we must stay faithful to the transformation.

Death:
The Archetype of Ego-Dissolution

Life is a constant process of dying.
—ARTHUR SCHOPENHAUER

Death is the most feared card of the tarot. It grabs us by the throat, demanding that we contemplate the greatest horror of living: its end. It is unfortunate when contemporary decks try to brush away the black tunnel of our mortality by renaming it things like *Rebirth*, *Metamorphosis*, or *Change*, because, being the only thoroughly universal experience of life, Death deserves the seriousness its name implies. This is not at all to say that Death should be taken literally, or that it is not also about rebirth, metamorphosis, and change, which of course it is. Simply, to achieve transformation, we must first endure disintegration.

The best expression we have of the psycho-spiritual process of Death comes from nature herself via the metamorphosis of the butterfly. As children we all learn how the little ugly caterpillar goes into its cocoon and molts into the resplendent butterfly, but we are spared the full horror of this ordeal. The caterpillar begins as a tiny larva, stuffing itself with nutrients, growing hardy and fat. When it reaches its plumpest potential, the caterpillar hangs itself from a branch (like the Hanged Man) and spins itself into a silken chrysalis. Within the chrysalis the caterpillar dissolves itself, literally liquifying in its own digestive juices until it is nothing more than a thin goo. Every bit of tissue is melted down with the exception of a handful of clustered cells called imaginal discs, which are essentially sacs of genetic material that hold the code for each new body part.* After an

---

* As a fun note, these discs are called *imaginal* from the Latin root *imago*, meaning "image," because what they hold is the potential of the butterfly's forms. We could just as well call them archetypal sacs.

average of thirteen days (Death's number) the soup of caterpillar protein is at last remade into a butterfly and the transformation is complete.

Death promises rebirth, but is itself the archetypal process of ego-dissolution. It is the breakdown of who we are. The Hanged Man sacrifices his ego-control for the opportunity to learn more about his sacred nature, but that sacrifice ends the way it must: with the perishing of the self as he knew it. In this stage of the katabasis, the Hanged Man sheds his earthbound body so that he may enter the world of only spirit, which, as we know from all our myths and fairy tales, is forbidden to the living (metaphorically, those still vested in their ego-identities). To travel through the underworld, we must first in some way "die" to our mortal life. If we turn back now, we nullify all the psycho-spiritual effort we've put in thus far. The only path forward is down.

This is not to paint the Death card as a hopeless pit. On the contrary, in the Waite-Smith deck we see the Death skeleton riding in on his white horse bearing what Waite calls the Mystic Rose, the symbol of purified life. In the background dawn blares between two great pillars, signifying the illumination to come if we can successfully complete the quest that Death has initiated. Though far on the horizon, that is the threshold we are soon to meet.

In many older decks, Death holds a scythe, a symbol of cyclical nature, being at one moment a tool of harvest and in the next a weapon to slice us up. It is a symbol of the natural process of psychic dismembering that we all must pass through to facilitate real renewal. As Edinger writes, "Dismemberment can be understood psychologically as a transformative process which divides up an original unconscious content for purposes of conscious assimilation."[3] Dismemberment signifies the dismantling of the entangled parts of our psyche—with its numerous complexes, wounds, and unconscious patterns—so that we may sort ourselves out, distinguishing the decay from what still has life. This is a process that brings great grief, but also, eventually, great relief. Nichols says it beautifully:

> Whoever mourns the amputation of an unconscious reaction which has been a part of him since childhood, or whoever bemoans the loss of some rigid projection which has long served as support for the tottering ego, these may consider themselves blessed. They will

ultimately be comforted with more valid insights and more enduring support.[4]

Death destroys what has already begun to erode in the psyche. It comes to sever us from that which impedes our individuation, whether it be a failing relationship, a festering belief, a crumbling dream, or any other source of rot. Within our tombs, we must suffer this mortification of the parts of us that are incompatible with the emerging authentic self, but we must also remember that those imaginal discs remain intact. When we are ready, they will guide us into our highest expression of selfhood.

When Death comes, it must be faced. We must not bargain, flee, or refuse. If a part of us must die—and it must—let us shed it freely so that a truer part is planted in its place. Blessed are those who are cut down by Death's scythe or fall beneath its black banner, for they alone will know the sanctity of true transformation.

In a Reading . . .

Death comes to tell us something within us is dead or dying. Maybe it comes to open us to the wail of grief or tell us to build a funeral pyre for something we've left to corrode in a compartment in our hearts. But Death also signals a moment to do the work of psychic dismemberment and cut away the gangrenous content. Perhaps projections have been recalled within a relationship and suddenly the love has been lost; perhaps a talent that once flourished has begun to fade; perhaps a complex that kept us fierce has withered and we are wondering where our strength has gone. Whatever is in a state of decomposition, we must amputate it and make room for new psychic growth.

Death comes when we are mourning a lost part of ourselves, but it can also nod toward the external pressures of failure and disappointment. Perhaps you have received yet another rejection letter or are debating, again, a hopeless reconciliation with an old lover. Death urges us to let the thing die, to work your gentlest magic of conclusions and rituals of lamentation to release it. The dead things in our lives and in our psyches will not heal or disappear on their own. If we do not take the opportunity to follow Death's lead, the rot will be removed in the sweeping destruction of the Tower.

When Reversed . . .

When Death is reversed, we can imagine ourselves like Drew Barrymore in *Scream*, frantically and futilely running to escape the masked predator breaking his way in. When we flee Death and the change it's promising, the result is psychic atrophy. We become fixated on "saving" things or double down on antiquated moralism or launch into bitter, self-deprecating tirades. As Karen Hamaker-Zondag puts it, "Clinging to the old brings out every negative thing that Death can produce."[5]

We know what we must let die, but when we refuse the purge of Death, we become energetically inert, stuck in our pitiable ways, and our souls turn sterile. The psyche forfeits its libidinal drive to develop, diminishing into lethargy, rigidity, and cowardice. Not only do we lose the connection to the emerging Self, but even our ego identities feel reduced to the level of the persona with no real "I" behind it. Though we resist the dying, we still become corpse-like, and there is no fertile ground to facilitate the rebirth that is promised. To finish with a little Jung: "Without death, life would be meaningless, since the long-lasting rises again and denies its own meaning. To be, and to enjoy your being, you need death, and limitation enables you to fulfill your being."[6]

Temperance:
The Archetype of the Mediating Psychopomp

> *He leads me beside quiet waters,*
> *he refreshes my soul.*
> *He guides me along the right paths*
> *for his name's sake.*
> *Even though I walk*
> *through the darkest valley,*
> *I will fear no evil,*
> *for you are with me.*
>
> —PSALM 23, NIV

With her ethereal robes and tranquil expression, Temperance may seem out of place squeezed between the horror of Death and the monstrosity of the Devil. However, Temperance's place in the sequence is mythically ordained and teaches us several essential lessons that will bring both psychic harmony and spiritual fortification for the trials to come.

As one of the four cardinal virtues, Temperance serves as the guardian of moderation, restraining carnal desires and impulses through chastity, sobriety, and self-discipline. Yet to the premodern world built upon these virtues, temperance was more than mere self-control—it was the virtue that refined the soul. As sixteenth-century philosopher Michel de Montaigne wrote, "Greatness of soul consists not so much in mounting and in pressing forward, as in knowing how to govern and circumscribe itself; it . . . demonstrates itself in preferring moderate to eminent things."[7] Essentially, temperance does not demand the relentless perfection of self but rather the *governing* of self to foster a state of balance that is attuned to something higher.

While this is a powerful lesson to take from the Temperance card, her archetypal guidance is less about practical *moderation* and more about psycho-spiritual *mediation*. Moderation asks us to subdue ourselves; mediation urges us to find a middle way through. This distinction is reflected in some of her earliest depictions, where the maiden holds a fiery torch in one hand and a jug of water in the other—elements that cannot be mixed, only balanced. Over time, as Christian virtue skewed puritanical, the torch was replaced with a cup of wine, signifying the dilution of indulgence (a shift preserved in the imagery of the tarot). Yet the original symbolism evokes a deeper paradox, one central to ancient alchemy: that true temperance is not suppression, but the fusion of opposites, tempering their extremes into a new, harmonized state.

This work of mediation is what the Temperance angel accomplishes. She stands with one foot in the water and one on land, signaling her equal presence in the inner and outer worlds. She takes what is fervently opposed in us—our mundanity and spirituality, our ferocity and mildness, our idealism and cynicism—and performs the alchemical ritual that brings them into balance. Through her help, we find harmony within the polarity.

Finally, her most significant act of mediation may be her role as an intercessor between the conscious and unconscious sides of the psyche, embodied in her function as the tarot psychopomp. Mythologically, the psychopomp is the archetypal soul-ferrier who guides our passage in and out of supernatural domains, manifesting in figures such as Hermes, Anubis, and the Valkyries. An example of a psychopomp that resonates deeply with the Temperance archetype can be found in the medieval poem "Pearl." In this poignant narrative, a father mourns the loss of his beloved daughter, symbolized by his precious pearl. As he drifts into sleep, his spirit is transported to a verdant landscape beside a rushing stream. There, across the water, stands an angelic maiden adorned in pearls—an apotheosized representation of his daughter—who imparts a vital message: hope must never be surrendered to grief, for all things die, much like "a rose that flowered and withered as nature allowed it."[8] She reassures him that, although death feels excruciatingly final, the journey of the soul continues, and the holy city of New Jerusalem awaits on the distant shore.* Upon waking, he realizes

---

* New Jerusalem is a popular medieval metaphor for heaven, and often appeared as the image on the World card in the oldest decks.

Figure 15. Fortitude and Temperance, bottom right, in the Psalter of Robert de Lisle, 1308

that though he is not yet ready to embrace the golden state of wholeness and complete his individuation journey, his encounter with the psychopomp has rekindled his courage to carry on.

The Temperance angel is this same inner soul-guide who restores our contact with the numinous, the divine. Like the pearl maiden, she reminds us that Death strikes us all, and temporal things rise and fall away. In her presence, we are cleansed of our last clinging attachments. She purifies our hearts of grief and nudges our eyes, once again, toward the sublime city of the Self as its radiant crown lifts over the valley.

This, ultimately, is the purpose of Temperance as psychopomp. She guides us to our immutable depths untouched by our external concerns, a holy message held on her lips. She is depicted as an angel, because this is the task of angels—to announce our potentiality, bring us to sacred places, and act as our guardians through our confusion and despair. What Temperance ultimately offers us is the blessing of a new devotion to life.

In a Reading . . .

We can think of Temperance as the invitation to find a new stance or new intentionality in our forward path. We have been woken from the death slumber where we could do little more than cower and cover our heads, and now we can look toward the shining future with clarity and tranquility. Our internal guidance changes from *what do I even want from life?* to *I'm ready to accept what life is guiding me toward*, and we approach living with a tempered openness. We are not swallowed by passions or fears or wrapped up in egoic desires. We can be still, patient, and receptive.

With one foot solidly in the real, earthen world and the other dipped into the pool of inner sacred experience, now is the time to weigh how we moderate and mediate life between these spaces. There is a middle way between all things, and our task is to blend our oppositions until we discover it. This is a time of many considerations: Do we need more moments of activity or sanctity? Are we motivated by fear or by longing? Do we need sips of solitude or more solidifying support?

Death has completed the alchemical work of *separatio*, and now Temperance holds our different parts in her cups, ready to help us merge them back together. Rather than force rigid compromises, Temperance invites us to reach for dynamic solutions. Temperance of the Christian world encouraged moderation by pacifying our passions, but the Temperance of the tarot shows us that balance is possible if we find the serenity between the opposites.

When Reversed . . .

Reversed, Temperance loses her connection to the centermost place. We feel jostled, constantly asking: *am I this or am I that?* The psyche dismembered by Death has not found its healing guide or resists it. Old habits that were meant to pass away resurface frantically. Unusual patterns of voracious indulgence or monastic abstinence surface. The angel looms there, somewhere in the distance, but we cannot see her clearly.

Temperance reversed tells us to calm down and center. If we continue the journey in a state of oscillation, we will not be sturdy enough to withstand the tests of the Devil. There is an urgent push to mindfully moderate our polarities. Have we erred too far toward the mundane, becoming lost in the minutiae of our jobs? Or have we thrown away our bills and decided to live a shaman's life, denying the realities of the world? Do we feel swept up by the promises of our specialness and greatness? Or do we feel lost to mediocrity, believing we are not even worthy of a prayer? If we are not thoughtful and attuned to equilibrium, we can easily become too one-sided. As our guardian, Temperance helps us navigate the liminal place, protecting the boundaries between the sacred and mundane to prevent the embellishing or flattening of life.

The Devil:
The Archetype of the Inner Enemy

> *The only devils in this world are those running around in our own hearts, and that is where all our battles ought to be fought.*
>
> —MAHATMA GANDHI

We arrive at the threshold we have dreaded. We have gone through so much to get here, and yet, as we stand naked at the gate as Inanna did, we know the greatest ordeal lies within.

Like Death, we tend to minimize the Devil, assuaging our nerves by reducing its meaning to addictive tendencies and sexual liberation. Still, we are undeniably afraid, and perhaps we should be. Throughout history, the devil has held the projection of our most appalling truths, and thus has become something hideous and horrifying, with goat's legs and vulture's talons, green- and red-skinned with mouths and tongues unraveling from every unnatural orifice. The devil is made up of the most repulsive potentials of our humanity, and the more we push them away, the more monstrous they become from afar. The only possible reactions are to deny, run, or cower at the gruesome thing before us.

The devil we're discussing here is not the lord of hell but the face of our own shadow. As Jung says, "We can swallow anything else, but not our own shadow because it makes us doubt our good qualities."[9] The ego cannot bear the loss of being "good," being the worthy hero, and so everything within us that we deem evil and vile must be suppressed or rejected into the unconscious. When we are blind to our shadow and its subterranean influence, we are incapable of managing it. This is when evil takes us over or, psychologically, when the shadow eclipses the ego and acts out its dark, repressed personality.

Figure 16. Lucifer Waiting for the Last Judgement, Livre de la Vigne nostre Seigneur, *c. 1450–70*

We naturally deny that we possess any evil, but it is a psychological fact that we all have the capacity for it and we all add to its presence in the world. While most of us are not criminals, brutes, or sadists, we possess a vein of evil that is subtler. Real evil in the psycho-spiritual sense is not a lack of goodness, but the host of countless malignant deeds and thoughts that we perpetrate all the time but cannot acknowledge. As M. Scott Peck writes, "We become evil by attempting to hide from ourselves. . . . Evil originates not in the absence of guilt but in the effort to escape it."[10] When we refuse to see these parts of ourselves, they rule us from the underworld. When we ignore the devil's grip, it tightens. (As Charles Baudelaire famously wrote, "The neatest trick of the devil is to persuade you that he does not exist."[11])

The Devil keeps us chained, simultaneously bound to the fear of who we really are and the futility of trying to escape it. He taunts us not with lies but truths, for he is both the great adversary and the light-bringer. Perhaps he whispers that our generosity is motivated by vanity or that our ambition is a cover for our incompetency or that our true gift is manipulation, not kindness. As difficult as it is, our task in the Devil's lair—as Jung reflects in *The Red Book*—is to listen:

> If you ever have the rare opportunity to speak with the devil, then do not forget to confront him in all seriousness. He is your devil after all. The devil as the adversary is your own other standpoint; he tempts you and sets a stone in your path where you least want it. Taking the devil seriously does not mean going over to his side, or else one becomes the devil. Rather it means coming to an understanding. Thereby you accept your other standpoint. With that the devil fundamentally loses ground, and so do you. And that may be well and good.[12]

If we turn away from the Devil, we will continue to unconsciously enact our shadow, but in turning toward him we must be careful not to succumb to our dark nature. Instead we must remain open to the Devil's truths and seek understanding above all else. Then our inner antagonist loses power over us, and we release the useless fallacy of our perfect goodness. We grow in both insight and humility and are prepared for the coming transformation.

And it must be said that when the individual shadow is not met and integrated, it is added to the collective. Our small demons of bias, fear, and belittlement pool into the global demons of racism, climate denial, and misogyny that have been passed through the generations. Whatever we refuse to see in ourselves we see everywhere else in the world. As depth psychologist Anthony Stevens writes, "confronting the brutal, destructive elements of the Shadow has become . . . the inescapable destiny of our species: if we fail, we cannot hope to survive."[13]

This is not to be alarmist, but when we're talking about the Devil, a little alarm is in order. When we meet the Devil, we should do so "in all seriousness," for it is in our personal work of knowing our darkness and holding its tension that we can protect the world from its harm and bring that much more peace into existence.

In a Reading . . .

Our tendency with the Devil is to project it onto others or refuse it altogether, but the Devil represents our other standpoint—our inner antagonist and saboteur. Any psychic impulse that is locked in shadow and not consciously known to us has the potential to act autonomously, invisibly influencing and corrupting our choices and behaviors. The Devil's power is to make us slaves to our own unconscious appetites.

The Devil's invitation is to do real shadow work and courageously examine our inner nature. This may look like investigating our jealousies and manipulations or admitting to our callousness and narcissism. Our instinct will be to blame or dig for childhood wounds to pardon ourselves, but in working with the Devil, we are not searching for excuses or reasons (there will be a time for that later). We are opening ourselves to uncensored truth, and merely listening.

Hearing the Devil's secrets can, in a way, be a medicine. In meeting the Devil we may finally break open our stultifying front of perfection or repressive virtue. We may see that our humanness is messy and complex, and that being the perpetual hero is both impossible and suffocating. There is not a small amount of freedom won from accepting our darkness. Examining our shadow does not mean we look and then push it back down or condone our devilish desires. It allows us simply, as the Temperance angel encouraged, to find a more moderate path.

When Reversed . . .

Traditionally, the inverted Devil may be associated with addiction crises, abusive relationships, criminal situations, or reckless sexual behavior, but all of these are symptoms of a greater problem. After a long chase fleeing from the Devil, he may overtake us and strap on the shackles, binding us to our shadow impulses. We may turn toward his darkness, acting out the worst of ourselves. Now is not the time for breakthroughs or interventions, as the Devil is too persuasive in his denial. Be tender, forgiving, and patient in your attempt to understand this darker side. Now may be the time to seek outside guidance and support.

Alternatively, the inverted Devil may point to a refusal to pass through his threshold, trapping us just outside but uncomfortably close to him. This may be a period of hyperconsumerism, hedonism, chaotic behaviors, and compulsive self-soothing. Turning our backs on the Devil creates the illusion of his disappearance, but in this willful ignorance of our shadow, our psychic temperature turns hot, cranky, and erratic. We become superficial and fixated on the outer world so that we have an excuse to blind ourselves to the inner one. This instinct lowers us to the base level of our humanity, sacrificing our sense of depth and fulfillment for worthless gratification.

The Tower:
The Archetype of Catastrophic Change

Only to the extent that we expose ourselves over and over to annihilation can that which is indestructible in us be found.
—PEMA CHÖDRÖN

We have come now to the final threshold of the katabasis. Although it is an undeniably formidable archetype, the Tower is one of the simplest cards in the tarot deck to understand. We all know the Tower's catastrophic potential because we've all experienced being tossed out of the solidity of our lives and forced into free fall. It's an image we all hold intuitively—the crashing down of what we built, brick by brick.

History and mythology both teach us that towers always fall. Since humankind first discovered its power to build and the great heights it could achieve, it has overestimated its reach. The most famous example is perhaps the Tower of Babel, which was felled by God himself. The Book of Genesis tells us that humans were once a united people with a singular home and language. When they found a hospitable place to settle, they said, "Come, let us build ourselves a city, with a tower that reaches to the heavens, so that we may make a name for ourselves." Enraged, God destroyed the tower and scattered the people, confounding their speech so they could never unify again. While God seems quite the villain in this story, his anger is not incited by the people's ingenuity as much as their hubris. Their aims were set too high, invading the territory of his own heavenly kingdom.

When we draw up the blueprints for our towers, we aren't initially motivated by psychological hubris. Our only aim is to build something worthy of our effort. We want to test our powers and possibilities, shaping something indomitable and lasting. However, when the towers we build (metaphorically, the lives we construct) become enmeshed in our inflated ego-identity, we arrogantly lay a crown upon them. We fortify them, making them impenetrable not only to threats from below but also illumination from above. Our towers, so high above the earth, become structures made up of our unyielding belief that we have successfully built a life that is impregnable by change. Then, over time the Tower becomes more prison than palace, and its rigidity prevents all possible remodeling without demolition.

After our confrontation with the Devil, who revealed the essential though uncomfortable truths we had previously denied, we return to the life the charioteer once strived to build—the life we once were sure would bring us power, success, or meaning—and find ourselves trapped. We may at last see that we only chose this life to fulfill others' expectations or that we constructed it to compensate for some shadowy wound or that, whether out of fear of failure and shame, we ignored the windswept whispers of our soul's true desires. Whatever kept us building, cementing our egoic grip, warding ourselves against vital change, now makes us captive to the inauthentic life. This is when we need God's lightning bolt to strike, or rather, we need the synchronistic intervention of the universe to help us do the work we can't muster with our own will.

We tend to view the Tower as something that happens *to us*, but it is often something that happens *through us*. A client once described a harrowing "Tower period" in her life in which she'd gotten divorced and was forced to give up on a career. When I'd asked her to identify the inciting incident, she insisted that it was all a terrible surprise. When she finally revealed the truth, she spoke the words as quietly as she herself must have heard them: "I guess one day, out of nowhere, I just thought, 'Does any of this really matter to me anymore?'"

In the Tower we are experiencing the same energetic charge that the Magician channels with his baton, but what we lack is his power of conscious manifestation. Without this power, the lightning symbolizes, as Jung puts it, "a sudden, unexpected, and overpowering change of psychic condition."[14] The lightning zaps us; the crown is knocked off; and we finally see that we cannot continue living this way. Whether coming down from the heavens or coiling up our spine, we have the sudden revelation of change.

When we see the Tower only as the callous hand of God, we are missing its sacred opportunity. After we settle from the shock and rage, we must remember that the universe will not allow us to remain in our lofty towers, so disconnected from the world and ourselves. The debris must be sorted. A new, truer path will emerge.

In a Reading . . .

When the Tower shows up on the table, we can almost smell the electricity in the air. There is no way to deflect the lightning bolt, nor should we try to. We can only prepare ourselves for it and—more radically—choose to welcome it.

Now is the time of sudden change as well as sudden release. Maybe it manifests as the loss of a job, a health crisis, or a breakup, or perhaps it is a subtler or interior experience such as giving up a long-term project or letting go of the effort to rekindle a friendship. However it strikes us, we know our life is being broken down into its simplest, most fundamental parts, and this can be a great gift. When our lives are split open and scattered, we can move through each piece of debris with intentionality and honesty. We can, like Psyche and so many other mythological heroines, sort through the mountain of seeds and pick out the ash, carefully examining the pieces with which we will rebuild.

Though crushing, the Tower is a moment of opportunity. If we have confronted and negotiated with our shadow with utmost sincerity, what we are hit with is the enlightening flash of awakening. We are liberated from our rigid egocentrism and the need to control and are forced into a more pliant and fertile position. We prime ourselves for rapid transition and psychological growth, allowing that which no longer represents our goals and identities to crumble away. Our turmoil and panic are momentary, and as soon as the bubble is burst, relief will enter and hope will be on the horizon.

When Reversed . . .

The Tower arrives reversed when we rage against God's thunderbolt. This happens when we lose the job we hated but ask them to reconsider or get dumped by the neglectful boyfriend and then claw our way back. Essentially, we reject the call to deconstruct the life that we were never meant to live and instead recommit to it because it's the only thing we know.

We should not waste our energy trying to minimize or reverse the Tower experience; we should seek to learn from it. A friend of mine was stuck in a dead-end job that he hated but was terrified to leave. When the Tower finally struck and he was fired, his rage and confusion channeled all his energy into demanding to know why rather than considering how he might move on and claim his greater potential. When we cling to the rubble, trying to uselessly stack the pieces back together, we cannot see that the Tower has broken things down externally so that something could be liberated internally. Then we may miss the opportunities eager to come.

The inverted Tower can also point to phases of stagnation in which we are dodging necessary change. We may become avoidant, refusing any circumstance that would make us vulnerable, or we may make ourselves *in*vulnerable by impulsively jumping out of the Tower before we can be thrown out. In both cases we are inhibiting the natural process of growth, because we subconsciously know its threat to our fragile egos.

— CHAPTER 11 —

APPROACHING WHOLENESS— ARCHETYPES OF TRANSCENDENCE

Transcendence constitutes selfhood.
—MARTIN HEIDEGGER

We finish our journey now on the macrocosmic plane, in the expanse of the heavens. We have traversed great heights and depths over the last sixteen cards, moving from the High Priestess's underworld temple all the way to the jagged mountain peak of the Tower. Now we find ourselves, naked and purified, drifting through the celestial realm. Here we shall navigate our way through the stars, moon, and sun, headed toward our resurrection, and then, finally, wholeness.

This is the anabasis following our katabasis—a sudden rise to compensate for our dramatic fall. This arc will lead to our apotheosis, our glorification into our highest self. We have sacrificed and strived with heroic effort, and at last the golden city is in sight. From this height, as we gaze back at our humanness and the microcosmic realm below, we can finally see the meaning in it all. Since the Magician first whipped out his baton, we have been reminded over and over *As above, so below*, and now, after such long journeying through the below, we can fully gaze upon the above: the transcendent and transpersonal experiences of selfhood.

From the Latin prefix *trans*, meaning "the other side of, beyond," transcendent or transpersonal experience ascends beyond the subjective self and crosses into the broader "other side" of the objective self. In other words, it expands beyond the limited margins of our personal ego and connects to the greater Self, whether through spiritual, archetypal, or metaphysical experience. These are our moments of breakthrough, illumination, and rapture, when suddenly the seams of the lower world split open to reveal the beckoning radiance of the higher one.

However, when we think of psychological transcendence as a state of "rising above" or "surmounting" our humanness, we unintentionally intensify the psychological schism between ego and Self. Therefore, as Woodman so beautifully puts it: "Do not try to transform yourself. Move *into* yourself."[1] In this way, we may even say that psycho-spiritual transcendence is synonymous with its opposite—immanence. We do not want to *overcome* ourselves to transcend into a higher being; we want to *encounter* the transcendent waiting within.

Of course, transcendent experience is not something we can force through egoic will. It is something that unfolds, often arriving by way of visions, dreams, and symbols. The archetypes of the tarot—and all archetypes—are such portals to transcendence. They cross beyond time, space, and individual experience, drawing us into that sublime and ineffable "other side." As Joseph Campbell writes, they "point beyond the phenomenal field toward the transcendent. A mythic figure is like the compass that you used to draw circles and arcs in school, with one leg in the field of time and the other in the eternal."[2] At this stage of the journey we can see how the archetypes of the tarot now wink at us, exposing their transcendent nature, revealing how they've unconsciously ushered our lives toward the eternal within.

The core purpose of these final six cards of the Major Arcana is to reach beyond ourselves and welcome the transpersonal experiences that will guide our approach toward wholeness. Here we complete the long struggle of oscillation between the inherent opposition of our conscious and unconscious halves and find them reconciled. We are approaching unity with the Self, the soul, the divine (or whatever you choose to call it), and so this last phase of our tarot individuation is the holiest and most profound.

Of course, we never really finish the individuation process. As long as we are living, we are bound to the individuation spiral. However, that does not mean we do not get to experience this transcendence. In fact Jung called these moments when we encounter the sudden shock of nearness to the Self "the transcendent function." While he was adamant that this function was not mystical, Jung describes its path as "an individual destiny" in which one transcends the tension of opposites to discover a new psychological attitude. He writes:

> The transcendent function does not proceed without aim and purpose, but leads to the revelation of the essential man.... The meaning and purpose of the process is the realization, in all its aspects, of the personality originally hidden away in the embryonic germ-plasm; the production and unfolding of the original, potential wholeness.[3]

The transcendent function is the process of revelation. When the conscious and unconscious face that impassable tension of opposites, something must break through. A new realization of the true personality "originally hidden away in the embryonic germ-plasm" of the soul instantaneously appears and reconciles the tension. Put simply, we experience an awakening, the constitution of a transfigured state of selfhood. These final cards of the tarot depict the moments of this sudden change, when we are opened to a new, transcendent perspective of self that was also immanent and destined to be discovered.

The Star:
The Archetype of the Inner Light

> *Man must first cry out that there is no health in him. He must be consumed with horror. This is the pain of purgatory. ... In this disturbance salvation begins. When man believes himself to be utterly lost, light breaks.*
>
> —MARTIN LUTHER

As the clouds of debris settle over the felled Tower, we can once again see the great light that had been blocked out by the edifice of our false life. At last, the Star rises.

The Star marks a tremendous shift in the tarot journey. For fifteen cards we made ourselves and made a life, and then the Tower's single calamitous strike demolishes it all. It is now that we are at our weakest, our most unsure, our most afraid, and we ask what, in all this mess, could possibly be left for us?

Let us meander, momentarily, out of the realm of intellect and into the contemplative imagination. Imagine a vast plain under an empty, slate-colored sky. All around is the rubble of the fallen tower: jagged stone bones scattered among a sea of dust and ash. There is a cavernous silence, so deep it seems impossible that any world-creating word could ever be uttered. It is as if in all the universe there is no one and nothing but you, bruised and stunned and alone as you are, unable to find a horizon through the haze. There is no hope. There is no home. All that has been is destroyed. All that could be is lost to the dark.

And then—something. Far off in the black sky a spot of light blooms, shimmers, until it becomes a beacon of silver luminescence. There is something familiar about this light. It is ancient and infinite, and yet somehow you know it is only yours. You recognize it as the light that drew you through the wonder of your childhood and the longings of your youth.

You feel it as your birthright, a gift you've never dared to name, a promise of meaning and hope. And now, as the light swells and rises, you can hear it singing your name. The star beckons you to follow.

I prefer to speak of the Star through the imagination because that is where it lives. It is the wondrous light that inspires the sanctified pursuit of living fully and truly. The Star is the symbol of our yearning to find our place in the cosmos. It is the archetype of the inner light of potential—not the potential of the ego's mastery but of the soul's destiny. It is the sacred gleam of our specialness, which is both universal to all and unique to us alone. It follows the Tower because, at last, after we have rid ourselves of the egoic constructs of a life that we were not meant to live, we can see the true potential we had forgotten.

Mythologically, stars are meant to be followed. It is the radiance of immanence cast outward into transcendence. (The light we pursue is the light we possess.) It shines with the numinous essence that the Hanged Man first sacrificed himself to and Temperance let us spy over her shoulder, reinspiring our yearning. The Star pours out the deep psychic contents that were hidden away in the Tower's shadowy cellar, reinfusing them into the pool of the collective unconscious, and we see now how our story reflects our long mythic heritage, and how those myths and archetypes have come alive in us. There is a reawakening to that paradox that we simultaneously own a mighty destiny and also are but a single speck in the design of the cosmos. We all have our very own star, and we are all deserving of it. No matter who we have been or what failures we've suffered, the light of the Star never sputters out. It is only obscured. Our task is to search for it in the dark skies above and follow.

Though it is decentralized, this is a moment of renewal for the defeated ego. Stripped of all identities and fallacies as Inanna was, the star-maiden bares her most essential self. We release rigid attachment to earthly ambitions, recognizing a higher purpose our lives serve. This is a moment of hope, not because we're promised safety and satiety, but because we're reminded that it is our naked truth that makes us precious to this world. After such destruction there is freedom to imagine new frontiers of potentiality.

What we must not forget is that the Star's hope only comes when we lift our eyes to seek it. If we linger too long in this dark wreckage, our vision fills with the black abyss of despair. Despair is the experience of meaninglessness and alienation from the Self that Jung called the "loss of soul." Despair teaches us the beauty of faith, encouraging a new, more authentic connection to the inner light. It offers us the glorious experience of remembering the precious essence of who we are and recommitting to the vocation of our deepest longing. As Jung writes, "While the man who despairs marches towards nothingness, the one who has placed his faith in the archetype follows the tracks of life."[4] When we are in the pit of despair, believing the light has gone out, our salvation comes through our faith in the archetype of the Star.

In a Reading . . .

The Star comes to remind us of our potential and higher purpose. Now is the moment to claim—without a word of rebuttal—*I am special and I have meaning in this world*. With the Star risen before us, we are invited to develop the serenity that only comes when we are at peace with ourselves. We may feel a silent promise, though soft, that everything will be okay. Hope is in abundance.

Now is not the time to rebuild the fallen Tower. In fact, now is not the time to act at all. Now is the time to find solace in the stillness of your being. Here is an opportunity to go within and speak to the child you once were, born under this Star. Healing is initiated, but it is not meant to be consciously directed. Remember your longing and reclaim it in whichever direction it illuminates. Something sublime might come into focus if you keep your eyes fixed on the night sky.

There is something important to remember about the Star: we must not speak of it with others or try to discern its meaning. The Star is too precious and too personal to be named or analyzed. Do not waste your time describing and defending this light that only you can see. Just feel it and live it.

When Reversed...

With the reversed Star we are likely in the pit of despair. The shock of the Tower may have sent us into a depression, or we bitterly decide to reject faith in something as unscientific as hope. In these cases we may become arrogant and rigid, denying our need to be soothed and healed.

By refusing this light, we may suffer specific symptoms: chronic minor health issues, a relentless tension in the chest, scoffing at stories of dreams coming true, resisting cathartic tears at a movie. What we are refusing is the sanctity of our lives, which makes them feel meaningless. We become angry and mean, regressing back from the Tower to the Devil, existing solely in the cranky, dank world of bleak mundanity.

We cannot allow ourselves to remain here. We must surrender to the breakthrough of the unconscious and the enormous depth of feeling we are keeping at bay. Accept your brokenness; seek the shattering. Allow the soothing waters to wash over you so that the Star might rouse you back to the great meaning of your life. Cling to the faith that although you cannot spot it now, the light has not and will never go out.

The Moon:
Lunar Consciousness and the Archetypal Dark Night of the Soul

> *We all have forests in our minds. Forests unexplored, unending. Each one of us gets lost in the forest, every night, alone.*
>
> —URSULA K. LE GUIN

After encountering the brilliance of the Star, we are eager to meet the exuberant illumination of the Sun, but there is a final passage we must make. Having reimmersed ourselves in our unconscious depths, we become lost in them. After setting foot in the Star's pool, we find ourselves suddenly out at sea.

The Moon is often feared as a card of confusion, lunacy, and all that is hidden and dark, but truly it sustains the Star's silver thread of hope. Behind the crawfish slithering up out of primordial ocean, and the dog and wolf howling in harmony, two gray pillars stand a short distance away. The first time we spotted these pillars was in Card 13—Death—then far on the horizon, the distant sun rising between them. Now we wander in those solemn hours before dawn, moonlight dimly lighting our way toward the winding path that passes through and beyond. The Moon, as an ancient symbol for the great gateway, shows that at last we have journeyed to the final threshold of rebirth Death had promised.

As we find so often in myth, right as the end comes into sight the hero encounters a "Dark Night of the Soul." This moment is described as a crisis of despair and meaninglessness, but St. John of the Cross, the sixteenth-century Spanish mystic who coined the term in his eponymous poem, describes himself wandering sorrowlessly through the dark:

In that happy night,
In secret, seen of none,
Seeing nought myself,
Without other light or guide
Save that which in my heart was burning.[5]

This burning light of the heart shines with his own contemplative longing for his beloved God (or in our lens, Self). Though he is shrouded in looming shadows, it is this interior light that guides him "more surely than the noonday sun," not toward clarity but *truth*. This is the same power of the Moon. In the landscape of unconscious oblivion, the light of ego-consciousness is snuffed out. What we follow instead is, as St. John of the Cross suggests, the burning intuition of our unconscious truth.

In archetypal study, the moon and sun are common symbols for the distinct domains of psychic experience, particularly in their more spiritual aspects. We find this prominently in the alchemical tradition, where the polarity of inner light and dark is presented as the marriage of Sol and Luna—natural opposites whose mysteries complement and complete each other. We see the same marriage of opposites in the tarot, no longer as gendered archetypal figures as in the first six trumps, but as the cosmic realms of lunar and solar consciousness.

Figure 17. Marriage of Sun and Moon from Emblem 30 of Atalanta fugiens *by Michael Maier, 1617*

Unlike solar consciousness which is clear, bright, and rational, lunar consciousness is pulsing and wild, located not in the intangible lights of the mind but in the cellular rhythms of the body. It is the consciousness of the dreamscape and the imagination, where the endless rambling rationales of the ego at last go silent. It speaks to us through riddles and questions, forcing us to journey toward our answers. As the orb of lunar consciousness, the Moon represents our rich, unconscious landscape that calls us to learn our own symbolic vocabulary and adapt it into our waking life.

Jung himself encountered the Moon when he fell into his own Dark Night of the Soul after cutting ties with Freud. For several years he mostly secluded himself in his attic library, surrendering to his own fantasy world. From this endeavor came his famous *Red Book*, in which he recorded his numerous dreams and visions.[*] As Jung writes in his autobiography, "I was being compelled to go through this process of the unconscious. I had to let myself be carried along by the current, without a notion of where it would lead me."[6] To those around him (and even to himself), it seemed that Jung was lost in a psychosis. However, as Jung himself has argued, this sort of insanity is merely an invasion of lunar content that overwhelms our conscious ability to discern reality from fantasy. Such invasions can be engulfing, but also illuminating. From this period of confrontation with the unconscious, Jung discovered the core principles of his psychology. It was not via rigid research and analysis that he learned of the nature of the soul, but from his willingness to encounter his own.

This may well be why the Moon is sometimes vilified as the scariest point of the Major Arcana sequence. As archetypal scholarship argues, lunar consciousness has become uncomfortably foreign to us. Within our narrow, linear rationality upheld by the patriarchal paradigm, we cannot make sense of a more irrational and intuitive understanding of ourselves and the world. When we enter the vacuum of

---

[*] The *Red Book*, formally titled *Liber Novus*, is neither a diary nor dry psychological text. Although deeply philosophical, the *Red Book* is a project of art and fantasy. Hand-calligraphed and filled with rich, vibrant imagery, Jung crafted something deeply personal, confessional, and rich with intuitions.

total night, we feel lost in the terror of the unknown and the senseless. If we can seek relationship with our unconscious wisdom, that "night that hast united / The lover with His beloved," we may be reconciled with the depths of the soul. Then, at last, we may cross the threshold into true dawn.

In a Reading...

The Moon reveals that we are churning through the primordial waters of unconsciousness. This may be a period of intense dreams, hypersensitivity, or delirium. It is natural to feel dazed or overwhelmed in the Moon space. You may encounter powerful archetypal forces or be easily swept away by fantasy. Old complexes and past fears may rise to flood you anew, this time with claws or wings or magic wands. Strange sensations, intuitions, and daydreams may barrage your waking mind, making you feel thoroughly unstable and even a little crazy.

Like Jung, we can take advantage of this powerful moment by allowing our conscious mind to give way to unconscious breakthroughs. This is a time to prioritize imagination, dream, and intuition. Give the unconscious the opportunity for expression in the way it likes to communicate, through art and fantasy. Allow yourself to relax your grip on life and get a little lost. Make room for childishness, play, and the freedom for deep feeling.

While it's true that the Moon can curse us with confusion, and that we often feel more frightened and lost than free in this phase, have faith. This leg of the journey can be long, but it's crucial. We must allow ourselves to be lost. We must welcome this moment as an opportunity to embrace that burning of the heart. If you try to avoid it, you will only be turning away from the threshold, which is in reach.

When Reversed...

When we are too lost in the inverted Moon's wilderness, we may actually fall victim to our lunacies and wander from the path. This may be a time of paranoia and neurosis, but we must not assume ourselves lost. In the Moon's domain we can be easily engulfed by her shadow, which can disorient us and make us anxious for the solace of sunlight and clarity. If we do not remain alert and focused on our pursuit of the threshold, we can be distracted by intense emotions and archetypal images, becoming enthralled to the dark.

When we encounter the Moon inverted, with its tides pulling us back into our unresolved truths and then sweeping us out toward the horizonless future, we feel impossibly dazed. We may feel as if, like Odysseus, we've been lost here for decades, wandering from shore to bewildering shore when all we want is to return home. It's important to remember that now is not the time to push for decisions or resolutions. Relationships, projects, and healing journeys may stall out and suffer. It may indeed be a Dark Night of the Soul, but it is nonetheless an encounter with the soul. Let this be a full-blooded experience of yourself. The path is not yet visible, but trust that the wandering won't be forever.

The Sun:
Solar Consciousness and the Archetype of Enlightenment

> *Truth at last cannot be hidden.*
> *Dissimulation is of no avail. . . .*
> *Nothing is hidden under the sun.*
>
> —LEONARDO DA VINCI

At last we have passed through that imposing gate and step fully into the light of the Sun and the new dawn. Most tarot references describe the Sun as a card of optimism and joy, but there is a profound psycho-spiritual cause for this brightness. Just as the Moon symbolizes lunar consciousness, the Sun represents solar consciousness, which depth psychologist Murray Stein explains this way:

> In what we may call solar consciousness, to distinguish from lunar consciousness, the ego is the center of consciousness and holds the levers of control. . . . Solar consciousness can proceed by logical thinking rather than by [lunar consciousness's] association, metaphor and image.[7]

While lunar consciousness draws us down and in, connecting us to the unconscious world of symbol and intuition, solar consciousness pulls us forward and up, awakening us to the bright and buoyant clarity of the ego. The Sun's joyfulness does not come from static optimism but from the dynamism of enlightenment, by which we mean the act of bringing light to all things. Illumination is ecstatic. To make this psychological passage out of the dense, drowsy darkness and into the clean, crystalline air of true vision is an exuberant thing.

Again, we should not villainize the Moon and venerate the Sun. They each play their essential role in our becoming. While the Moon waxes and wanes according to her own rhythms, teaching us about mutability and cyclic flow, the Sun's blessed constancy gives the entire universe its primordial structure. This is perhaps why the eighteenth-century philosophers studying the principles of reason, empiricism, and natural order became "Enlightenment" thinkers; the Sun was their symbolic mentor, inspiring them to understand—coherently and completely—the universal laws governing all it shines its light upon.

The Sun is about the illumination of the conscious mind, but it is often experienced as an eruption from the heart. This sudden enlightenment arrives in Technicolor, as an experience of effervescent joy and childlike awe, which is demonstrated by the sun-child bouncing happily on his steed, arms outstretched to the world. While the Moon gives us no human figures (because the unconscious contains the instinctual, archetypal world), the Sun presents us with the ego-hero reborn, fully conscious, openhearted, ready to live.

The child in the Sun card is an Eternal Child. Such child archetypes, as Jung stresses, symbolically bring light, enlarge consciousness, and "overcome darkness, which is to say that they overcome the earlier unconscious state."[8] This Eternal Child gathers all that was rediscovered in our descent into shadow and all that was hidden in the Moon's gloomy wilderness and brings it into the light. With such unobstructed vision of all that had previously been veiled, we finally, fully see ourselves and understand why we are who we are. Through this understanding we may indeed achieve true consciousness, thus transcending all our previous conflicts of opposites.

In the gnostic creation story, it is said that during the Fall (a tragedy caused not by Eve and her apple but by the aeon Sophia and her child the demiurge) God was split into infinite fragments and implanted in the souls of each human being. These shards of God's light—metaphorically, pieces of higher consciousness—were imprisoned in the matter of our bodies, and each individual's task was to liberate it so that the divine unity could be restored. A similar idea was held in medieval alchemy, which maintained that the true goal of the magnum opus was to liberate the deity trapped in the prima materia, the essential matter of all life. What we can draw from these stories is that the light of the Sun is not about manufacturing enlightenment, but *releasing* it. Throughout this long and harrowing journey, that shard of God, that trapped essence of our divine clarity, that experience of transcendence, has been slowly shining its way to the surface. We see the immanent light of the Self glinting through us, illuminating everything, and the result is joy. The bliss of the Sun is truth coming to consciousness: knowing ourselves, understanding ourselves, accepting ourselves, loving ourselves.

However, as effervescent as the Sun might feel, Jung warns, "One does not become enlightened by imagining figures of light, but by making the darkness conscious."[9] We cannot forget what is required to arrive here. We cannot know the brilliance of the light without first encountering the shadows around it. When we become too fixated on the knowledge and clarity of the Sun, we become Moon-deniers (as the patriarchal West has been for several thousand years), and we lose touch with the unconscious. The key to the light is in the dark. To arrive at the Sun rising on the far horizon, we must journey toward it through the depth of night.

In a Reading . . .

The Sun does not simply promise happiness or tell us to be optimistic. It orients us toward the illumination we have fought hard to earn. It encourages us to reflect and revel in what we have learned about ourselves, how we have changed, and the feeling of life bursting from our hearts.

Sometimes the message of the Sun is direct and simple: *go outside; don't think too much; trust the clarity that comes*. Or perhaps it is an invitation to more consciously reflect on recent revelations about the person you've become. Either way, this card is about seeing things as they are. My own first experience with the Sun archetype came on a warm May afternoon when I was sixteen. As I walked home from school, ruminating and moping as teenagers do, I glanced up and saw the sun emerging from behind a cloud. I suddenly thought: *Oh, I see. I will figure it all out. I am smart and strong and I'm alive, and that's all I need.* That small whisper of illumination tore through me with a joy I had never before experienced, and it quite literally brought me to my knees. I felt thoroughly cleansed by the sun, and sometimes that is exactly the point of the Sun's arrival on our tables.

Another possibility is to reconnect to that Eternal Child archetype within you, embracing its innocence and potential. This is not about the heavy inner child work of unloading your traumas. Instead, it's an opportunity to feel the brilliance of the divine child in a way that is neither inflated nor weighted with expectation, but at once simple and infinite.

When Reversed...

When inverted, we may be numbed to the revelatory power of the Sun. We may feel dull, depressed, or desperate for the light. This is when we most wish the Sun will appear, hoping it might extend the gift of unburdened happiness, free and ripe for the taking. However, when inverted, we should not expect a sudden ray of light to release ourselves from frustration and dejection. We must first part the clouds of our own willful blindness and self-neglect. We must look for the light.

This reversed Sun also directly correlates with Jung's archetype of the Puer Aeternus, who refuses development and responsibility for his individuation. Symptoms of a Puer Aeternus complex include feeling that the blessings of our lives are not quite what we wanted, insisting on waiting for some perfect image of life to magically manifest, or leading a sort of "provisional life" in which we numbly accept what life hands us and never take agency to seek what we desire. Rather than feeling youthful and hopeful, we feel this dark side of the Eternal Child, becoming petulant, cynical, and even hostile. Now is the time to release cynicism and self-pity and to question whether we are indeed meekly living this provisional life. Enlightenment is a conscious power, a choice to live as authentically and fully as possible.

Judgement:
The Archetype of Psycho-Spiritual Redemption

*He will wipe every tear from their eyes.
There will be no more death or mourning or crying or pain,
for the old order of things has passed away.*

—BOOK OF REVELATION, NIV

Judgement is perhaps the most psychologically intense and transformational card in the tarot series. Though many modern decks soften this card by retitling it Resurrection or Awakening, Judgement is indeed loyal to its name. What it shows is a scene of Judgement Day, when, according to the Christian tradition, humanity will be lined up at the gates of heaven to receive God's final judgment. Although salvation is promised, it is contingent upon our worthiness. We may only enter heaven if our sins are truly repented and forgiven.

Contemporary tarot study tends to distance the deck from its Christian roots, but these roots are essential to understand Judgement. Since the tarot's conception, Judgement has most consistently depicted that famous biblical scene with the looming angel, sounding horns, and the dead standing in their graves. Symbolically, this scene depicts how we experience the transcendent function, that "revelation of essential man" when we resolve our tension of opposites and genuine transformation becomes possible. This is not the result of deliberate effort so much as a spontaneous, archetypal eruption. After such a long journey suspended between our conscious attitude and unconscious wisdom, there's a sudden breakthrough of a third way, often accompanied by a sense of awe or sublimity. This is represented by the soaring angel: an archetypal messenger and a manifestation of what Jung called the *numinosum*. This new psychic energy "grips" us, just as the angel's horn grips the people with its urgent call. In essence, we are seized by something greater than ourselves and awakened to a new way of life. Whether with awe-filled hope or bone-rattling desperation, the people rise, no longer cowering as they had with Death but erect and attentive to the angel's pronouncement, ready for change.

This is the moment of resurrection, but their open arms and eagerness to be judged show a more enthusiastic participation in the process. Therefore, we might more accurately call this a scene of *redemption*. Etymologically, *resurrection* comes from the Latin *resurgere*, "to rise again," while *redemption* comes from the Latin word *redimere*, meaning to "buy back" or "ransom." As Nichols writes:

> Individuation is *au fond* a redemptive process. Its aim is not to create something entirely new—something beyond and foreign to ourselves. But, rather, simply to redeem and liberate aspects rightfully belonging to ourselves which have been held hostage in the unconscious.[10]

After the journey we have made, the shadows we have faced, the scars we have earned, there is no simple return to our old selves. We cannot replace the crown on the Tower, nor regress back to the Chariot. To unify ourselves into wholeness we must "ransom" those virtues that had been locked away—all those golden truths buried in our depths—which requires us to acknowledge and "repent" the ways we refused, failed, and betrayed them in the past.

Redemption cannot happen if we do not allow ourselves to be judged. This is why preserving the original title of this card is important. The word may sound critical and threatening, but this judgment is not done by some outside, faceless critic. It is our ego being judged, and it is the Self who is the judge. As Edinger writes:

> The evidence is quite clear that one phenomenological aspect of the activated Self is the generation of the ego experience of being judged: 1) as to how it is living its life; and 2) with regard to the psychological attitude with which that ego is living.[11]

When the Self—the highest expression of our being—suddenly blows its horn, beckoning us to rise, we cannot help but keenly examine the lives we've chosen to live and the attitudes we've held while living them. For many, this is the most intimidating moment of the sequence. To earnestly, even brutally account for the way we have lived (and the ways we have failed to live) is so frightening that we experience it archetypally as inner apocalypse.

We fear being judged, but we must not forget the transcendent function in action. When we accept the redemptive process of Judgement, we can judge ourselves not with animosity but with honesty, responsibility, and forgiveness, reconciling who we've been with who we now are called to become. This is the last test of our individuation quest. Transcendence is here, if we can rise above the reluctance of the ego and answer the blaring call to embrace the true soul.

In a Reading . . .

Judgement is a sign that all the powers of the psyche are in support of meaningful change. We are moving beyond the ego-centeredness of the Chariot pursuing the life it desires, and instead placing our faith in the life the Self has destined for us.

This is a time of psychological accountability, when we examine how we have lived our lives and the attitude with which we lived them. Now is the time to confront those proverbial sins: our wasted time, the neglect of our dreams, all those self-betrayals and excused cruelties. It is important that we release blame and face all that we have shunned or ignored with love, especially that which is painful or uncomfortable. This is not the nigredo stage in which we first begin to confess our sins, but the rubedo stage in which we fully own the part of ourselves that committed them. If we are honest and brave, if we can withstand the heartbreaking yet valid self-judgments, we will see that we can ransom our virtue and make dramatic, lasting change.

Judgement also heralds the moment of the transcendent function, when the tension between our conscious orientation and our unconscious wisdom is reconciled. We may experience it as an awakening, a sudden "getting it," a sigh of instant change chased by those trembling tears of understanding. We might also experience it more gradually, noticing that soft spots are strengthened and previously constrictive inner crossroads feel wide and easy. However it occurs, stay humble, honest, and faithful to the transformation.

When Reversed . . .

Often Judgement comes reversed when we are reluctant to change or continue to blame the world for our failings. If the ego cannot bear to read its entry in the Book of Judgement, it merely pounds at heaven's gate, demanding salvation while refusing repentance. In this case, redemption is impossible.

A client came seeking an explanation for why, after a year of intentional and dramatic change, she still felt "dead" in her life. She had broken up with an abusive partner, quit her suffocating job, and moved far away from her controlling family. She was proud of her courage, but frustrated that cutting all this out was somehow not enough. When I pulled Judgement reversed, I asked if, with all these changes, she had attempted to reconcile what also needed to change within herself. She blinked at me, somewhat affronted, and answered a resounding *no*.

Though she had not created her unfortunate circumstances, in refusing to investigate how she (consciously or unconsciously) participated in them and herself needed to change, she was missing the opportunity for self-understanding and the transcendent, enlivening breakthrough of the path forward. In this way, we unwittingly refuse rebirth by closing the casket lid so that we can continue wallowing and denying, stopping our ears to the horn's blaring call.

If we seek the promised resurrection of Judgement Day, we must be ready to be judged. We must be willing to see all of ourselves and to list everything in the book. Only then will we become true candidates of redemption and wholeness.

The World:
The Archetype of Wholeness

> *Where we had thought to travel outward, we shall come to the center of our own existence; where we had thought to be alone, we shall be with all the world.*
>
> —JOSEPH CAMPBELL

The journey has at long last reached its end. Everything we have experienced since that initial spark channeled through the Magician's wand, everything that has made us and unmade us and remade us, folds into a unified story of who we are. With the World, we arrive at the archetype of wholeness, the full integration of all parts of our selfhood, the true unification of the psyche. It is the moment when that elusive Self, which has thus far been only a promise, a glimmer in the distance, is now everywhere.

The World is arguably the most abstract and mystical card of the deck, and so the best route to comprehending it is through its symbols.

At the center of the card is the World-dancer, a depiction of the anima mundi, the world soul. Drawing from ancient Greek philosophy, the anima mundi is described simultaneously as the center of all life and the animating force of supreme loving intelligence. Though typically depicted as a woman, the anima mundi could equally take shape as Mercurius or Christ, exemplifying its ineffability and androgyny (hinted at by the World-dancer's hidden genitals). The World-dancer bears breasts filled with the High Priestess's milk of wisdom as well as the Magician's baton of divine inspiration, marrying the soul's infinite unconscious mystery with the spirit's spark of cosmic consciousness. This is the product of the alchemical coniunctio in earnest, what the alchemists depicted as the rebis. This is the sacred conjoining of the opposites, the miraculous blending of the disparate elements into the holy gold, the goal of the magnum opus and our individuation.

Figure 18. Rebis from Theoria Philosophiae Hermeticae *by Heinrich Nollius, 1617*

Figure 19. Shiva Nataraja, Southern India, Tamil Nadu, Chola dynasty, c. 900–1100

With the figure's raised foot, we are reminded of the Hanged Man's fruitful sacrifice, showing that the egoic fixations of life have been transcended. Like Nataraja, a form of the Hindu god Shiva, the figure dances to the entwining rhythms of creation and destruction, while maintaining the tranquility of the Atman, the transcendent Self. It symbolizes not only our ability to move with grace through life, but the joyful immediacy of presence with the Self, in which all answers break through in a sudden rapture of movement. As Nietzsche's Zarathustra says, "Only in the dance do I know how to speak the parable of the highest things." This dance symbolizes not only the motion and flow of life, but communion with the greater rhythms of the macrocosm, the universe.

Figure 20. Vesica piscis *in door of the Chalice Well in Glastonbury and Christ in the mandorla enthroned amongst the four evangelists, Speyer Pericopes, 1220*

Outside the dancer, a wreath of leaves is woven into a mandorla (also known as the *vesica piscis*), an ancient symbol of containment. The mandorla is the space between overlapping circles that holds the meeting of the opposites, mimicking the shape of the vulva, the seed, and 0, the number of the Fool (to whom the World is bound, as we will soon see). This is the womb of the emergent, unified self. It is the sanctuary and shield in which the dancer experiences their totality. It is the space of eternity, which, as Joseph Campbell reminds, is not the expanse of unending time but a dimension of the here and now.

Around the mandorla are the four zodiacal symbols we first spotted in the Wheel of Fortune, grounding us back into the four corners of human experience. The eagle, angel, ox, and lion represent the four evangelists of John, Matthew, Luke, and Mark; the signs of Scorpio, Aquarius, Taurus, and Leo; the elements of water, air, earth, and fire; the functions of feeling, thinking, sensation, and intuition; and the experiences of connection, discernment, being, and meaning. They show us life in balance, harmonizing around the World-dancer who flows effortlessly between them all.

Immersed in the ecstatic dance of existence, encased in the eternal womb of life, and contained by the four corners of creation, we have achieved wholeness, the realization of Self. Of course, we know that we can only experience this glorious moment not as lived reality but as symbol, as Jungian Aniela Jaffé writes:

> The goal of individuation, the realisation of the [S]elf, is never fully attained. Because it transcends consciousness, the archetype of the [S]elf can never be wholly apprehended, and because of its boundlessness never completely lived in actual life. "Successful individuation" is never total, it is only an optimal achievement of wholeness.[12]

As long as we are living, we are seeking. Even when we achieve some level of wholeness, we still want, fear, and wonder. We must not be tricked into believing we will ever fully "get there," but the World represents the (likely brief but nonetheless profound) moment when we are truly free to be all of who we are. It is the union of ego and Self, which is always experienced as liberation. As Jung puts it, being one with the Self:

> means that you are always conscious of your own identity and know that you can never be other than yourself. You can never lose yourself, you can never be alienated from yourself, because you know that the Self is indestructible; it is always one and the same, it cannot be dissolved nor can it be exchanged for anything else, and thus it enables you to remain the same through all conditions of life.[13]

In a Reading . . .

The World signals the close of the journey and the completion of our individuation, but of course, we never actually experience it this way. To read this card, we need to pull it down from mystical abstraction into practical experience. The World interrupts our monotonous lives and reminds us that the ultimate goal is not getting the promotion, not winning the award, not finding your soulmate. The goal is union with the Self that "enables you to remain the same through all conditions of your life." It is an opportunity for transcendence. It is a moment in which we should zoom out and imagine ourselves in the expanse of the macrocosm, looking down upon the microcosm of our daily lives with a new perspective. If we can imagine ourselves as the World-dancer, full and free and whole, we can reorient ourselves to the true psycho-spiritual end of our journeying.

The World can herald things coming to fulfillment, chapters of our lives arriving at their natural close, or aspects of ourselves finally being integrated. As Plato might put it, it is an indicator that the outcome is of the highest good. It is an opportunity to loosen our grip on the what comes next and become receptive to a more mystical experience of being, simply by participating in the dance.

When Reversed . . .

Reversed, this card often points toward an inevitable end, and sometimes an uncomfortable one. We may resist the natural close of something, be it a relationship, role, or phase of life. This is not the necrotic resistance of Death, but a sort of willful obstruction of closure and integration. It may also indicate that things are stagnating, like water circling the drain, and we must reevaluate our agency to move the story forward. Our task is to examine this experience with greater consciousness, weaving all the dangling threads into a completion.

Another possibility is that we refuse to accept the end of the story and thus sabotage our individuation. In our modern world that overvalues progress and positivity, we expect that all ends must be "happy," that it's only over when we overcome suffering or achieve bliss. Of course, this is not the way of life. The point of the journey is, as Jung said, to experience the fullness of who you are in any circumstance, not to be freed from strife or promised prosperity. Our goal should be the intimacy with the soul that fortifies us to accept and embrace it all, so that we may say, as Joseph Campbell puts it so well, "life is pain and life is suffering and life is horror, but by God, you're alive and it's spectacular."[14]

The Fool:
The Archetype of the Individuated Self

> *Life is not a problem to be solved, but a mystery to be lived.*
> *Follow the path that is no path, follow your bliss.*
> —JOSEPH CAMPBELL

The Fool stands at the cliff's edge, his eyes pointed not toward the jagged rocks below but up at the open sky. He is the Fool because that is what the world has named him, scorning the strange and reckless path he travels. Above, the conscious illumination of the Sun guides his path, while behind the Moon's canine guardian acts as a daimon—the guiding spirits of ancient Greece said to shepherd souls to their destiny. Heedless of any danger or disappointment, he walks on, living in his own way, following what Campbell would call his "bliss."

We are ending our discussion of the trumps with the Fool because he is the destination we've pursued all along. We have serenely held the primordial opposites, walked the path of the ego-hero, crossed into the underworld of shadow, and risen back into the transcendent firmament. Now, having integrated all these lessons with the World, we are at last ready to reinitiate ourselves into life.

This card is commonly associated with taking leaps and pushing past comfort zones, but this is only a fraction of its wisdom. The Fool fears neither societal scrutiny nor the changing conditions of life. He accepts the promise of failure, and never betrays his fidelity to hope. He knows the only way for him to live is the way defined by his unique, individual, authentic self. From the vantage point of the world around him, he walks the road to doom; from his own view, it is the road of liberation.

I place the Fool at the end of the journey because it is only by going through all our terrible and miraculous trials of individuation that we discover the true nature of our authentic self. The challenge of the

Fool—and it is indeed a challenge—is to actually live it. This is the practical realization of our individuation: to withdraw from the mass and center the individual self. As Campbell tells us:

> What is in process right here, now, as your world, affirm it and live it. That's all there is to this mythological mystery. It sounds so simple but it's very, very difficult: to dissociate yourself from concepts, from authority, from the fear of what they'll do to you, from the isolation that will come—and it will. Everybody says think for yourself, and if you do, you're finished.... All that can be done is to live your own way.[15]

The Fool is on the quest of self-actualization, which is both an external and internal pursuit. The Ten Ox-Herding Pictures, an ancient Zen allegory of enlightenment, depicts this quest. The first picture presents us with a well-dressed, self-important youth who has abandoned his life to search for an ox, a symbol for his own vital self. Through the following eight pictures we see a journey of seeking, struggling, and transcending, much like the first twenty arcana of the tarot. In the final picture, however, the youth does not brush the dirt off his fine clothes (which symbolize his attachment to society) and return to his previous place in the world. Rather, we find him in humble rags, standing across from an older, plumper fool who radiates as much joy and ease as the World-dancer.

This is the same archetypal negotiation of the World and the Fool. Like the Fool, the youth's bundle is meager and light, while, like the World, the older man's girth carries all the wisdom digested through his faithful individuating. As von Franz describes him, "barefooted and naked of breast," the youth (the Fool) has learned that the purpose of his efforts is to empty himself without forgetting himself—in other words to divest his prescribed pursuits and attachments in order to liberate the seed of authenticity buried underneath. We don the dress of who society tells us we are, who we thought we should be, but eventually we must be willing to shed it and bare our true skin. Thus, this actualization of our individuation is a rebellion which supplants *who-we-are-supposed-to-be* with *who-we-uniquely-are*. As von Franz continues, "Uniqueness springs from him as a creative act, but it is not intentionally on his mind. He does not feel unique; he is unique."[16]

The Fool, unnumbered, ever-present within us, is a perpetual initiate. He is always being led onto the truer path, always accepting foolishness as the cost of living his unique bliss. He is poised between the reckless naivete and profound faith needed to leap into newer and greater experiences. He is committed entirely to his own radical truth and growth.

The Fool takes us out of society and onto our own winding path, but we should always be wary of ignoring our grasp on reality and forgetting our humility. When we become too enmeshed in the Fool as this archetypal clown or outsider, we either neglect our instinctive senses or mistake anticonformity for authenticity. Then, as Jungians Ann and Barry Ulanov would put it, he "falls back time after time to the lonely place where his grandiose fantasies inhabit him, undelivered but for him always present."[17] The ultimate realization of the Fool is that to bring the dream to life it must be ready to meet the conditions of life. We are only fools after all, learning how to live with each singular step.

In a Reading . . .

The Fool is the instinct that hums *yes* in us. Beneath all our anxious wonderings and reluctant wanderings, he rallies us to embark upon the journey that is already in process. It is not a card simply about bravery or desire, but about being willing to live life in whatever unique way it calls to us, in whatever honest way we must.

The Fool reminds us that we can always choose to live our own way, that by our birthright we have permission to step away from societal expectation and put our bare feet on our own path. We are not stuck where we are; we simply need to begin by choosing the authentic life. As the mystics often point out, it is when we make this foolish choice that everything aligns and the path ripples forth, as if it had been waiting for us all along. As Jung himself wrote in one of his letters: "I had to follow the ineradicable foolishness which furnishes the steps to true wisdom."[18]

Now is indeed the time to take the leap, make the bold choice, follow the less-trodden path. Do not balk when you find that the way is full of stones and brambles, as it has not been walked before. Nor

APPROACHING WHOLENESS 257

Figure 21. Pictures 1 and 10, Ten Oxherding Pictures, Tenshō Shūbun, fifteenth century

should you heedlessly jump off the cliff unless there is a strong intuitive knowing that tells you you must. The Fool never leaves us, but when he arrives on the table now, more than ever, we must sincerely *live*.

When Reversed . . .

Reversed, the young man's foolishness comes not from his authenticity but from his folly. We may claim to follow our inner intuition, but in reality are only pursuing passing whimsy and ego-driven ambition. Or we may continue to prioritize societal or external validation and expectation, muting the voice of inner knowing yapping at our feet. When the archetypal Fool is not truly realized, it meanders, never satisfied, until it calcifies into the isolating experience of the unlived life. And this, as Jung identified, is the great tragedy of modern human existence.

Another possibility with this reversal is that your life has turned more artificial than authentic, built as a sort of "mock" life that is a placeholder for a real one. In this way we're disengaged with the authentic self, and possibly even afraid of it. This may look like overbooking ourselves with online writing classes that eat up the time we actually have to write or centering our lives around "wellness" while also refusing to quit that job that makes us sick. We may find ourselves ever-stuck in mindsets of comparison, envy, and futility. In this case we may believe ourselves the initiate, but act only as the clown, stuttering on the path we are too frightened to actually follow.

PART 4

READING WITH A PSYCHO-SPIRITUAL LENS

―― CHAPTER 12 ――

THE RITUAL OF THE READING

*Any ritual is an opportunity for transformation.
To do a ritual, you must be willing to be transformed
in some way. The inner willingness is what makes
the ritual come alive and have power.*

—STARHAWK

We think of ritual as creating a sacred setting or performing a religious routine, but ritual is really about cultivating psycho-spiritual containers—interior spaces that, as Woodman tells us, "make a firm demarcation between the profane and sacred, between what is us and what is not us."[1] In ritual we step out of the flatness of the mundane and into the richness of our depth, opening to both our familiar comforts and the revelation of something new. Reading tarot is just such an exercise in which we enter this inner container that holds both our profundity and mystery. Therefore, we should think of drawing cards not as a routine or a practice but as a ritual—one that has no set guidelines and requires no special ceremony. It is a covenant with the oracle in which we listen, wonder, and trust, seeking not directives, but deepening support for our psycho-spiritual wellness and wholeness.

In this chapter we will explore the ritual practice of reading the cards, beginning with the moment we pick up our decks through the following days and weeks of contemplation. Tarot is all about asking questions, but I encourage you to let go of the need for arid clarity and instead wade around in the fertile waters of confusion. This is where real revelation waits.

Preparing to Read

The conditions you set both internally and externally are vital in fostering grounded, soul-centered readings. So I recommend creating a space that feels *contained*, meaning it is free from distraction and invulnerable to outside interruption. Go somewhere quiet where pets, children, or strangers won't disturb you, and leave phones and devices in another room. Take a moment to clear away clutter, and light candles or spread out some crystals. Being raised Catholic, I can't help but think of laying out a tarot spread the way I used to consider taking holy communion; there should be a sense of presence, reverence, and sanctity about the moment. Once you are settled and ready, you can move through these four stages of preparation to facilitate deep and powerful readings.

1. Be in the Right Psycho-Spiritual Orientation.

The right time to engage in any divinatory practice is when the archetype at the center of our question or intention is activated, but we are not overcome by its intensity. If we turn to the cards in a state of desperation, we may be less receptive to the cards' soberer counsel—which any professional reader will tell you the tarot loves to dole out. Wait until you are more curious than anxious, and then consider what it is drawing you to the oracle. If you are demanding reassurance (or if you are simply following a prescribed routine), now may not be the best time to pull cards. Return when you feel as if there is a sense of open interest about this moment in your life or yourself. I like to tell my students that the time to pick up our decks is when the door of the heart feels as though it's creaked open. When you can sit in silent contemplation with the archetype (by which we mean the fear, the feeling, the symbol—whatever is at the heart of this moment) and release yourself to that little tug indicating you're ready to listen, that is when you know you are in the right space.

Take a moment to redirect your focus inward. You might journal beforehand, do a meditation, or simply take some grounding breaths. If you are giving someone else a reading, it's important to help your querent find this contemplative space as well, maybe by lighting a candle together at the beginning or guiding them through a body scan. Whatever you choose to do, the goal is to disentangle yourself from your outer reality so that the inner one can be as receptive as possible. We are crossing from the realm of the worldly—the profane—and into the space of the soul—the sacred.

2. Ask the Question or Set the Intention.

Once you have crossed that liminal line, you can present your question. Make sure you pose it in a way that is exploratory and open-ended, as we discussed in chapter 2. If your question remains too narrow or unclear, set an intention instead, always focusing on what change you hope the reading will bring. Perhaps you realize that you desire a firmer resolve or need to shift a pattern that's keeping you stuck. Once you feel settled on your question or intention, I recommend speaking it aloud to solidify it for both yourself and your deck.

When reading for others, spend a few moments before the reading talking through not only the circumstances that have brought them to the table, but their deeper feelings, concerns, and desires. Then, together, establish what it is the querent most needs to draw from the reading. For example, if the querent asks if they should shift careers, you might discuss their indecision and arrive at an intention like, "The querent needs to understand the source of their hesitation so they can feel at peace with their choice." With this intention, the reading shifts from solutions to explorations, and the cards will have a much deeper personal resonance for how the querent might achieve the inner resolution they seek.

3. Enter the "Lowered Level."

As we discussed in chapter 2, before reading we want to bring ourselves into a state of suppressed consciousness in which we are more receptive to the unconscious. There is no set way to enter this lowered mental level, but the most successful technique I've developed is a simple visualization. I begin by imagining the sun at the apex of the sky and then watch as it slowly sinks into total night. This symbolizes the light of the conscious mind surrendering to the darkness of unconscious wisdom—the clarity-driven Sun giving way to the intuitive realm of the Moon. Then I call in the question or intention, seeing it arrive as a tapestry of light or sometimes as a star falling down to me. Once I feel grounded in this space and open to what wishes to come, I know I'm ready to begin drawing my cards.

There are many other possibilities to encourage this lowered mental level, of course. You can take a few breaths that drop you down into the base of your spine or imagine your active mind receding while another, wiser version of yourself steps forward. Whatever helps that conscious chatter settle and that unconscious depth spread out, embrace it in the ritual. It will make your readings clearer, your intuition louder, and the wisdom you receive much more deliberate.

4. Engage the "Archetype of the Magical Effect."

Shuffling and drawing your cards should be the most thrilling part of your reading ritual. It is the moment when you touch skin to paper and magically call forth what most needs to come. This is often the point in which readers become the most nervous, but your energetic state is crucial here and can impact the success of a reading.

In Jung's studies of precognition and psychic receptivity, he theorized that it was not the individual's psychic gift that determined success but their state of mind. He saw that when a subject maintained a hopeful expectancy of guessing the right image behind a card, they were more likely to guess correctly. Therefore, it was the subjects' engaged participation that activated their unconscious insight, and he called this phenomenon "the archetype of the magical effect." Most tarotists have experienced this, and very likely in that first encounter with the cards. When we are brimming with that undeniable sense of awe, anticipation, and archetypal wonder, something miraculous comes through.

By intentionally engaging the archetype of the magical effect while shuffling, we both activate the archetype at the center of our readings and prime ourselves for the cards that will come. Eliminate any distractions that undermine this state of excitement or unfocus you, such as worrying over how to shuffle or how many cards to pull. Commit to a method of shuffling before you begin, whether you like to wait for an intuitive "click," repeat a standardized pattern, or just let the cards jump out on their own. It's also best to have your spread preselected (if you use one), so that you can remain concentrated and resist that itch to just keep pulling. Then, as you shuffle, focus on that magical expectancy, feeling it as a rush of wonder flowing through you into the cards. Once you've completed your shuffling and laid out your spread, do not question it again. Protect your faith in the oracle.

Interpreting the Cards

With the cards now laid out, this is the point in which we are most prone to discomfort, confusion, and even panic. Some cards will feel clear and true, while others will puzzle us. It's inevitable that we'll glance down at the assortment of symbols and figures and despair of how we will make any sense out of them. Remember that the work of reading the cards, like all inner work, is process not progress. To find the treasure a card holds, we must be willing to suspend understanding and engage the unknown.

In the archetypal approach, interpreting a card is not simply reciting its meaning by rote. It is a three-part exercise of **contextualization**—considering our current circumstances and past patterns; **personalization**—exploring our unique feelings, thoughts, experiences, and responses; and **amplification**—investigating the relevant symbolic elements and archetypal significances. When we draw a card, we should consider each of these factors while contemplating what aspect of the psyche it has come to convey.

Just as the Magician's full creativity engages all four suits on his table, we should engage all four of our functions in our interpretations. Beside the basic analytical approach of the thinking function, we can apply emotional, imaginary, and symbolical methods of interpretation via the feeling, intuition, and sensation functions respectively. When a card comes that does not immediately click, this is not evidence of your failure as a reader or the invalidity of the tarot. It is a request to listen in other ways and seek other pathways to discover the card's wisdom.

Thinking Analysis

Rational analysis is the typical approach to interpreting the cards. We think of it as basic addition, combining a cards' keywords with our personal circumstances to get its unique meaning for us. But we can use a more thorough and intimate process of analysis that makes for much richer interpretations.

First, we gather whatever meanings or keywords we ascribe to the card, whether these are ones from a guidebook or our own established knowledge. (Do not be afraid to use multiple resources or to pick and choose; just be wary not to throw away meanings because they are unfavorable.) Next, we move beyond these meanings and collect those personal associations we've uncovered as we developed our relationship with the card. Perhaps it reminds you of a childhood memory or brings up strange feelings of melancholy or contains a symbol that has always been meaningful to you. Don't worry if what comes up seems trivial or irrelevant—we do not yet know what will be important.

Blending these together, we can now analyze how the card applies to us, considering first what it reveals that we already know and, second, what it reveals that may be new or surprising.

Let's consider an example. Perhaps we come to the cards asking why we feel so suffocated with stress, and draw the Three of Cups. Initially we might be confused by this card, seeming so positive and carefree, but, as always, trust the oracle. As we move through the beginning steps of gathering meanings and associations, we might arrive at the following reflections:

> *My guidebook tells me that this card is about community and joy, and I once pulled it for my friend who is lighthearted and loves to have fun, and it just seems so her. She always tells me not to take things so seriously, but with all the responsibilities in my life right now, I don't have the luxury of being as carefree as she is.*

Already we have a strong foundation for interpreting the card. Though the guidebook's meanings are positive and encouraging, the personal association is tinged with frustration. The friend clearly embodies that joyful nature of the Three of Cups, but our reaction to her joyfulness is somewhat cynical. Now we can reflect on what the card says that we already know and might arrive at the following:

> *This card shows the joy and ease that I want in my life but don't have. Unlike my friend, I can't just drop my burdens to go have fun.*

With this established, we can investigate new insight, asking what the card might say that we *don't* already know. Keep in mind that an answer may come instantaneously or not at all. The key is patience, as we cannot rush the response from the unconscious. After some contemplation, maybe we arrive at this conclusion:

> *My friend can so easily embrace the joy I'm missing, and the truth is that I am jealous of that. As much as I resist it, maybe she's right. Maybe I can follow her lead and take things a little less seriously. I might have more freedom than I like to admit. Without joy, everything is too overwhelming. Maybe I need to recognize my power to change that.*

Now we can locate the disconnection between the conscious orientation that longed for joy but clung to its narrative of being trapped in responsibilities and the unconscious one that projected this forbidden joy onto the friend. The Three of Cups, which at the start may have felt shallow, out of place, or confusing, now illuminates a deep disconnect and a path to healing it.

Feeling and Emotion

Often our initial emotional responses to the cards offer the most illuminating points of interpretation. Emotions are spontaneous expressions of unconscious energy. Though it may seem irrational or have no clear reason behind it, emotion proves that the unconscious is engaged and responsive. Our task is to use the emotion like a diving line, following it down to its place of origin to discover its deeper significance.

In exploring your emotional reactions, you might meditate on questions like:

What does this card make me feel and why?

What's the thought/fear/belief supporting this feeling?

What might resolve this feeling or transform it?

What is the key emotion in this card, and how do I respond to it?

You can pass through these questions swiftly and lightly or break out the journal. The goal is to release the lumbering effort of analysis for something more fluid and instinctive. Returning to that Three of Cups, perhaps we recognize that our initial emotion was irritation, and we move through the following reflection:

This card makes me feel irritated, but when I question why, I only feel more upset. I am afraid that I can never have the joy of the Three of Cups because I am weighed down with burden and that will never change. More deeply, I feel an underlying sense of hopelessness. I feel exhausted, as if I have given in to believing I will never be free to just dance. The resolution is to permit myself the joy I feel is forbidden to me. Why is this so hard to allow?

Here we have opened a portal to deeper exploration. Notice that we have not arrived at what the card *means* or how we can *fix* things, because the goal of this sort of feeling exploration is not to solve but to *connect* to a deeper truth within.

Intuitive Imagination

Years ago I worked at a specialized learning center supporting children with reading and comprehension issues. Their remarkably successful program was built on studies which showed that both memory and comprehension are much stronger when we have activated our faculty of cognitive visualization. Essentially, if we can *picture* what we're reading, we can understand it.

This applies equally to our understanding of the cards. If we can draw the card into our imagination, expanding it beyond its static frame to observe its dynamic potential, we will more thoroughly get its depth of meaning. We can approach this method through the first or third person, either placing ourselves in the card or watching its scene unfold. It's important to allow this to be purely intuitive and uninhibited so that the unconscious may speak freely.

To begin, simply describe the scene of the card and then allow the imagination to insert itself and carry it forward. Returning to our example, this might look like:

> *Three women are dancing and laughing. They are celebrating life. Their wine may pour over their raised cups, but they don't care. They feel so free, as if this one day is eternity. As I watch I feel the strong urge not to disturb them. After years of exhausting work, they have earned this dance. I wish I could join them, but I know I'm not welcome. I will only bring a dark cloud over this bright moment.*

In just a short reflection we have learned so much. The imagination has focused on the sense of freedom in the card, as well as our unworthiness of it. We've illuminated the psyche's simultaneous feeling of alienation from joy and the need to reconcile with it. If we approach via the third person, exploring the card as a scene from the unconscious, our reflections may look like this:

> *These three women are celebrating after an exhausting harvest. They are human, but it's not mortal wine in their cups. They drink the wine of the gods, which they've earned because of their tireless efforts. The gods are well-pleased, and now they are allowed to rest.*

Here we do not have a direct reflection of our personal experience, but rather a story to extrapolate into metaphor. The women's exhaustive labor may very well mirror our own tireless work ethic, and the gods' gift of wine may be a symbolic gift from the psyche that at last permits us reward and rest.

Again, there are no exact answers here, but many fertile questions. By following such questions, deep meaning may indeed come through.

Sensation and Symbol

Symbols are containers of great power, and though they seem abstract, a symbolic approach to a card can actually give our sensate side something more concrete to work with. By focusing our attention on particular symbols presented in the cards, we can draw concentrated meaning.

Working with symbols requires us to develop our own symbolic literacy, meaning that we must actively learn about the symbols we encounter in our dreams, synchronicities, and stories. We can do this both on an individual and collective level, exploring symbols' personal meanings as well as their mythological significance. It's always good to have a vetted symbol dictionary on hand or to keep a journal to record the symbols that connect in a more individual way.* Also, when working with symbols, it's important not to confuse them with signs, which have *fixed* meaning (such as a red light meaning stop or believing that a dove means peace). Symbols are fluid and cannot be exhausted. They may direct our attention to certain ideas, but ultimately they are alive, evocative, and always remain elusive to some degree.

Returning again to our Three of Cups, we might find that our attention is locked on the fruits of the harvest and explore their symbolic significance as follows:

> *The fruits of the harvest symbolize fertility and abundance in myth, and for me they symbolize the richness of life. But I always worry that I won't achieve this richness and that my efforts will never ripen. However, in the Three of Cups the harvest is clearly ready, which makes me wonder if I am actually ready to reap what I've planted. Perhaps abundant joy is available, and I simply need to feast and enjoy.*

As we can see, the symbol acts as a concretizing image. The abstract idea of opening to more conscious joyfulness is made real in the symbol of the fruit and the metaphor of reaping what we have sown.

---

* It's important to note that symbols can take on different meanings personally and collectively. I once dreamed of a crocodile, and though all my resources mentioned the role of the crocodile as a threshold guardian, in my dream it clearly symbolized the aggressive nature of anxiety. Though it's important to trust in the symbolic potency of the collective unconscious, be flexible with your interpretations.

Continuing the Work

It is a disappointing habit that after staring at the cards for ten or fifteen minutes, most tarotists take only the crust of what came through and leave the real nutrients of wisdom on the table. The truth is that, like a dream, the meaning will likely come into focus days or even weeks later. The real work of a reading begins after we've put our cards back in the deck.

We do not need to drown ourselves in complex exercises or waste time with compulsory journaling. Rather, continuing our work with the cards is a practice of mindfulness and contemplation. When we pull out our cards, we are initiating a conversation with the unconscious, with the soul, and in the ensuing days we should keep listening and speaking. In addition to using the techniques we discussed in chapter 2, I highly recommend that you engage these prompts in the days following your reading:

> *What new question, feeling, or understanding has entered since I first pulled these cards?*
>
> *How has the meaning of these cards shifted for me?*
>
> *What small seed of truth have these cards helped to plant?*

Beyond these questions, here are more suggestions on how you might continue your work after a reading.

1. Pay Close Attention to Your Dreams.

The unconscious speaks most openly through the dreamworld, and so it's important to watch for what arises after a reading (or even before). Symbols and motifs may be replicated, expounded, or clarified in dreams, which can help alchemize the reading's messages.

This will rarely ever be direct. You likely won't pull the Magician and then dream of a cloaked wizard strolling around your childhood home. Instead, the cards will return as symbol, shifting dramatically in form but holding to their archetypal center. Several years ago, after pulling the Hermit for myself, I dreamed that I was alone in an abandoned Parisian apartment, wistfully staring out at the Eiffel Tower twinkling in the distance. There was no old man with a lantern, but what the Hermit and the dream shared was the central archetypal experience of deep solitude and the shimmering light of beauty and hope. Though pulling the Hermit had already offered much insight, adding the personalized symbolism in the dream deepened my understanding of its significance in that moment.

2. Notice Synchronicities.

With any charged inner work, after a breakthrough or the concretization of a symbol, synchronicities may follow. As with dreams, these meaningful coincidences can pull our attention to a particular theme or element of a reading. You might draw the Six of Cups and then find yourself seated beside two adoring sisters on a plane or pull the Moon and suddenly become inundated with wolf imagery. We tend to strangle these synchronicities for meaning, but the sense of them usually only comes when our ego-minds can step out of the way. Simply be curious about how they focus your attention or what else they reveal about what the cards had presented.

3. Explore Action Points Inspired by the Cards.

Homework can be helpful, and while there's no set list of activities prescribed by the cards, their imagery and themes can guide us to some possibilities. For example:

- Take the swords off the wall in the Nine of Swords by listing out our anxious thought patterns (possibly nine of them) so that they no longer hover over us.
- Go for technology-free walks with the sole purpose of basking in the sunshine to manifest the brilliance and joyfulness of the Sun card.
- Transcribe the internal argument between the cold, analytical Queen of Swords and the bright, enthusiastic Knight of Wands.
- Contemplate what may have died in you with the Death card. Then write a eulogy to that part of you on a piece of paper, and reverently bury or cremate it.

Not every card will present such an opportunity, but allow yourself to be creative and intentional in making the abstraction of the cards real and actionable in some way. This will help alchemize their wisdom more quickly and proactively.

More Questions, Fewer Answers

One of our favorite requests of the cards is to bring *clarity*, but I have learned to become suspicious of this intention. Clarity means removing ambiguity and obscurity so that things become transparent, and this is indeed what we want from a reading. But I have witnessed countless clients and students move through deeply potent readings only to say at the end, "I see things more clearly now, but I still don't know *what to do*." When we ask the cards for clarity, what we often mean is a prescription. We want to be told what to do, when to do it, how to do it. We want to resolve the tension of living, but the tarot does not have this power, nor is it meant to. As we've established throughout this book, the wisdom the tarot offers is the wisdom we ourselves hold.

If we seek sincere self-knowledge, confusion is more useful than clarity. Of course, there are times where an intuitive breakthrough will clarify the path forward, but instant clarity typically confirms the ego-perspective and thus shuts out the unconscious information trying to enter. Just as we must wander in the haze of the Moon before truly accessing the illumination of the Sun, we must let the cards confuse us so that we may voyage toward expanded understanding. True, lasting clarity is best won through contemplation of our confusion.

Therefore, I again urge you to orient your readings to arrive not at answers but the *better questions*. There are no true answers in life, and questions are not our crises but our hope. They are the stepping stones of the journey that only becomes truer and more precious. Poet Rainer Maria Rilke puts it better than anyone:

> I want to beg you, as much as I can . . . to be patient toward all that is unsolved in your heart and to try to love the *questions themselves* like locked rooms and like books that are written in a very foreign tongue. Do not now seek the answers, which cannot be given you

because you would not be able to live them. And the point is, to live everything. *Live* the questions now. Perhaps you will then gradually, without noticing it, live along some distant day into the answer.[2]

Love the questions and have faith in the mystery. Embrace the tension of living, and let it expand the strength of the soul. The more you ask about who you are, the more you learn and the further you journey toward the sacred Self within.

— CHAPTER 13 —

ARCHETYPAL TAROT SPREADS

In the universe, there are things that are known, and things that are unknown, and in between, there are doors.
—WILLIAM BLAKE

Reading tarot with a psycho-spiritual lens is, as Jung and the author of *The Cloud of Unknowing* would undoubtedly agree, an exercise in *Self*-contemplation. The archetypal approach rejects answers and shifts our focus to the questions themselves—the truer questions, the questions drawn from the soul. If we can, as Rilke encourages, learn to *live* those questions, exploring and refining them through the cards' direction, we may indeed individuate our way into the answer.

A successful tarot reading is not about mastery but receptivity, as Jung wrote, "I have always said to my pupils: 'Learn as much as you can about symbolism; then forget it all when you are analyzing a dream'."[1] The skill of reading does not only come from our training and intuitive gifts, but from being able to spontaneously and uniquely weave our knowledge of the cards with what is evoked from the unconscious. In this way, reading the tarot is, ultimately, an exercise in unfolding a moment in our individual mythology. We must saturate the external images with internal depth so that the cards expound the inner myth hidden in this moment of our lives.

We will walk through three spreads developed for the archetypal approach, but keep in mind that as much as spreads can focus the scope of our readings they can also limit them. The most illuminating readings are grounded not in precision but in interpretive adaptability. When we try to squeeze a card into a position that doesn't seem to suit it, mental acrobatics ensue. Rather than worry over how the cards fit, always consider how they respond to the initial question or intention we set for our readings or what they spark *within you*. No matter the position, every card can inspire a new conversation with the unconscious.

The Tension of the Opposites Spread

One of Jung's richest insights was that true change only comes when we can hold that tension of inner opposites:

> The repressed content must be made conscious so as to produce a tension of opposites, without which no forward movement is possible. The conscious mind is on top, the shadow underneath, and just as high always longs for low and hot for cold, so all consciousness, perhaps without being aware of it, seeks its unconscious opposite, lacking which it is doomed to stagnation, congestion, and ossification. Life is born only of the spark of opposites.[2]

When we can sit in between our conscious and unconscious opposites, we do not waste energy struggling for truce but await the collision which will produce a spark—a new psychological orientation or revelation of truth. In many of my classes, students are encouraged to develop a tolerance for this tension by pulling the Tension of the Opposites Spread each week and no other cards in between. Though simple, it taps us into this tension of opposites and may indeed strike the necessary charge between them.

Card 1 represents your conscious attitude, situation, or ego-orientation. This may be something that you are currently experiencing, contemplating, or even resisting, but it is identifiable by the conscious mind.

Card 2 represents something lingering in the unconscious that may offer deeper understanding or unblock the psyche. This might appear as internal conflict, repressed wisdom, or shadow material. Keep in mind that this card is presenting something that is unconscious, meaning you

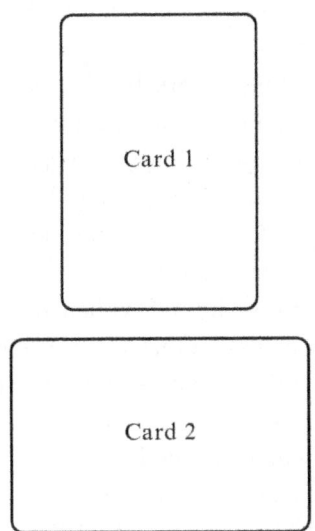

Figure 22. Tension of the Opposites Spread

Figure 23. Tension of the Opposites Spread Example

should not expect to get it right away. If you do, consider what hidden truth may be beneath it.

Let's examine a reading I workshopped with one of my students. Feeling increasingly frustrated by the lack of growth at her new job, my student—we'll call her Sally—wanted to reflect on what was agitating her so deeply and how she could shift things. Pulling the Page of Swords as card 1, Sally quickly recognized it as the side of her personality that was intellectually stimulated and engaged, describing it as her "inner apprentice" striving to prove herself. When we discussed this Page as part of her persona, she expressed that she suspected her coworkers scrutinized her as if she were the immature, indecisive Page of Swords, which only made her want to prove herself more. At the same time, she was aware that she was very much in the Page phase of typological development, still building her confidence and skill at this new workplace.

Seeing the Hanged Man, Sally was initially sure that she understood the message to go with the flow more and wait for things to change on their own. Though helpful advice, I encouraged her to remember that card 2 points to the *unconscious* orientation and she should continue to meditate on it. After a few days in contemplation, Sally reported that though the Page of Swords at the forefront was active and eager for development, the truth was that underneath she felt immobilized. She had imagined herself dangling from a branch, just waiting there for someone to come and tell her that she was ready to be put on her feet again. This brought up intense anger, and she was itching for someone to blame. Sally wondered if this furious, frustrated energy was what was motivating that Page of Swords to keep pushing harder, even though logically she knew she was too new at the job to progress forward. This led to a series of important questions: Why was she trying so hard to prove herself? What about this state of waiting made her so angry? Was her desire for growth at the job a remedy for the tension of not being in control? What would change if the Hanged Man were set upright and she centered acceptance rather than resistance?

By asking these questions inspired by the cards (which would not have occurred to her before pulling them), Sally saw that while the Page of Swords in her had been striving to move up at her job and prove her competency, it was an unconscious compensation for the deeper feeling of being out of her depth. Interestingly, over the following weeks Sally wondered if the Hanged Man had forced a pause in her growth so that she could face the truth that she wasn't actually sure she wanted to move forward at this job at all.

The Inner Work Spread

In situations where there is something pressing that we feel called to work on, the Inner Work Spread can be very helpful. Begin by clarifying the focal point at the heart of the struggle and write it down or speak it aloud. You may even want to put it on a piece of paper and place that at the center of the spread. As always, be wary of writing questions seeking definitive answers. Rather choose a question or intention that supports the change or understanding you hope the reading will bring.

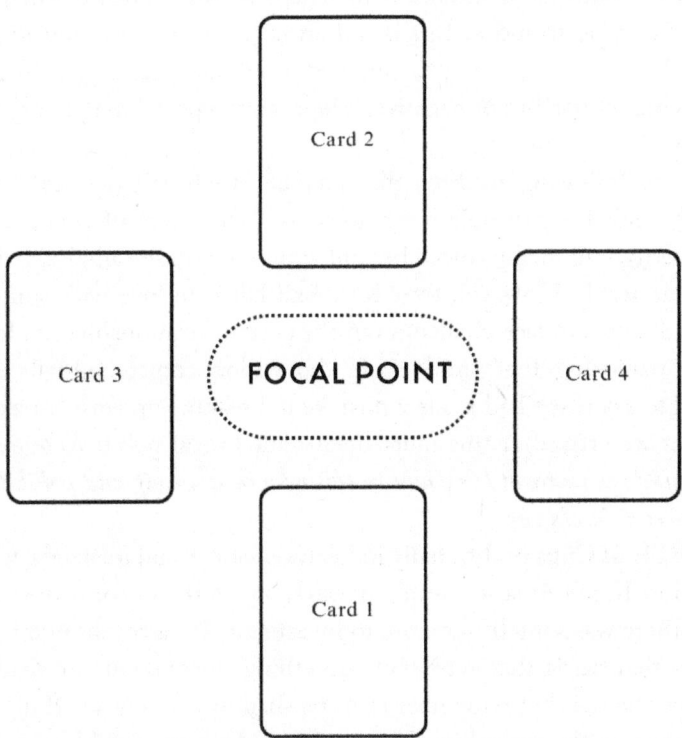

Figure 24. Inner Work Spread

Card 1 begins with what unconscious or shadow material lies beneath the focal point. It represents a hidden factor in the psyche or an aspect of shadow affecting the situation.

Card 2 highlights what is above the focal point. Sometimes it shows a higher calling, drawing you above the situation to gain a new perspective, and sometimes it indicates a mental fixation that blocks or preoccupies the ego. For example, if we draw the Star card, we'd likely read it as a higher point of illumination, but if we draw the Ten of Swords, we might see it as the anxiety blocking our progress.

Card 3 represents what is behind the focal point, or what past experiences or psychological patterns are influencing the current situation. For example, drawing the Emperor reversed may represent our longtime battle with our belligerent father, or drawing the Seven of Wands may point to a pattern of becoming combative when we feel threatened.

Card 4 points our attention to what's ahead, showing where the energy is trying to move. This is not an outcome, but an indication of where the psyche is leaning to empower resolution, healing, or integration. Whether positive or negative, it represents a portal to the next stage of our individuation.

In the following reading, the querent—we'll call her Kate—had recently ended a passionless relationship. After years of silent disappointment, she'd finally voiced her unhappiness, and she and her partner parted amicably. However, after Kate had fallen in love with someone new and began to face challenges in the current relationship, she found herself panicking that she'd made the wrong choice. Initially Kate wanted to ask if she had made a mistake in breaking up with her ex, but together we arrived at this more open-ended focal point: *Kate seeks to understand the source of her doubt in this new relationship and validate her choice to end the old one.*

The Six of Cups traditionally indicates memory and nostalgia, which applied to Kate's situation in many ways, but as the unconscious experience there was something more to investigate. It's a common misconception that cards that represent something unconscious or shadowy must be negative, but remember that the shadow contains anything that is unknown to the ego, which can equally be the beauty inside of us. The focus here was not her longing to return to the past, but her nostalgia for what she had once shared with her ex. The more "bad" she discovered in her new partner, the more she appreciated the "good" in her old one. This was not an indication that she had made a mistake giving up the relationship, but that in recalling the value of their love, real healing was happening inside her. Reflecting on this, Kate admitted that she had spent a long time resenting her ex, and these emerging memories of appreciation and tenderness were making her uncomfortable. Rather than explore them, she was suppressing them, which forced them to break through, especially in intimate moments with her new partner.

Because of its inversion, we explored the King of Wands as a disruptive complex in Kate's psyche. Kate prided herself on being a confident

Figure 25. Inner Work Tarot Spread Example

leader in many areas of her life, but she admitted that in the past relationship this capable part of her would bump into her ex's passiveness and she'd turn from confident to domineering. She had originally blamed her ex's weakness for bringing this side out of her, but now that it was flaring up with her new partner, she could no longer diagnose it as a symptom of the old relationship. When we dug a little more into that King of Wands' side, Kate confessed that she felt only a strong man could be worthy of her, and the new partner was failing that standard just as the old one had. Naturally, this brought us to question whether this complex was setting up an impossible expectation for her partners that they (and everyone) were doomed to fail.

Card 3 turned our attention backward to an internal pattern Kate had encountered many times before. The Seven of Pentacles, especially when inverted, indicates hesitation and distrust of our senses. Kate easily connected it to her need for the conditions to be just right before taking action (a common struggle for the sensation function), which is why she had not ended the old relationship earlier. She felt that she had wasted years stuck in this hesitation and feared she was repeating the same pattern with her new partner. This fear was pushing her to consider ending things, but when we questioned what exactly was creating all this pressure, Kate realized it was again the King of Wands who demanded a "strong" decision. The guidance seemed to point in two directions: first, that she examine that pattern of waiting for those just right conditions more critically, and second, that she investigate how the King of Wands complex overcompensated by urging her to act before she was ready.

Lastly, Temperance came as the way forward. Temperance indicated mediation, suggesting that both orientations (the one nostalgic for the old relationship and the one eager for the new) must be understood and blended together. As always, this was not a solution to the problem but a doorway to pass through. Temperance encouraged Kate to temper the domineering criticisms of the inverted King of Wands and embrace the tender appreciation in the Six of Cups. It also showed the fruit of the Seven of Pentacles blooming in her garden, hinting that though Kate had hesitated, she'd followed the most fruitful path. This was clearly an invitation to find a sense of balance and peace through her reflections before taking action. Overall, Temperance suggested that both things were true: Kate had left something that was once beautiful and was right to choose a new path seeking greater love.

The complaint we might now have is that we did not arrive at a specific answer saying to go back to her ex or stay with her new lover, but by now I hope you can see how much richer this archetypal approach is. With just four cards, Kate engaged in serious inner work, facing her repressed feelings, rigid complexes, and past patterns. She more clearly understood her deeper desires and the cause of her psychological discomfort. As the Temperance angel shows, it was in mediating these tensions that the path into the horizon opened before her.

The Archetypal Tarot Spread

Drawn from the Celtic Cross, the Archetypal Tarot Spread, shown on page 277, is a complex spread best used in those potent moments in life when we need to see our myth laid out before us. Because of its depth and intensity, I generally recommend that this spread should not be used more than a few times a year.

Card 1 begins by representing the conscious attitude, situation, or ego-orientation in the present moment, and card 2 crosses it with what I call "the thing on the altar," be it an obstacle, opportunity, or any experience immediately pressing on us. Though typically an unconscious element, it can be positive or negative and represents a challenge for the ego to either overcome or embrace.

The following four cards are much like the positions in the Inner Work Spread. Card 3 represents unconscious or shadow material needing to rise to the surface; card 4 represents an inner or outer experience from the past; card 5 represents either a higher calling or a mental fixation; and card 6 represents an archetype or energy to be anticipated on your individuation path.

Cards 7 through 10 can be read either formulaically (the combination of column + row) or as amplifications of the surrounding cards. These amplifications can manifest as enhancements, clarifiers, or connecting elements, as we'll see in the following example.

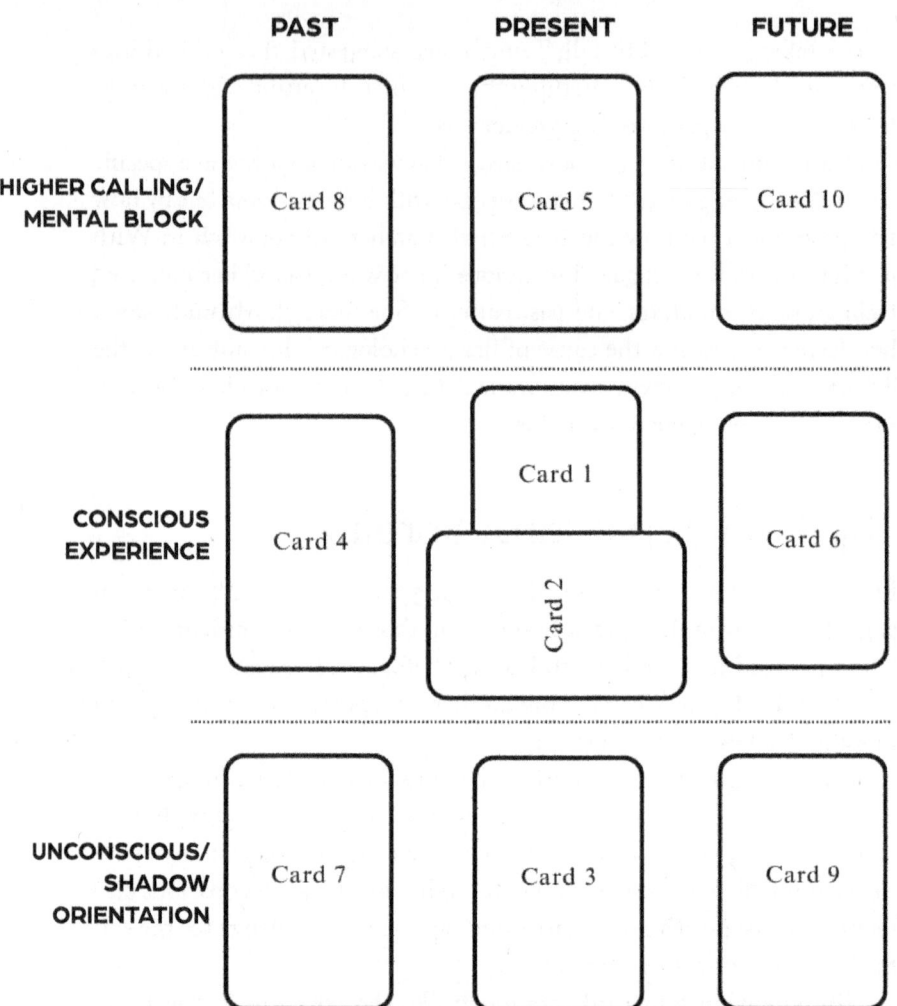

Figure 26. The Archetypal Tarot Spread

The querent—John—was two weeks away from retirement after a multidecade career as a respected professional in his field. He anticipated this shift with both excitement and fear and came to the reading seeking to sort through these conflicting feelings and focus his newfound freedom in life.

As the conscious ego-orientation, the Page of Wands was an excellent encapsulation of John's wide-open feeling facing retirement. He was flooded with ideas for his "what's next?" considering opening community

ARCHETYPAL TAROT SPREADS

Figure 27. The Archetypal Tarot Spread Example

centers and joining spiritual groups. Though this wide-open feeling was exciting, it was also a bit overwhelming for John, who, after nearly forty years as an expert, now had no idea what he was doing. He was suddenly a Page again, staring out at the limitless unknown.

The crossing card showed the true significance of this moment. He was not simply ending a career; he was closing an entire stage of his individuation. The World suggested a moment of integration and intimacy with the Self, which moved John deeply. He revealed that for years he had felt divided: one half was the everyday professional who needed to be good at his job; one half was the spiritual seeker in pursuit of the Self. He had suppressed the spiritual half to preserve the professional one, and seeing the archetype of wholeness validated his feeling that his halves were at last being reconciled. He described a powerful spontaneous symbol that appeared in his mind's eyes: the world egg being cracked open and the dancer within being released.

The Tower brought a sudden, shadowy jolt to the reading. John explained that though he had wished to retire for years, he'd constantly put it off. (Even at the time of our session he had still not submitted the last of the paperwork.) What we discovered was that while John was consciously eager for change, he unconsciously cowered from the resulting destruction he knew this Tower decision would cause. With his ego so intertwined with his professional persona, he instinctively knew its fragility and potential for collapse. It became clearer how truly split John was. While the spiritual seeker within him saw the end of his career as a moment of sublime culmination, the professional side of him saw it as ego-obliteration.

The Ten of Pentacles inverted in the past offered more information to understand the repression of the Tower. The Ten of Pentacles is a card of success and abundance, but inverted it took us in two directions. The first suggested that John's past focus on the material side of life had distracted him from the spiritual journey he now felt he had to catch up on, and the second highlighted John's feeling that he had never really achieved the height of the success he'd strived for. Fearing this disappointment, he unconsciously kept the Tower—the breakdown of his old identity—at bay.

The Nine of Cups as the higher calling was a welcome shift toward a new perspective. With such fear of the Tower locked in the shadow, here was an invitation to more thoughtfully consider the value he had cultivated in his life—how he had filled his cups. Connecting emotionally to this card, John recognized how much sincere satisfaction his long career had brought him. The higher calling, therefore, was to shift the focus off his unfulfilled external achievements and onto the great inner rewards he had earned. If he could indeed hold this calling, then the effort to sort through the debris of the Tower would be much more meaningful.

The Fool in the future suggested that if he could allow the Tower to bring down the last vestiges of his old self, and thus embrace the transcendent close of the World, then he would undoubtedly feel opened to a brilliant new destiny. There was a clear harmony between the symbols of the World and the Fool—the end and the beginning. Ahead was the wide, sun-dappled road into authentic selfhood. This was truly an auspicious glimpse into the promise awaiting him.

Now let us turn to the corner cards and understand the various ways they both expand and specify the reading. Beginning with card 7, the Knight of Cups inverted pointed to a potent complex from John's past. He described himself as always being openhearted and eager to connect with the world in meaningful ways, but also related that when he felt rejected, he could quickly become demoralized and defensive. He explained that he heard a "Queen of Swords type" in his head, criticizing his dreams of pursuing his true values. (We are never locked into only the cards that are on the table, and bringing in other elements for exploration—be they cards, dreams, or personal symbols—can be extremely useful.) John confessed that he had wanted to shift toward the Knight's heartfelt pursuits long ago, but that level of vulnerability made him too nervous and he refused the call (which clarified, also, the intensity of that split he felt in the World).

This led us to the Ace of Swords inverted as card 8, which we read formulaically as the past higher calling or mental block. With all the cards of the past column being inverted, there was a pattern of interior stagnancy, possibly indicating the individuation work he'd avoided. Although the discerning, active blade of the Ace of Swords was on the table, it seemed as if it had not been used. He had avoided taking action, afraid of triggering the Knight of Cups' feelings of rejection. This guided us beyond our more analytical method of interpretation and toward the symbolic and imaginary. We agreed that the Knight of Cups' quest (his grail quest, we might say) was to make a new relationship with this Queen of Swords anima figure, viewing her not as warden but goddess, accepting her sword as a gift he is finally ready to use. Though he had not wielded it in the past, the Ace of Swords was still within reach.

The Three of Pentacles as card 9 seemed to appear as a bridge between the Tower and the Fool. Sorting through the Tower's debris to clear the way for the Fool would be a task of real labor. The Three of Pentacles, therefore, presented the advice of going about this work more practically. First, John would need to gather all his inner allies—the Knight of Cups' sense of longing, the Ace of Swords' clarity of will, the Page of Wands' perseverance—and craft a blueprint for how he might "do the work." This card encouraged John to remain focused on his practical goals and trust his skills so that he might rebuild on the sacred ground of authenticity.

Finally, the Two of Wands between the Nine of Cups and the Fool highlighted a potential challenge for John. Living as the Fool, the world would now be his for the taking, but with the Nine of Cups seated and satisfied with what was already present, a new tension of opposites was introduced. The dreams of the Fool might pull John one way, the couched contentment of the Nine of Cups another. John admitted this tension was already something he felt. A part of him wanted to give up on the Page of Wands' burgeoning dreams because he was getting older and things were already "good enough." The Two of Wands pointed to a coming paralysis between his inspiring visions for the wide world "out there" and the simple, predictable life already in John's control. John knew he wanted to pursue the Page's big visions, and so he would have to learn to hold this tension until the Three of Wands—the ability to persevere without attachment to outcome—could synthesize in him.

Overall, with the World and the Fool, it was clear that this was a profound moment in John's myth. Here was the great culmination and liberation, or as Campbell might put it, the "freedom to live." Though all the other cards were rich with information about John's psyche, these two encapsulated it all, and told him to go off, know himself, embrace himself, and live the truth of himself as fully as possible.

AFTERWORD

The only thing that makes life possible is permanent, intolerable uncertainty: not knowing what comes next.
—URSULA K. LE GUIN

We cannot help but revolt against the unknown, to emphatically refuse the horizonless *what's next?* This is why we go to our decks: to soothe the ego desperate to see and know all things, to defend ourselves against feeling alone, unsure, blind in the dark. But what the tarot teaches us is that we cannot control the meandering course of our lives; we can only remain faithful to our goal. This goal is not—and has never been—to spare ourselves uncertainty or doubt, nor to get the answers that would take the living out of life. (Remember, as Rilke tells us, *we must live everything.*) Doubt is the force that urges us to find our Self at the center. Without doubt there would be no mystery, no quest toward wonder, no discovery of meaning, no cultivation of faith. Our goal is not to dissolve doubt but walk hand in hand with it, always asking, as I said in the very first pages of this book, *How am I meant to live?*

As we glance over our cards, we are desperate to understand how they answer this question and what they mean. But meaning is not determined by sterile analysis. Rather, as Mary K. Greer writes, it is defined in "full participation with what it signifies."[1] To demand neatly packaged, easily discernible meaning is to deny ourselves vibrant participation with the depth of what the cards *signify*. Each card is a metaphor for a part of our personal mystery, and it is within the mystery, not the card, that we find meaning.

If we use it with reverence and responsibility, the tarot can guide us through the story of our lives *as we live it*. It can unveil the characters, plots, and themes animating our psyches. It can offer a red thread through the labyrinth of our complexities. It can put us in immediate contact with our personal divinity, whether that be God or universe or soul. It can direct us toward the moonlit road to the treasures of our being. It can even inspire the Foolish unfolding of our bliss, guiding us to harmonization with the World within.

Who could send us off with better encouragement using these seventy-eight cards in our pursuit of Self than our beloved fourteenth-century mystic, who speaks of discovering God's love in contemplation the way we might speak of discovering the soul's wisdom in the cards:

> Do not give up then, but work away at it till you have this longing. When you first begin, you find only darkness, and as it were a cloud of unknowing. You don't know what this means except that in your will you feel a simple steadfast intention reaching out towards God.... . Reconcile yourself to wait in this darkness as long as is necessary, but still go on longing after him whom you love.... And if you will work hard at what I tell you, I believe that through God's mercy you will achieve this very thing.[2]

Every weeping wound, every tender insight, every dizzied question that draws us to the tarot is a cloud of unknowing that opens us to a lesson on this blissful path. Perhaps now, with the Fool's long shadow still visible in our imagination, there is a whisper of response to the question of how you are meant to live. Perhaps there is a sense, distantly, of what wild road you are meant to follow and how the cards might guide you along it. May you be steadfast in your intention. May you reconcile yourself to waiting in the darkness of uncertainty. May you go on loving You whom you love. May you embrace the cloud of unknowing, trusting in this seventy-eight-faced oracle to present the holy wisdom that will guide you to achieve the wholeness that is your birthright and destiny.

ACKNOWLEDGMENTS

The first dream that ever blossomed in me was to author a book. I remember staring up at the moon with my mother at three years old, telling her how badly I wanted to write about it. What I really meant is that I wanted to write about the mystery of life and the wonder of the soul. It is with immeasurable gratitude that I can now say that dream has come true.

First and foremost, I'd like to thank my late mother, whose faith in me was the most precious kind of love. Thanks, as well, to my sister Persephone for being my biggest adorer no matter what I do.

Thank you to my agent Kara Rota for guiding me through the ins and outs of this process. And a tremendous thank you to the Weiser team—Amy, Christine, Ashley, Eryn, and the others who midwifed this book into life. I am so honored to be counted among your extraordinary authors.

Thank you to the friends and colleagues whose expertise and support I have so deeply appreciated. In particular a fervent thanks to Cristina Farella, Alyssa Polizzi, Emma Frey, Nina and Anton Leksin, and Elisabeth Pomès. And thank you most of all to my exceedingly patient husband Stephen.

I must thank those who have pioneered this study of card, archetype, and soul: Carl Jung, Joseph Campbell, Marion Woodman, Marie-Louise von Franz, James Hillman, Mary K. Greer, Rachel Pollack, Sallie Nichols, A. E. Waite, Pamela Colman Smith, and countless others. The world is blessed by their brilliance and courage.

And last but very much not least I'd like to thank my students. It is your zeal for wisdom, your open-hearted yearning that has been my greatest inspiration. I have learned more about the holy power of the tarot from you than anywhere else. Thank you for trusting me to be a mentor on your path.

Though strange—I know—my final word of appreciation is for that ineffable force in my psyche that, in the greatest periods of confusion and pain, has still urged me toward the greater potential. As Rilke put it, my blood is indeed alive with many voices, all telling me I am made of longing. I thank those voices now, with humility and reverence.

NOTES

Introduction

1 Sallie Nichols, *Jung and Tarot: An Archetypal Journey* (Samuel Weiser, 1980), 5.
2 James Hillman, *Revisioning Psychology* (Harper Perennial, 1975), xii.
3 Marie-Louise von Franz, *On Divination and Synchronicity: The Psychology of Meaningful Chance* (Inner City Press, 1980), 57.
4 Carl Jung, *Two Essays on Analytical Psychology*, trans. R. F. C. Hull (Meridian Books, 1960), 182.
5 Rollo May, *The Cry for Myth* (W. W. Norton and Company, 1991), 15.
6 *The Cloud of Unknowing and Other Works*, trans. Clifton Wolters (Penguin Books, 1978), 51.
7 *The Cloud of Unknowing and Other Works*, trans. Clifton Wolters, 52.

Chapter One

1 Jung, *Psychology and Religion: West and East*, volume 11 of *Collected Works of C. G. Jung*, ed. Gerhard Adler and trans. R. F. C. Hull (Princeton University Press, 1969), 263.
2 Jung, *The Structures and Dynamics of the Psyche*, volume 8 of *Collected Works of C. G. Jung*, ed. Gerhard Adler and trans. R. F. C. Hull (Princeton University Press, 1988), 158.
3 Von Franz, *On Divination and Synchronicity*, 39.
4 Von Franz, *The Interpretation of Fairy Tales: Revised Edition* (Shambhala, 1996), 3.
5 Von Franz, *The Interpretation of Fairy Tales*, 1.
6 Von Franz, *On Divination and Synchronicity*, 50.

Chapter Two

1. Ursula K. Le Guin, *The Language of the Night: Essays on Writing, Science Fiction, and Fantasy* (Scribner, 2024), 137.
2. Connie Zweig and Steve Wolf, *Meeting the Shadow: A Guide to Soul Work for a Vital, Authentic Life* (Ballantine Books, 1999), 5–6.

Chapter Three

1. Joseph Campbell, *Pathways to Bliss: Mythology and Personal Transformation*, ed. David Kudler (New World Library, 2004), 113.

Chapter Four

1. Jung, *Jung Speaking: Interviews and Encounters*, ed. William McGuire and R. F. C. Hull (Pan Books, 1980), 404.
2. A. E. Waite, *The Pictorial Key to the Tarot* (U.S. Games System, 2000), 194.
3. Jung, *The Archetypes and the Collective Unconscious*, volume 9, part 1, of *Collected Works of C. G. Jung*, ed. Gerhard Adler and trans. R. F. C. Hull (Princeton University Press, 1959), 96.

Chapter Five

1. Jung, *Aion: Researches into the Phenomenology of the Self*, volume 9, part 2, of *Collected Works of C. G. Jung*, ed. Gerhard Adler and trans. R. F. C. Hull (Princeton University Press, 1975), 9.
2. Robert Johnson, *Inner Work: Using Dreams and Active Imagination for Personal Growth* (Harper & Row, 1986), 45.

Chapter Seven

1. Pierre Delattre, *Tales of the Dalai Lama* (Houghton Mifflin, 1971), 33.

Chapter Eight

1. Plato, *Symposium*, trans. Alexander Nehamas and Paul Woodruff (Hackett Publishing, 1989), 27.
2. Delattre, *Tales of a Dalai Lama*, 33.
3. Jung et al., *Man and His Symbols* (Anchor Press, 1964), 195.
4. Jung, *Archetypes of the Collective Unconscious* in *CW* vol. 9, pt.1, 255.
5. Nichols, *Jung and Tarot*, 50.
6. Michael Maier, *Atalanta fugiens*, trans. Hereward Tilton (1617), alchemywebsite.com.
7. Marion Woodman, *The Pregnant Virgin: A Process of Psychological Transformation* (Inner City Books, 1985), 23.
8. Erich Neumann, *The Fear of the Feminine and Other Essays on Feminine Psychology*, trans. Boris Matthews et al. (Princeton University Press, 1994), 171.
9. Nichols, *Jung and Tarot*, 103.
10. Mircea Eliade, *The Sacred and the Profane: The Nature of Religion* (Harcourt, Brace & World, 1959), 11–12.
11. Jung, *Modern Man in Search of a Soul*, trans. W. S. Dell and Cary F. Baynes (Harcourt, Brace and Company, 1934), 57.
12. Neumann, *Amor and Psyche: The Psychic Development of the Feminine: A Commentary on the Tale by Apuleius*, trans. Ralph Manheim (Princeton University Press, 1973), 85.
13. Kahlil Gibran, *The Prophet* (Senate, 2003), 16.

Chapter Nine

1. Tung-shan, "If you look for the truth outside yourself," in *The Enlightened Heart: An Anthology of Sacred Poetry*, ed. and trans. Stephen Mitchell (Harper Perennial, 1989), 37.
2. Jung, *Two Essays on Analytical Psychology*, 62–63.
3. Jung, *Psychology and Alchemy*, volume 12 of *Collected Works*, ed. Gerhard Adler and trans. R. F. C. Hull (Princeton University Press, 1968), 480–81.

4 *Meditations on the Tarot: A Journey into Christian Hermeticism*, trans. Robert A. Powell (Jeremy P. Tarcher/Putnam, 1985), 226.
5 Rumi, *Rumi: The Big Red Book: The Great Masterpiece Celebrating Mystical Love and Friendship*, trans. Coleman Barks (Harper One, 2011), 209.
6 Boethius, *The Consolation of Philosophy*, trans. Victor Watts (Penguin Books, 1999), 25.
7 Boethius, *The Consolation of Philosophy*, 105.
8 Friedrich Nietzsche, *Thus Spoke Zarathustra: A Book for All and None*, trans. Thomas Common (Thrifty Books, 2009), 172.
9 Joseph Campbell and Bill Moyers, "Sacrifice and Bliss," episode 4 of *Joseph Campbell and the Power of Myth*, PBS television broadcast, June 24, 1988, approx. 56 min., *billmoyers.com*.
10 Woodman and Jill Mellick, *Coming Home to Myself: Daily Reflections for a Woman's Body and Soul* (Conari Press, 1998), 22.
11 Jung, *Aion* in *CW* vol. 9, pt. 2, 71.
12 Waite, *The Pictorial Key to the Tarot*, 115.

Chapter Ten

1 Johnson, *Owning Your Shadow: Understanding the Dark Side of the Psyche* (HarperCollins, 1991), 17.
2 "Odin's Rune-Song" from *The Elder Eddas of Sæmund Sigfusson and The Younger Eddas of Snorre Sturleson*, trans. Benjamin Thorpe and I. A. Blackwell and ed. Rasmus B. Anderson and J. W. Buel (Norroena Society, 1906), Project Gutenberg, *gutenberg.org*.
3 Edward Edinger, *Ego and Archetype: Individuation and the Religious Function of the Psyche* (G. P. Putnam and Sons, 1972), 140.
4 Nichols, *Jung and Tarot*, 229.
5 Karen Hamaker-Zondag, *Tarot as a Way of Life: A Jungian Approach to the Tarot* (Samuel Weiser, 1997), 158.
6 Jung, *The Red Book: Liber Novus*, ed. Sonu Shamdasani and trans. Mark Kyburz and John Peck (W. W. Norton & Company, 2009), 275.

7 Michel de Montaigne, *The Essays of Michel de Montaigne, Complete*, ed. William Carew Hazlitt and trans. Charles Cotton (1877). Project Gutenberg, May 28, 2001, *gutenberg.org*.
8 *The Poems of the Pearl Manuscript*, trans. Malcolm Andrew and Ronald Waldron (University of Exeter Press, 2007), 6.
9 Jung, *Nietzsche's Zarathustra: Notes of the Seminar Given in 1934–1939*, ed. James L. Jarrett (Princeton University Press, 1988), 1090.
10 M. Scott Peck, "37. Healing Human Evil," in *Meeting the Shadow*, ed. Zweig and Abrams, 179–80.
11 Charles Baudelaire, *Paris Spleen: Little Poems in Prose*, trans. Keith Waldrop (Wesleyan University Press, 2009), 60.
12 Jung, *The Red Book*, 261.
13 Anthony Stevens, "4. The Shadow in History and Literature," in *Meeting the Shadow*, ed. Zweig and Abrams, 28.
14 Jung, *The Archetypes of the Collective Unconscious* in *CW* vol. 9, pt.1, 295.

Chapter Eleven

1 Woodman and Mellick, *Coming Home to Myself*, 65.
2 Campbell, *Pathways to Bliss*, xiii.
3 Jung, *Two Essays on Analytical Psychology*, 120–21.
4 Jung, *Memories, Dreams, Reflections*, ed. Aniela Jaffé (Pantheon Books, 1961), 306.
5 St. John of the Cross, "The Dark Night of the Soul," trans. David Lewis, Poetry Foundation, *poetryfoundation.org*.
6 Jung, *Memories, Dreams, Reflections*, 196.
7 Murray Stein, *Minding the Self: Jungian Meditations on Contemporary Spirituality* (Taylor and Francis, 2014), 35.
8 Jung, *Archetypes of the Collective Unconscious* in *CW* vol. 9, pt 1, 169.
9 Jung, *Alchemical Studies*, volume 13 of *Collected Works of C. G. Jung*, ed. Gerhard Adler and trans. R. F. C. Hull (Princeton University Press, 1968), 265.
10 Nichols, *Jung and Tarot*, 344.
11 Edinger, *Archetype of the Apocalypse: Divine Vengeance, Terrorism, and the End of the World*, ed. George R. Elder (Open Court, 1999),

148.
12 Aniela Jaffé, *The Myth of Meaning: Jung and the Expansion of Consciousness* (Penguin Books, 1975), 83–84.
13 Jung, *Visions: Notes of the Seminar Given in 1930–1934, volume 2*, ed. Clare Douglas (Princeton University Press, 1997), 1078.
14 Campbell and Moyers, "Sacrifice and Bliss."
15 Joseph Campbell and Brad Olson, host, episode 1, "The Masks of God," *Pathways with Joseph Campbell* (podcast), March 1, 2021, 60 min., 10 sec., *pathways-with-joseph-campbell.simplecast.com*.
16 Von Franz, *Alchemy: An Introduction to the Symbolism and the Psychology* (Inner City Books, 1980), 160.
17 Ann Ulanov and Barry Ulanov, *The Witch and the Clown: Two Archetypes of Human Sexuality* (Chiron Publications, 1987), 244.
18 Jung, *Selected Letters of C. G. Jung, 1909–1960*, ed. Gerhard Adler (Princeton University Press, 1984), 190.

Chapter Twelve

1 Woodman, *The Pregnant Virgin*, 19.
2 Rainer Maria Rilke, *Letters to a Young Poet*, trans. M. D. Herter Norton (W. W. Norton and Company, 1993), 34–35.

Chapter Thirteen

1 Jung et al., *Man and His Symbols*, 56.
2 Jung, *Two Essays on Analytical Psychology*, 64.

Afterword

1 Mary K. Greer, *21 Ways to Read a Tarot Card* (Llewellyn, 2016), 239.
2 *The Cloud of Unknowing and Other Works*, 61–62.

BIBLIOGRAPHY

Abrams, Jeremiah, and Connie Zweig, eds. *Meeting the Shadow: The Hidden Power of the Dark Side of Human Nature.* J.P. Tarcher/Putnam, 1991.

Baudelaire, Charles. *Paris Spleen: Little Poems in Prose.* Translated by Keith Waldrop. Wesleyan University Press, 2009.

Boethius. *The Consolation of Philosophy.* Translated by Victor Watts. Penguin Books, 1999.

Campbell, Joseph. *The Hero with a Thousand Faces.* Meridian Books, 1956.

———. *Pathways to Bliss: Mythology and Personal Transformation.* Edited by David Kudler. New World Library, 2004.

Campbell, Joseph, and Bill Moyers, interviewer. *Joseph Campbell and the Power of Myth.* Episode 4, "Sacrifice and Bliss." PBS television broadcast, June 24, 1988. Approx. 56 min. *billmoyers.com.*

Campbell, Joseph, and Brad Olson, host. Episode 1, "The Masks of God." *Pathways with Joseph Campbell* (podcast). 60 min., 10 sec. The Joseph Campbell Foundation, March 1, 2021. *pathways-with-joseph-campbell.simplecast.com.*

The Cloud of Unknowing and Other Works. Translated by Clifton Wolters. Penguin Classics, 1978.

Delattre, Pierre. *Tales of a Dalai Lama.* Houghton Mifflin, 1971.

Edinger, Edward. *Archetype of the Apocalypse: Divine Vengeance, Terrorism, and the End of the World.* Edited by George R. Elder. Open Court, 1999.

———. *Ego and Archetype: Individuation and the Religious Function of the Psyche.* G. P. Putnam and Sons, 1972.

The Elder Eddas of Sæmund Sigfusson and The Younger Eddas of Snorre Sturleson. Translated by Benjamin Thorpe and I. A. Blackwell, edited by Rasmus B. Anderson and J. W. Buel. Originally published by Norroena Society, 1906. Project Gutenberg. *gutenberg.org.*

Eliade, Mircea. *The Sacred and the Profane: The Nature of Religion.* Harcourt, Brace, & World, Inc., 1959.

Gibran, Kahlil. *The Prophet.* Senate, 2003.

Greer, Mary K. *21 Ways to Read a Tarot Card.* Llewellyn, 2016.

Hamaker-Zondag, Karen. *Tarot as a Way of Life: A Jungian Approach to the Tarot.* Samuel Weiser, 1997.

Hillman, James. *Revisioning Psychology.* Harper Perennial, 1975.

Jaffé, Aniela. *The Myth of Meaning: Jung and the Expansion of Consciousness.* Penguin Books, 1975.

Johnson, Robert A. *Inner Work: Using Dreams and Active Imagination for Personal Growth.* Harper & Row, 1986.

———. *Owning Your Shadow: Understanding the Dark Side of the Psyche.* HarperCollins, 1991.

Jung, Carl. *Aion: Researches into the Phenomenology of the Self.* Vol. 9, part 2, of *Collected Works of C. G. Jung,* edited by Gerhard Adler and translated by R. F. C. Hull. Princeton University Press, 1975.

———. *Alchemical Studies.* Vol. 13 of *Collected Works of C. G. Jung,* edited by Gerhard Adler and translated by R. F. C. Hull. Princeton University Press, 1968.

———. *The Archetypes and the Collective Unconscious.* Vol. 9, part 1, of *Collected Works of C. G. Jung,* edited by Gerhard Adler and translated by R. F. C. Hull. Princeton University Press, 1959.

———. *Jung Speaking: Interviews and Encounters.* Edited by William McGuire and R. F. C. Hull. Pan Books, 1980.

———. *Memories, Dreams, Reflections.* Edited by Aniela Jaffé. Pantheon Books, 1961.

———. *Modern Man in Search of a Soul.* Translated by W. S. Dell and Cary F. Baynes. Harcourt, Brace and Company, 1934.

———. *Nietzsche's Zarathustra: Notes of the Seminar Given in 1934–1939.* Edited by James L. Jarrett. Princeton University Press, 1988.

———. *Psychology and Alchemy*. Vol. 12 of *Collected Works of C. G. Jung*, edited by Gerhard Adler and translated by R. F. C. Hull. Princeton University Press, 1968.

———. *Psychology and Religion: West and East*. Vol. 11 of *Collected Works of C. G. Jung*, edited by Gerhard Adler and translated by R. F. C. Hull. Princeton University Press, 1969.

———. *The Red Book: Liber Novus*. Edited by Sonu Shamdasani and translated by Mark Kyburz and John Peck. W. W. Norton & Company, 2009.

———. *Selected Letters of C. G. Jung, 1909–1960*. Edited by Gerhard Adler. Princeton University Press, 1984.

———. *The Structures and Dynamics of the Psyche*. Vol. 8 of *Collected Works of C. G. Jung*, edited by Gerhard Adler and translated by R. F. C. Hull. Princeton University Press, 1988.

———. *Two Essays on Analytical Psychology*. Translated by R. F. C. Hull. Meridian Books, 1956.

———. *Visions: Notes of the Seminar Given in 1930–1934, volume 2*. Edited by Clare Douglas. Princeton University Press, 1997.

Jung, Carl, Marie-Louise von Franz, Joseph L. Henderson, Jolande Jacobi, and Aniela Jaffé. *Man and His Symbols*. Anchor Press, 1964.

Le Guin, Ursula K. *The Language of the Night: Essays on Writing, Science Fiction, and Fantasy*. Scribner, 2024.

Maier, Michael. *Atalanta fugiens*. Translated by Hereward Tilton. 1617. alchemywebsite.com.

May, Rollo. *The Cry for Myth*. W. W. Norton & Company, 1991.

Meditations on the Tarot: A Journey into Christian Hermeticism. Translated by Robert A. Powell. Jeremy P. Tarcher/Putnam, 1985.

Mitchell, Stephen, ed./trans. *The Enlightened Heart: An Anthology of Sacred Poetry*. HarperPerennial, 1989.

Montaigne, Michel de. *The Essays of Michel de Montaigne, Complete*. Edited by William Carew Hazlitt and translated by Charles Cotton. Originally published 1877. Project Gutenberg, May 28, 2001. gutenberg.org.

Neumann, Erich. *Amor and Psyche: The Psychic Development of the Feminine: A Commentary on the Tale by Apuleius.* Translated by Ralph Manheim. Princeton University Press, 1973.

———. *The Fear of the Feminine and Other Essays on Feminine Psychology.* Translated by Boris Matthews, Esther Doughty, Eugene Rolfe, and Michael Cullingworth. Princeton University Press, 1994.

Nichols, Sallie. *Jung and Tarot: An Archetypal Journey.* Samuel Weiser, 1980.

Nietzsche, Friedrich. *Thus Spoke Zarathustra: A Book for All and None.* Translated by Thomas Common. Thrifty Books, 2009.

Plato. *Symposium.* Translated by Alexander Nehamas and Paul Woodruff. Hackett Publishing Co., 1989.

The Poems of the Pearl Manuscript. Translated by Malcolm Andrew and Ronald Waldron. University of Exeter Press, 2007.

Rilke, Rainer Maria. *Letters to a Young Poet.* Translated by M. D. Herter Norton. W. W. Norton and Company, 1993.

Rumi. *Rumi: The Big Red Book: The Great Masterpiece Celebrating Mystical Love and Friendship.* Translated by Coleman Barks. Harper One, 2011.

Stein, Murray. *Minding the Self: Jungian Meditations on Contemporary Spirituality.* Taylor and Francis, 2014.

St. John of the Cross. "The Dark Night of the Soul." Translated by David Lewis. Poetry Foundation. *poetryfoundation.org.*

Ulanov, Ann, and Barry Ulanov. *The Witch and the Clown: Two Archetypes of Human Sexuality.* Chiron Publications, 1987.

von Franz, Marie-Louise. *Alchemy: An Introduction to the Symbolism and the Psychology.* Inner City Books, 1980.

———. *The Interpretation of Fairy Tales: Revised Edition.* Shambhala, 1996.

———. *On Divination and Synchronicity: The Psychology of Meaningful Chance.* Inner City Press, 1980.

Waite, A. E. *The Pictorial Key to the Tarot*. U. S. Games Systems, Inc., 2000.

Woodman, Marion. *The Pregnant Virgin: A Process of Psychological Transformation*. Inner City Books, 1985.

Woodman, Marion, and Jill Mellick. *Coming Home to Myself: Daily Reflections for a Woman's Body and Soul*. Conari Press, 1998.

Zweig, Connie, and Steve Wolf. *Meeting the Shadow: A Guide to Soul Work for a Vital, Authentic Life*. Ballantine Books, 1999.

IMAGE CREDITS

Page 5. The cards "rise for judgement," "fortitude," and "charity" from the Visconti di Modrone tarot, Milan, 15th century. Cary Collection of Playing Cards, Beinecke Rare Book and Manuscript Library, Yale University. Public domain via Wikimedia Commons.

Page 7. The Magician, The Lovers, and Death from the Tarot de Marseille by Nicolas Conver (circa 1760, Marseille). Reproduced via Tarot World Project, 2020, via Wikimedia Commons CC0 1.0 Universal license.

Page 7. The Magician, The Lovers, and Death from the Rider-Waite tarot deck, 1909, illustrated by Pamela Colman Smith. Scans from the original by Holly Voley. Public domain via Wikimedia Commons.

Page 154. Mercurius, "Clavis": the second key from the *The Twelve Keys of Basil Valentine* (Basilius Valentinus), engraved by Matthaeus Merian, 1618. Roy G. Neville Historical Chemical Library, Courtesy of Science History Institute. Public domain via Wikimedia Commons.

Page 158. Sophia or Sapientia from Emblem 26 of *Atalanta fugiens* by Michael Maier, engravings by Matthäus Merian, published in Oppenheim, 1617. Public domain via Wikimedia Commons.

Page 163. Battle between Marduk and Tiamat, drawn by Faucher-Gudin based on the excavated bas-relief from the Temple of Ninurta, c. 865 BC. From *Monuments of Nineveh*, Second Series'plate 5, London, J. Murray, 1853. Public domain via Wikimedia Commons.

Page 176. Chemical Marriage of Sun and Moon from *Rosarium Philosophorum* by Jaroš Griemiller, 1578. Public domain via Wikimedia Commons.

Page 218. The Psalter of Robert de Lisle. England circa 1310. Source: Arundel 83, f.129. British Library/Alamy.

Page 222. Lucifer Waiting for the Last Judgement, from *Livre de la Vigne nostre Seigneur*, fol. 067v. France ca. 1450–70. Public domain via Wikimedia Commons.

Page 237. Marriage of Sun and Moon from Emblem 30 of *Atalanta fugiens* by Michael Maier, engravings by Matthäus Merian, published in Oppenheim, 1617. Public domain via Wikimedia Commons.

Page 250. Rebis from *Theoria Philosophiae Hermeticae* by Heinrich Nollius, 1617. Public domain via Wikimedia Commons.

Page 250. Shiva Nataraja, Southern India, Tamil Nadu, Chola dynasty, c. 900–1100. Photograph by Daderot, public domain, via Wikimedia Commons.

Page 251. *Vesica piscis* in door of the Chalice Well in Glastonbury, England. Photo by the author.

Page 251. Christ in the mandorla enthroned amongst the four evangelists. From the Codex Bruchsal, Speyer Pericopes, 1220. Medieval. Public domain via Wikimedia Commons.

Page 257. Pictures 1 and 10, Ten Oxherding Pictures, Tenshō Shūbun. These are two of a series of ten images, generally known in English as the Ox-herding (or Bull-herding) pictures or Ten Bulls, by the 15th-century Japanese Rinzai Zen monk Shūbun, copied from the originals, now lost, traditionally attributed to Kakuan, a 12th century Chinese Zen Master. Public domain via Wikimedia Commons.

INDEX

A

abaissement du niveau mental, 39
absolute knowledge, 22, 29, 157
action points, 272–273
active imagination technique, 39–41
Adler, Alfred, 106
alchemical shadow work technique, 41–43
    albedo, 44
    citrinitas, 44
    nigredo, 44
    rubedo, 44
alchemy, 43, 151, 217, 242
amplification, 41, 265
anabasis, 207, 229
anima/animus, 25, 27, 151, 154, 157–158, 160, 165, 169, 176, 178, 249, 287
anima mundi, 249
archetypal motifs, 5
archetypal numerology, 55
    1 (unity and purity), 56
    2 (tension of opposition), 56
    3 (synthesis and dynamism), 56
    4 (stasis and containment), 57
    5 (humanity and conflict), 57
    6 (harmony and evolution), 57
    7 (mystique and paradox), 57–58
    8 (auspice and action), 58
    9 (arrival at the threshold), 58–59
    10 (totality and completion), 59
archetypal spreads, 275
    Archetypal Tarot Spread, 283–288
    Inner Work Spread, 279–283
    Tension of the Opposites Spread, 276–279
Archetypal Tarot School, 25
archetypes
    anima/animus, 25, 27, 151, 157–158, 160, 165, 176, 178, 249, 287
    of descent, 205–228
    developing ego, 181–204
    ego, 25, 26
    Feminine principle, 150–152
    gender constructs and, 149
    of the magical effect, 264–265
    Masculine principle, 150–152
    persona, 25, 26–27
    puer aeternus, 195, 244
    Self, 25, 28
    Senex, 195
    shadow, 25, 26
    theory of, 22–24
    transcendence, 229–258
    the Wise Old Man, 192

B–C

Boethius, 196–197

cards. *See specific cards*
carte da trionfi, 5
the Chariot, 144, 181, 184–187
clarity, 273
cognitive functions, 51–52
    rational/irrational pairings, 50–52
collective unconscious, 6, 8, 10, 17, 20 21, 23, 59
complexes, 106–112
consciousness, 19–20
    citrinitas, 44
    complexes and, 106–107
    ego and, 26
    ego-consciousness, 237
    lowering of, 39, 263–264
    lunar, 237–238
    solar, 237–238, 241–244
    the Sun, 242
contemplation, 13–14
contextualization, 265

court cards, 103
    and complexes, 106–112
    Kings, 4, 132–137
    Knights, 4, 120–125
    maturity, 105–106
    Pages, 4, 114–119
    persona and, 105
    projection and, 104
    Queens, 4, 126–131
    typological maturity, 105–106
Cups, 71–76

D

"dark night of the soul", 236–240
Death, 146, 206, 212–215
depth psychology, 3, 8–9
the Devil, 146, 173, 179, 206, 221–224
divination, 10–11
    psychoid unconscious and, 21–22
    synchronicity and, 30
dreams, 271–272
    Jung's, 238

E

ego, 20, 25
the Emperor, 144, 162, 167–170
the Empress, 5, 144, 162–166
Eros (god), 150, 177–178
eros, 126, 144, 150–152, 171, 175
extraversion/introversion, 113

F–G

feeling function, 50–53
Feminine principle, 126, 150–152
the Fool, 148, 254–258
Freud, Sigmund, 8, 55, 104

gender constructs, archetypes and, 149
grail, 70–71, 72, 168

H

the Hanged Man, 145, 182, 206, 208–211
the Hermit, 145, 181, 192–195
hero's journey, pips and, 59–68

the Hierophant, 25, 144, 171–174, 179, 193
hieros gamos, 143
the High Priestess, 2, 5, 144, 157–161, 202
Hillman, James, 9

I

imaginal realm, 40
Inanna, Queen of Heaven, 167, 168, 205–206
individuation, 10–11
    alchemical stages, 43–44
    ego strength and, 182–183
    goal of, 230–231, 252
    Major Arcana and, 49, 141–150
    pips and, 60
    process, 18–19
    synchronicities, 30
inflation, 185–187
intention setting, 263
intuition function, 50–52, 55
intuitive clarity, 36–37

J–K

journaling, 35
Judgement, 5, 245–248
Jung, Carl
    individuation and, 11, 18–19
    psychology, 8, 17–22
    Red Book, 194, 238
    The Undiscovered Self, 1
Justice, 145, 200–204

Kabbalistic Tree of Life, 93, 200–201
katabasis, 206, 229

L

libido, 55, 87, 101, 184–187
logos, 126, 144, 150–152, 171, 172
the Lovers, 144, 175–179
lunar consciousness, 237–238

M–N

macrocosm (divine world), 143–144, 153, 251

INDEX

the Magician, 144, 153–156
Major Arcana, 4, 141
    archetypes, 142–143
    the Chariot, 144, 181, 184–187
    Death, 146, 206, 212–215
    the Devil, 146, 173, 179, 206, 221–224
    the Emperor, 144, 162, 167–170
    the Empress, 5, 144, 162–166
    the Fool, 148, 254–258
    the Hanged Man, 145, 182, 206, 208–211
    the Hermit, 145, 181, 192–195
    the Hierophant, 25, 144, 171–174, 179, 193
    the High Priestess, 2, 5, 144, 157–161, 202
    individuation and, 49, 142
    Judgement, 5, 245–246
    Justice, 145, 200–204
    the Lovers, 144, 175–179
    Magician, 144, 153–156
    the Moon, 147, 236–240
    primordial powers, 143–144
    the Star, 147, 232–235
    Strength, 5, 145, 188–191
    the Sun, 147, 241–244
    Temperance, 146, 200, 206, 216–220
    the Tower, 146–147, 206, 225–228
    the Wheel of Fortune, 145, 181, 196–199
    the World, 5, 147, 148, 249–253, 255
Marseille deck, 6–141
Masculine principle, 150–152
Mercurius, 154–155, 158
microcosm (human world), 143–144, 153
Minor Arcana, 4, 137. *See also* court cards; pips
    Aces, 61
    Cups, 70–77
    Eights, 65–66
    Fives, 63
    Fours, 62–63
    Kings, 4, 132–137
    Knights, 4, 120–125
    as lived realities, 49
    monomyth, 59–68
    Nines, 66
    Pages, 4, 114–119
    Pentacles, 86–93
    Queens, 4, 126–131
    Sevens, 64–65
    Sixes, 64
    Swords, 78–85
    Tens, 67
    Threes, 62
    Twos, 61–62
    Wands, 94–102
monomyth, 59–68
the Moon, 147, 236–240
Myers-Briggs Type Indicator (MBTI), 50
mysterium coniunctionis, 150, 176, 249
myths, 12–13

O–P

Odin, 209

Pentacles, 86–93
persona, 25, 26–27, 98
personality types, 50–52
personalization, 265
personal unconscious, 20
pip monomyth, 4
    Ace, 61
    Eight, 65–66
    Five, 63
    Four, 62–63
    Nines, 66
    Seven, 64–65
    Six, 64
    Ten, 67
    Three, 62
    Two, 61–62
Plato's Forms, 22–23
pneuma, 151
primordial powers, 143. *See also specific cards*
    Feminine principle, 150–152
    Masculine principle, 150–152
projection, court cards and, 104
Psyche (goddess), 177–178
psyche, 8, 17–18, 151
    and cognitive functions, 51–52

ego, 20
personal unconscious, 20
psychoid unconscious, 20, 21
strata, 19–22
psychopomp, 146, 207, 217, 219

Q

questions, 3
forming better questions, 37–39
reading preparation, 263

R

reading preparation
archetype of magical effect, 264–265
intention setting, 263
lowering the mental level, 263–264
psycho-spiritual orientation, 262–263
reading interpretation
analysis, 266–267
amplification, 265
contextualization, 265
emotion, 267–268
feeling/emotion, 267–268
intuitive imagination, 268–269
personalization, 265
sensation/symbols, 270
relationship building with cards, 34–36
Rider-Waite-Smith deck, 6

S

Self, 1, 4, 9, 25, 28, 34. *See also soul*
alienation from, 90, 187, 234
atonement with shadow, 44, 147
the Atman, 251
ego and, 183
Feminine principles, 150
the Fool, 254–258
the Hanged man, 182, 208–211
individuation and, 18–19, 147–148, 254–258
Judgement, 246, 247
mysterium conjunctionis, 150
persona and, 26–27
the Sun, 243

Temperance, 219
transcendence, 230–231
trump cards, 142
unified Self, 9
the Wheel of Fortune, 197
the World, 249, 252–253
selfhood
archetypes of developing ego, 181–204
individuation, 18–19
sensation function, 50–52, 54
shadow, 25, 26
complexes, 108, 111
descent, 205–207
the Devil, 221, 223
individuation, 142
projection, 104
shadow work, 41–46, 111
Smith, Pamela Colman, 6
solar consciousness, 237–238, 241–244
soma, 151
Sophia, 158–159
soul. *See also Self*
psychology and, 8–9
selfhood, 19
spirit and, 151–152
spreads. *See archetypal spreads*
the Star, 147, 232–235
Strength, 5, 145, 188–191
suits
cognitive functions and, 52–55
Cups, 4, 70–77
functions, 52–55
Pentacles, 4
Swords, 4
Wands, 4
the Sun, 147, 241–244
Swords, 78–85
synchronicity, 28–31, 155, 272

T

tarocchi, 5
tarot, description, 4–8
Temperance, 146, 200, 206, 216–220
Thecla, 188, 190

Themis, 202, 204
thinking function, 50, 51, 53–54
the Tower, 146–147, 206, 225–228
Tiamat, 163–164, 168
transcendence, 229–258
transcendent function, 231, 245, 247
trumps, 5

U–V

unconsciousness, 19, 21
    complexes and, 107
    the Moon, 239
    psychoid unconscious, 20, 21
    rubedo, 44
unus mundus, 29

Visconti-Sforza Tarot, 4–5

W–Z

Waite, Arthur Edward, 6
Wands, 94–102
the Wheel of Fortune, 145, 181, 196–199
the World, 5, 147, 148, 249–253, 255

ABOUT THE AUTHOR

After stumbling upon a copy of *The Undiscovered Self* by Carl Jung in her grandfather's attic library, Mariana Louis left behind a promising Broadway career to become one of today's leading tarot scholars and teachers. She devoted herself to the study of the psyche and the mystery of the soul, developing a unique expertise in Jungian depth psychology, archetypal theory, and occult philosophy. These threads alchemized into her archetypal tarot approach, which she has taught to thousands of students worldwide through her popular Archetypal Tarot School and other programs.

In addition to her own educational platform, Persephone's Sister, Mariana lectures with several Jungian organizations and other online learning communities. She is the cohost of the beloved *Soror Mystica* podcast, which explores the world's most enigmatic symbols through in-depth conversations. Mariana is also a published poet and lyricist and is based in her native Queens, New York.

TO OUR READERS

Weiser Books, an imprint of Red Wheel/Weiser, publishes books across the entire spectrum of occult, esoteric, speculative, and New Age subjects. Our mission is to publish quality books that will make a difference in people's lives without advocating any one particular path or field of study. We value the integrity, originality, and depth of knowledge of our authors.

Our readers are our most important resource, and we appreciate your input, suggestions, and ideas about what you would like to see published.

Visit our website at *www.redwheelweiser.com*, where you can learn about our upcoming books and free downloads, and also find links to sign up for our newsletter and exclusive offers.

You can also contact us at *info@rwwbooks.com* or at

Red Wheel/Weiser, LLC
65 Parker Street, Suite 7
Newburyport, MA 01950